SUPREME FICTIONS

Brian John

Supreme Fictions

Studies in the Work of William Blake,
Thomas Carlyle, W. B. Yeats,
and D. H. Lawrence

McGill–Queen's University Press Montreal and London 1974

© 1974 McGill–Queen's University Press
ISBN 0 7735 0213 0
LC 74 75973
Legal Deposit 4th quarter 1974
Bibliothèque nationale du Québec

Design by Peter Maher
Printed in Canada by The Hunter Rose Company, Toronto

This work has been published with the help of a grant from the Humanities Research Council of Canada, using funds provided by the Canada Council.

Acknowledgements

Grateful acknowledgement is made to Mr. M. B. Yeats, the Macmillan Co. of London & Basingstoke, the Macmillan Co. of Canada, and the Macmillan Publishing Co., Inc., for permission to quote from *A Vision* (copyright 1937 by W. B. Yeats, renewed 1965 by Bertha Georgie Yeats and Anne Butler Yeats), *Essays and Introductions* (© Mrs. W. B. Yeats 1961), *Autobiography* (copyright 1916, 1935 by the Macmillan Publishing Co., Inc., renewed 1944, 1963 by Bertha Georgie Yeats), *Mythologies* (© Mrs. W. B. Yeats 1959), *Explorations* (copyright © Mrs. W. B. Yeats 1962), *The Variorum Edition of the Poems of W. B. Yeats*, edited by Peter Allt and Russell K. Alspach (copyright 1940 by Georgie Yeats, renewed 1968 by Bertha Georgie Yeats, Michael Butler Yeats, and Anne Yeats), *The Variorum Edition of the Plays of W. B. Yeats*, edited by Russell K. Alspach (copyright © Russell K. Alspach and Bertha Georgie Yeats 1966); to Mr. M. B. Yeats and Oxford University Press for excerpts from *W. B. Yeats and T. Sturge Moore: Their Correspondence, 1901–1937* and *Letters on Poetry from W. B. Yeats to Dorothy Wellesley;* and to Mr. M. B. Yeats for excerpts from *The Letters of W. B. Yeats*, edited by Allan Wade. I am grateful to both A. P. Watt and Son and the Macmillan Publishing Co., Inc., of New York for their help in granting me permission to quote from the works of W. B. Yeats.

For permission to quote from the works of D. H. Lawrence, I am also indebted to Alfred A. Knopf, Inc., William Heinemann Ltd., Laurence Pollinger Ltd., and the Estate of the late Mrs. Frieda Lawrence for "Sun" and "The Woman Who

Rode Away" from *Complete Short Stories of D. H. Lawrence*;
for *Mornings in Mexico* by D. H. Lawrence; for *The Plumed
Serpent* by D. H. Lawrence; for "St. Mawr," "The Virgin
and the Gipsy," and "The Man Who Died" from *The
Short Novels of D. H. Lawrence*; and for *The Memoirs and
Correspondence* by Frieda Lawrence, edited by E. W. Tedlock,
Jr. (© the Frieda Lawrence Estate 1961. All rights reserved).
Excerpts from *Lady Chatterley's Lover* by D. H. Lawrence
(copyright © 1957 and 1959 by Grove Press, Inc.) are reprinted by permission of Grove Press, Inc., William Heine-
mann Ltd., Laurence Pollinger Ltd., and the Estate of the
late Mrs. Frieda Lawrence. And for *Not I, But the Wind*
by Frieda Lawrence, grateful acknowledgement is made to
Laurence Pollinger Ltd. and the Estate of the late Mrs. Frieda
Lawrence.

Excerpts from *The Collected Poems of Wallace Stevens*
(copyright 1954 by Wallace Stevens. All rights reserved) are
reprinted by permission of Alfred A. Knopf, Inc.; from
Cahiers by Paul Valéry (© Editions Gallimard) by permission
of Editions Gallimard.

I would like to thank Eóin McKiernan and the Irish American Cultural Institute for allowing me to reprint in slightly
changed form my discussion of "Crazy Jane Reproved,"
which originally appeared in *Eire-Ireland* (4: 4). I am de-
lighted to be able to quote from the unpublished autobiography of the late Rolf Gardiner, for which I am most
grateful to his son, Mr. S. C. Gardiner.

Finally, I am appreciative of the debt I owe to the late
John F. Danby, whose student I was in North Wales; to
my friend Paul West, for his constant urging and encourage-
ment; to my colleagues Drs. Maqbool Aziz and Michael
Ross, who have read various chapters and made valuable
suggestions; to Mrs. Carol Robinson for her careful typing;
to Beverly Johnston and Audrey Hlady of McGill-Queen's
University Press for their advice and editorial work; to the
Arts Division Research Advisory Committee, McMaster
University, for its support over several summers in the form
of Summer Research Stipends; to the Humanities Research
Council of Canada and the Canada Council for financial
support towards publication; but, above all, to Margaret,
Andrea, and Paul, my own "delight & comfort."

For Margaret

Contents

Abbreviations

WILLIAM BLAKE

DC	*A Descriptive Catalogue*
E	*The Poetry and Prose of William Blake*, ed. David V. Erdman, commentary by Harold Bloom (Garden City, N.Y.: Doubleday, 1965). Citations from Blake are, unless otherwise stated, to this edition.
EG	*The Everlasting Gospel*
FZ	*The Four Zoas*
GP	*For the Sexes: The Gates of Paradise*
J	*Jerusalem*
M	*Milton*
MHH	*The Marriage of Heaven and Hell*
NNR	*There Is No Natural Religion*
VLJ	*A Vision of the Last Judgment*

THOMAS CARLYLE

OC	*Oliver Cromwell's Letters and Speeches*, 4 vols.

CME   *Critical and Miscellaneous Essays*, 5 vols.
FR   *The French Revolution*, 3 vols.
HHW   *On Heroes and Hero-Worship*
LDP   *Latter-Day Pamphlets*
PP   *Past and Present*
SR   *Sartor Resartus*
Citations from Carlyle are, unless otherwise stated, to
The Works of Thomas Carlyle, ed. H. D. Traill, Cente-
nary ed., 30 vols. (London: Chapman and Hall, 1896–
1901).

W. B. YEATS

Auto   *Autobiographies* (London: Macmillan,
            1956)
E & I   *Essays and Introductions* (London: Mac-
            millan, 1961)
Exp   *Explorations*, selected by Mrs. W. B. Yeats
            (New York: Macmillan, 1962)
Letters   *The Letters of W. B. Yeats*, ed. Allan Wade
            (London: Hart-Davis, 1954)
LP   *Letters on Poetry from W. B. Yeats to
            Dorothy Wellesley*, introd. Kathleen Raine
            (London: O.U.P., 1964)
Myth   *Mythologies* (London: Macmillan, 1959)
V   *A Vision* (New York: Macmillan, 1961)
Var   *The Variorum Edition of the Poems of
            W. B. Yeats*, ed. Peter Allt and Russell K.
            Alspach (New York: Macmillan, 1966).
            Citations from the poetry of Yeats are to
            this edition.
Var. Plays *The Variorum Edition of the Plays of
            W. B. Yeats*, ed. Russell K. Alspach (Lon-
            don: Macmillan, 1966)
Y & TSM   *W. B. Yeats and T. Sturge Moore: Their
            Correspondence, 1901–1937*, ed. Ursula
            Bridge (New York: O.U.P., 1953)

D. H. LAWRENCE

Apo   *Apocalypse,* introd. Richard Aldington (New York: Viking, 1966)

CL   *The Collected Letters of D. H. Lawrence,* ed. Harry T. Moore, 2 vols. (New York: Viking, 1962)

CP   *The Complete Poems of D. H. Lawrence,* 3 vols.

EP   *Etruscan Places*

Fan   *Fantasia of the Unconscious*

Not I Frieda Lawrence, *Not I, But the Wind* (Toronto: Macmillan, 1934)

Letters *The Letters of D. H. Lawrence,* ed. Aldous Huxley (London: Heinemann, 1956)

MEH   *Movements in European History* (London: O.U.P., 1925)

Mem   Frieda Lawrence, *The Memoirs and Correspondence,* ed. E. W. Tedlock, Jr. (New York: Knopf, 1964)

MM   *Mornings in Mexico*

Nehls Edward Nehls, *D. H. Lawrence: A Composite Biography,* 3 vols. (Madison: Univ. of Wisconsin Press, 1957–59)

Ph   *Phoenix: The Posthumous Papers of D. H. Lawrence* (1936), ed. Edward D. McDonald (New York: Viking, 1968)

Ph. II *Phoenix II: Uncollected, Unpublished, and Other Prose Works by D. H. Lawrence,* ed. Warren Roberts and Harry T. Moore (New York: Viking, 1968)

PR   E. T. [Jessie Chambers], *D. H. Lawrence: A Personal Record,* 2d ed. by J. D. Chambers (London: Cass, 1965)

Psy   *Psychoanalysis and the Unconscious*

QR   *The Quest for Rananim: D. H. Lawrence's Letters to S. S. Koteliansky, 1914–1930,* ed. George J. Zytaruk (Montreal: McGill-Queen's Univ. Press, 1970)

YL   Ada Lawrence and G. Stuart Gelder, *Young*
        Lorenzo: Early Life of D. H. Lawrence
        (Florence: Orioli, 1931)
The Phoenix edition of Lawrence's works has normally
been used: *Complete Poems; Complete Short Stories,*
vol. II (for "Sun," "The Woman Who Rode Away");
Kangaroo; The Lost Girl; Mornings in Mexico and
Etruscan Places; The Plumed Serpent; The Short Nov-
els, vol. II (for "St. Mawr," "The Virgin and the Gipsy,"
"The Man Who Died"). Other editions used: *The First*
Lady Chatterley, foreword Frieda Lawrence (New
York: Dial Press, 1944); *Lady Chatterley's Lover*
(Harmondsworth: Penguin, 1960); *Psychoanalysis and*
the Unconscious and *Fantasia of the Unconscious,*
introd. Philip Rieff (New York: Viking, 1960).

Introduction

In grouping together in a single study the work of Blake, Carlyle, Yeats, and D. H. Lawrence, one becomes aware of a common tradition in which they all participate, of certain shared principles, attitudes, and values, and, despite the individual inflexion of voice, a common language. No matter how distinct each author may be—and the intrinsic individuality of each should not be underestimated—that tradition is obviously Romantic and, more particularly, vitalist. Moreover, as one sees the continuation of that Romantic vitalism, often to varying degrees and taking different forms, in more contemporary writers—from Dylan Thomas, Richard Eberhart, the American Beat writers of the fifties, to Ted Hughes and, more recently, the Children of Albion—one recognizes also that Yeats's prediction, "We were the last romantics,"[1] was too gloomy in its finality.

1. "Coole Park and Ballylee, 1931." Citations from the poetry of W. B. Yeats are to *The Variorum Edition of the Poems of W. B. Yeats*, ed. Peter Allt and Russell K. Alspach (New York: Macmillan, 1966). References by title and line number are in the body of the text; references to Yeats's Notes, Prefaces, and Dedications are given as *Var*, followed by the page number.

In using such terms as "Romantic" and "vitalist," one is at once confronted with the problem Arthur O. Lovejoy has properly identified as the "plurality of Romanticisms." "The word 'romantic' has come to mean so many things that, by itself, it means nothing."[2] However, despite the all-encompassing character of the term "Romantic," it is still possible to distinguish that element in the tradition which I call "vitalist," while recognizing also that not all Romantics subscribe to that element as an article of faith. Since "vitalist" as much as the broader term "Romantic" is the unifying principle of this study, it is necessary to provide a preliminary definition, which will be clarified further in subsequent chapters.

At the heart of the doctrine of vitalism, a doctrine deriving ultimately from the Logos of Heraclitus and the entelechy of Aristotle, is the principle of Force—which Blake called Energy—running through all things, cosmic and individual. Macrocosm and microcosm are bound up together in and by the principle of Force. The vital Force, with accompanying images of flame and fire, gives to existence as a whole a dynamic character; provides a dialectical pattern within which things progress; and indicates a direction which ends in revelation and, more often than not, apocalypse.[3]

The character, pattern, and direction are each intrinsic to the vitalist doctrine and denote a distinctive brand of Romantic belief. In its biological analogues, the doctrine parallels another element in Romantic thought, organicism, with which it has much in common. In its apocalyptic teleology, however, with roots in more esoteric traditions like cabbalism and neo-

---

2. "On the Discrimination of Romanticisms," in *English Romantic Poets*, ed. M. H. Abrams (New York: O.U.P., 1960), pp. 6, 8.
3. A fuller discussion of vitalism may be found in Evelyn Underhill, *Mysticism: A Study in the Nature and Development of Man's Spiritual Consciousness* (1911; rpt. London: Methuen, 1960), pp. 26–43.

platonism, it is probably closer to "the general tendency . . . to naturalize the supernatural and to humanize the divine," which M. H. Abrams has called, after Carlyle, "natural supernaturalism."[4] Consequently, in *Heroes and Hero-Worship,* a work in which both the organic and the apocalyptic loom large, one finds Carlyle declaring the vitalist faith: "Force, Force, everywhere Force; we ourselves a mysterious Force in the centre of that. 'There is not a leaf rotting on the highway but has Force in it: how else could it rot?' . . . this huge illimitable whirlwind of Force, which envelops us here; never-resting whirlwind, high as Immensity, old as Eternity."[5] Whether consciously or not, Carlyle is in direct descendance from Shelley, whose "Ode to the West Wind" likewise depends upon a dialectical vision of the "destroyer and preserver," employs imagery of wind and winged seed, and also attributes to the poet, as inspired interpreter, a prophetic role.

A similar vision, given a peculiarly Irish colouring, enabled Yeats in an early poem, "The Hosting of the Sidhe," to sing:

The host is riding from Knocknarea
And over the grave of Clooth-na-Bare;
Caoilte tossing his burning hair,
And Niamh calling *Away, come away:*
Empty your heart of its mortal dream.

4. *Natural Supernaturalism: Tradition and Revolution in Romantic Literature* (New York: Norton, 1971), p. 68. Carlyle's term is to be found in *Sartor Resartus,* 202–12. See also Abrams' earlier study, *The Mirror and the Lamp: Romantic Theory and the Critical Tradition* (New York: Norton, 1958), esp. chaps. 7 and 8, for further discussion of organic theories.
5. *HHW,* 8–9. Citations from Thomas Carlyle are, unless otherwise stated, to *The Works of Thomas Carlyle,* ed. H. D. Traill, Centenary ed., 30 vols. (London: Chapman and Hall, 1896–1901). References in the text are to abbreviated titles and page numbers or volume and page numbers.

The winds awaken, the leaves whirl round,
Our cheeks are pale, our hair is unbound,
Our breasts are heaving, our eyes are agleam,
Our arms are waving, our lips are apart;
And if any gaze on our rushing band,
We come between him and the deed of his hand,
We come between him and the hope of his heart.
The host is rushing 'twixt night and day,
And where is there hope or deed as fair?
Caoilte tossing his burning hair,
And Niamh calling Away, come away.

In a note to the poem, Yeats explicated his imagery
and recognized, in its Gaelic and medieval parallels,
sources older than any nineteenth-century vitalism:
"Sidhe is also Gaelic for wind, and certainly the Sidhe
have much to do with the wind. They journey in whirling winds, the winds that were called the dance of
the daughters of Herodias in the Middle Ages, Herodias
doubtless taking the place of some old goddess" (*Var,*
p. 800). Whatever source Yeats might wish to ascribe,
he was still at this time considerably under the influence of Shelley, and saw also in the work of the *fin-de-*
siècle Gustave Moreau and Oscar Wilde whirling
dancers like Herodias-Salome. Yeats is clearly working
with Romantic as well as Irish or medieval myth. The
very correspondence of the myths in meaning and
image would be part confirmation of their significance
and truth.

Without the principle of Force, however, all would
remain in Blake's world of Experience—a static and
stagnating world, bounded by horizons imposed by the
limited nature of a fragmented and arrogantly rational
self; that which Wordsworth, echoing Milton, summed
up as "a universe of death" (*The Prelude,* XIV, 160).
The new cosmology, emerging in the late eighteenth
century and firmly established by Blake, Wordsworth,
and other Romantic poets and theorists, was not
wholly new, not without roots in previous intellectual

traditions, yet was not necessarily the expression of a *philosophia perennis* surfacing again after an arid stretch of rationalism and analysis. Indeed, scientific thought, often misconstrued as the villain of Romanticism, reflects a corresponding shift—from the cosmic and mathematical constructions of Newtonian physics to the chemistry of things, the biological, botanical, and zoological, verifiable by observation of the particular and organically mutating. The age of evolution itself evolved over several generations of scientists and thinkers, Darwin being as much a product as a founding father. Romantic vitalism is an aesthetic expression of that same movement of mind and continues to influence art and thought down to the present.

We generally associate Romanticism with, among other things, a heightened emphasis upon the self. Taking a variety of forms, that emphasis showed itself in new, often politically inspired, assertions of the importance of the individual and in a parallel concern with psychology and self-introspection. And indeed here Romantic vitalism has its firm roots. For it was to counteract the Augustan faith in general principles, abstraction, intellect, and the mind's passivity in perception that the vitalist reasserted the particular and concrete, the revolutionary and individual, the suprarational and intuitive, and the mind's fundamentally creative character.

The problem's source, as A. N. Whitehead has argued, lay in the duality of mind and body inherited from the mathematician Descartes.[6] With evangelical zeal, the vitalist sought the reunification of self—mind and body, passions and intellect, in their essential and primordial unity—in order to avoid the fallacious and spiritually fatal Cartesian dualism. The Christian myth of the Fall and Redemption, used not only by Blake

6. *Science and the Modern World* (Cambridge: C.U.P., 1946), chap. 9.

but by other Romantic vitalists, proved conveniently relevant. In the hands of eighteenth-century empiricists, the Cartesian dualism resulted, after John Locke, in descriptions of the mind in the act of perception as a passive *tabula rasa* upon which the external world imprints its image through sense-data. What followed, in works like David Hartley's *Observations on Man* (1749), was the codification of mental processes into theories of association, which in turn described moral growth and development along mechanistic lines. The subsequent cosmology, labelled "cosmic Toryism"[7] and imaged as a Great Chain of Being in works like Pope's *Essay on Man*, was, to the Romantic, mechanical in nature and devoid of life. Like the mythical upas tree, such mechanism poisoned all growth and reduced all things to a fearful spiritual wasteland. "Bacons Philosophy has Destroyd all Art & Science," Blake commented in a furious annotation to Reynolds' *Discourses;* or again, to Berkeley's *Siris*, "God is not a Mathematical Diagram."[8]

However, such a cosmology, imaged as a machine and knowable through mathematics, had been promoted since the time of Descartes. In his *Treatise on Man*, Descartes describes the human brain and body as a machine, the structure of which he compares to the fountains of a French formal garden:

> The nerves of the machine that I am describing to you may very well be compared to the pipes of the machinery of these fountains, its muscles and its tendons to various other engines and devices which serve to move them, its animal spirits to the water which sets them in motion, of which the heart is the spring, and the cavities of the

7. Basil Willey, *The Eighteenth Century Background* (London: Chatto and Windus, 1957), chap. 3.

8. E, pp. 645, 653. Citations from William Blake are, unless otherwise stated, to *The Poetry and Prose of William Blake*, ed. David V. Erdman, commentary by Harold Bloom (Garden City, N.Y.: Doubleday, 1965). Where possible, references are to abbreviated titles, followed by plate numbers and/or line numbers.

brain the outlets. Moreover, respiration and other such functions as are natural and usual to it, and which depend on the course of the spirits, are like the movements of a clock or a mill.[9]

The recurrence of such imagery in later expressions of the mechanistic cosmology accounts for the dark Satanic mills of Blake, Carlyle, and Lawrence, while they will employ the image of the fountain, as in Yeats's "Meditations in Time of Civil War," not in any mechanistic way but as reflecting the vital brimming of the creative self. The obvious Romantic antithesis to Descartes' use of the symbolism is Coleridge's "Kubla Khan," where the planned garden gives way to a "deep romantic chasm" from which "A mighty fountain momently was forced."

By attending to the individual and particular and to the psychology of the self, the Romantic recognized both the source of the evil and the cure. Whether one attended to the Minute Particular without or the Intellectual War within, the Romantic saw that the traditional mechanistic explanations were refuted by the very dynamic nature of things themselves. Coleridge's own philosophic development—from a Hartleian associationism and Godwinian necessitarianism to a Kantian faith in Reason, the supra-rational faculty by which the absolute realm of spiritual reality is known—reflects the transition from eighteenth-century philosophical traditions to those of the nineteenth century. Coleridge was indeed, to use John Stuart Mill's distinctively Romantic image, a "seminal" mind.[10]

With his heightened and more precise awareness of the nature of mental processes, for example, the Romantic realized that, instead of a mechanical con-

9. *Selections*, ed. Ralph M. Eaton (New York: Scribner's, 1927), p. 353.
10. "Bentham," in *Mill on Bentham and Coleridge*, introd. F. R. Leavis (London: Chatto and Windus, 1950), p. 40.

struct, the mind was fundamentally an organism. Whether on the level of perception or on its more imaginative levels, the mind was neither passive nor a *tabula rasa*. Rather, in Coleridge's distinctive image in "Dejection: An Ode," the unifying or "shaping spirit of Imagination," whether in perception or aesthetic creation, echoes in its very creativity the Divine Creator. Nevertheless, however much he might insist upon the self's creativity—and few critics were as influential upon later aesthetic theory and philosophy—Coleridge remained certain of the distinction between man, no matter how creative, and God, the Creator of all things. A more thoroughgoing faith would lead Blake to assert, "God only Acts & Is, in existing beings or Men" (*MHH*, 16), a humanism rearticulated, though in strikingly different ways, by Carlyle, Lawrence, and Yeats. In any case, all were agreed that knowledge of reality was possible only when the mind itself was organically unified and actively creative. One conclusion to which this argument leads is a Berkeleyan subjectivism in which the external world's existence depends upon that very creativity of self. One creates the world in which one lives, the artist being quintessentially the maker. In "The Idea of Order at Key West," one of the great expressions in our own day of this Romantic principle, Wallace Stevens' singer, not unlike Wordsworth's solitary reaper, constructs and defines her world and vision in her song:

> It was her voice that made
> The sky acutest at its vanishing.
> She measured to the hour its solitude.
> She was the single artificer of the world
> In which she sang. And when she sang, the sea,
> Whatever self it had, became the self
> That was her song, for she was the maker.[11]

11. *The Collected Poems of Wallace Stevens* (New York: Knopf, 1964), p. 129.

This it was that made Coleridge assure Sara Hutchinson, "O Lady! we receive but what we give, / And in our life alone does Nature live" ("Dejection: An Ode"), or Blake assert, "Where man is not nature is barren" (*MHH*, 10: 68). On the other hand, eighteenth-century descriptions of the world depended, like those of Blake's Angel, upon their author's limited vision and fragmented self: "All that we saw was owing to your metaphysics" (*MHH*, 19). A mechanistic cosmology corresponded not to the reality of things but to the perverse and perverted nature of the perceiver.

When the mind is most vital and creative, then, it is capable of seeing a world in turn vital and creative. Because of its peculiarly dialectical nature, however, Force is both creative and destructive; in Blake's terms, is both the Prolific and the Devourer (*MHH*, 16). Such a tension of antinomies gives a distinctive pattern to things and provides for growth and development. The difference between the two cosmologies, mechanist and vitalist, is thus between a closed and an open universe. In the first, change within the Great Chain of Being must be limited to prevent the disastrous cosmic disharmony which would result from tampering with the divinely created "gradation";[12] in the second, change is sought as a manifestation of the regeneration which the vitalist seeks for all things. Rather than seeing the dialectic as negating, the Romantic vitalist concurred with Blake: "Without Contraries is no progression" (*MHH*, 3). What will become clear, as we proceed from Blake to Yeats, is the necessary war within the self and all things if growth towards fulfilment is to take place. Blake's state of Experience and the Zoas' fall into disunity, Carlyle's Everlasting No, Yeats's dialogue of self and soul, Lawrence's battles

12. See Pope, *Essay on Man*, I, 241–58. For a fuller discussion of this and related concepts, see Arthur O. Lovejoy, *The Great Chain of Being: A Study of the History of an Idea* (New York: Harper, 1960).

with himself, his characters, and with a philistine public, are all requisite to the fulfilment of the creative
self. What distinguishes the imaginative man, however,
is his refusal to pervert the contraries into what Blake
called "negations," an error which the analytical intellect persistently commits. On the level of moral choice,
the perversion takes the form of acceptance of suffering
and evil; in politics, the preservation of the status quo.
In his fundamentally tragic vision, in his elevation of
the heroic defeat or the disillusionment and frustration
known to poet and lover, and also in his political
conservatism, Yeats comes closest to this Urizenic
perversion.

Since the vitalist cosmology rejects the image of the
universe as a machine, the increased industrialism of
the last two hundred years becomes a suitable external-
ization of a similar scarring of the landscape of the self.
Blake, Carlyle, and Lawrence all agree on this point.
The industrial society is an emblem of the Fall and
epitomizes man's increasing reliance upon technology
and rational explanation. The awful industrial blight
upon a landscape; the stunted growth of the inhabitants; the increasing dependence upon the machine;
the subsequent commercialism, mammonism, profit-
eering; the reduction of persons to things; the lack of
contact between man and man, man and Nature, man
and God—all these and more were evidence not only
of the Industrial Revolution but of a whole world,
mental as well as physical, committed to a perversion
of spirit, to a fallen, inorganic, and fragmented vision
which lacks the moral and imaginative strength to
reverse the trend. The direction, therefore, is towards
apocalypse and revelation. Consequently, just as Blake
saw Newton and Locke as satanic forces leading mankind down an increasingly blind alley, so Yeats berated
Tyndall and Huxley for denying him the possibility of
an orthodox faith, and D. H. Lawrence conceived
Bertrand Russell as the epitome of contemporary man's
spiritual dilemma.

The artist's function, in his myth-making and in his imaginative vision, is then to redirect us to the old positives, the ancient vitalist wisdom known to less technologically corrupt peoples, whether the Mexican Indian or the west of Ireland peasant. The result is not only a form of primitivism, though both Yeats and Lawrence avoid full commitment to such a view, but also, for the artist, a prophetic mask and a hieratic voice. The evangelical character and insistence upon conversion are strong in the work of vitalists from Blake to Lawrence; even Yeats, in whom they are less explicit, has this side to him. There is a corresponding inclination towards arrogance and assertion which, in matters of style, takes the form of incantation, rhetoric, and aphorism, and, in political views, supports aristocracy and an élitism. The insistence upon heroic men, central in Carlyle, Yeats, and Lawrence, and sometimes taking on more nearly fascist colouring, begins with Blake: "those who envy or calumniate great men hate God, for there is no other God" (*MHH*, 23). When applied to epistemology or aesthetics, that élitism asserted the primacy of a transcendent reality over mere empirical ones and constructed a theory of symbols. The universe must be read symbolically, in the cabbalistic sense of the universe as the "signature" of God. The imaginative man thus becomes the priest capable of revealing the essence of things through his reading of symbols and his awareness of the transcendental nature of reality. Indeed, both the Symbolists and the Aesthetes of the late nineteenth century are indebted to the Romantic vitalist tradition for its upholding a transcendentalism and a corresponding faith in symbols. Appropriately enough, Arthur Symons dedicated his *Symbolist Movement in Literature* (1899) to W. B. Yeats and began with a quotation from Carlyle. The vitalist's insistence upon the organically mutating became, in its aesthetic form, a belief in transformation and metamorphosis. As Blake put it, the fourfold vision, attained only by the imaginative man possessed of an integrated, harmonious self, revealed a world humanized and not the myopic Urizenic world of time, space, and matter.

At its best, vitalism has made a major contribution to that "imaginative revolution" Northrop Frye has talked of, a revolution in man's vision of himself and his world "which has carried on until our own day, and has by no means completed itself yet."[13] It has provided the artist, as well as the philosopher and scientist, with a new cosmology; it has given new and imaginative directions to our historical consciousness and the ways in which we regard past, present, and future; it has reinstated the creative self and granted a stature and dignity to human nature. At its best it has made more possible that germination or spiritual growth the vitalists, from Blake to Lawrence, seek for men. It has also been used to justify some of the most vicious and inhumane aspects of our century. And at its worst it declines into a worship of physical violence and a self-defeating elevation of irrationality.

While upholding the continuity of a Romantic vitalist tradition, from Blake to the present, we must also, however, recognize the need for precise distinctions. For a study of Romantic vitalism reveals the peculiarly individual nature of its articulators. The fact should be obvious, even inevitable and desirable, given the characteristically subjectivist nature of vitalism. Yeats's tragic gaiety is thus vastly different from Blake's Joy,

13. *A Study of English Romanticism* (New York: Random House, 1968), p. 15. Cf. M. H. Abrams: "It is now becoming apparent that the esoteric view of the universe as a plenum of opposed yet mutually attractive, quasi-sexual forces—which was discredited and displaced by Cartesian and Newtonian mechanism, but was revived, in a refined form, in the *Naturphilosophie* of Schelling in Germany and of Coleridge in England—proceeded, by a peripety of intellectual history, to feed back into scientific thought some of the most productive hypotheses of nineteenth-century and modern physics" (*Natural Supernaturalism*, p. 171).

and Yeats continually misinterpreted or misrepresented Blake, as Blake had in turn misinterpreted or misrepresented Milton. The City of Jerusalem is nothing like Byzantium or St. Edmundsbury or Rananim. The vitalist insistence upon the intuitively revealed or instinctively known led Carlyle, Yeats, and Lawrence to assert the mysterious and finally incomprehensible nature of existence—what Blake, on the other hand, derisively called "Mystery" and persistently attacked as the Whore of Babylon. These and other distinctions will become clear as we proceed to look more closely at individual writers and their positions within the common tradition. Some of the distinctions derive from the personality of the individual writer and others from the character of the period in which he lived.

Nevertheless, whether viewed with the optimistic clarity of Blake's fourfold vision or with the deliberate and dramatic tension of Yeats's perpetual vacillation, at the heart of the vitalist vision is the dynamic fabricating self. Busy in the construction of "supreme fictions"—Wallace Stevens' terms[14]—the artist, like Yeats, can "hold in a single thought reality and justice,"[15] and can teach men how to live. For the supreme fictions construct an order out of the chaos of existence; the artist or imaginative man becomes, *par excellence*, the "Connoisseur of Chaos" (as in Stevens' poem of that name), while his myths and images "relate to reality and they intensify our sense of it."[16] There can be no higher aim.

14. "The Noble Rider and the Sound of Words," in *The Necessary Angel* (New York: Vintage, 1965), p. 31.
15. W. B. Yeats, *A Vision* (New York: Macmillan, 1961), p. 25.
16. Stevens, "Three Academic Pieces," in *Necessary Angel*, p. 78.

CHAPTER ONE

William Blake
The Poet as Mental Prince

Both in his own lifetime and in the long haul to his present status as a major Romantic poet, Blake suffered from the charge of eccentricity, a term sometimes synonymous with lunacy. Though no one today need seriously question his sanity, an issue more troublesome for his Victorian admirers and critics, Blake's position in the English poetic tradition is, for some, still suspect. In 1920 T. S. Eliot saw him as possessing a surplus of individual talent but lacking a tradition: "a framework of accepted and traditional ideas which would have prevented him from indulging in a philosophy of his own, and concentrated his attention upon the problems of the poet."[1] Eliot's arguments have worn increasingly thin but, curiously enough, echoed the previous view of W. B. Yeats, who remained more convinced of Blake's worth. "He was a man crying out for a mythology, and trying to make one because he could not find one to his hand. Had he been a Catholic

---

1. "William Blake," rpt. in *The Sacred Wood* (1920; London: Methuen, 1960), pp. 157–58.

of Dante's time he would have been well content with Mary and the angels."[2] The problem of a tradition, mythology, or "System" is indeed central to Blake, as it is in our time to Eliot and Yeats. Yet it is precisely that "digest of the numerous odd religious and pseudo-historical works current in his day" which in part accounts for Robert Graves' now finding Blake's prophecies "dated, tedious, and perverse."[3] Even admirers of the lyrical Blake believe the Prophetic Books, "with their sources and points of reference in Jewish mysticism, Renaissance alchemy, Early Christian heresies, Hindu religion, and eighteenth-century fantasies about the Druids, are exotic phenomena."[4]

One alternative has been pursued by Kathleen Raine and F. A. C. Wilson:[5] to argue that the neoplatonic tradition is The Tradition; that Blake's vision derives from sources which, while esoteric, remain so central to the European intellectual tradition that he is by no means eccentric. However, the extreme critical positions here—Eliot and Raine—are unnecessary if one sees the fundamentally Romantic as well as esoteric quality of Blake's work. Indeed, he is as comprehensible within the Romantic vitalist tradition as within any other: our reading of Coleridge and Keats, for example, proves as valuable to our appreciation of Blake's myth as might the study of Swedenborg, Boehme, or Plotinus.

2. "William Blake and the Imagination" (1897), in *Essays and Introductions* (London: Macmillan, 1961), p. 114.
3. *The Crowning Privilege* (Harmondsworth: Penguin, 1959), p. 81.
4. *Selected Poems of William Blake*, ed. F. W. Bateson (London: Heinemann, 1961), p. xxviii.
5. Kathleen Raine, *Blake and Tradition*, Bollingen Series, no. 35 (Princeton: Princeton Univ. Press, 1968). The neoplatonic she sees as "the central tradition of European poetic and pictorial symbolism" (I, 99). F. A. C. Wilson, *W. B. Yeats and Tradition* (London: Gollancz, 1958), chap. 1. Cf. the earlier work of Denis Saurat, *Blake and Modern Thought* (1929; reissued New York: Russell and Russell, 1964) and *Literature and Occult Tradition* (1930; reissued New York: Haskell, 1966).

A similar argument might be applied to another Romantic autodidact, W. B. Yeats. Valuable as the tracking down of occult references or cabbalistic sources might be, it is also necessary to place both Blake and Yeats within the Romantic and vitalist tradition, which includes writers as different as Carlyle and Lawrence.

A further problem confronting readers of Blake is that his poetry operates upon multiple levels of meaning. Poems like *The French Revolution* or *Europe* or *America* are to varying degrees political and social, moral and psychological, aesthetic and epistemological, and finally cosmological in reference. One may object, as F. W. Bateson has done, that Blake "was trying to say too many things at the same time."[6] Certainly the prophecies are not always successful and satisfying as poems, though I shall return to this question later in discussing *Milton*. Nevertheless, it remains equally true that the distinctive quality of Blake's work and achievement depends upon his attempt to concentre his vision—"Create a System"—in such a way that his vision more closely approximated the divine reality he saw plainly and often. The multiple or, more precisely, the fourfold vision Blake always strove for determined the nature of the prophetic utterance. The Prophetic Books were a necessary mode, their difficulty not a mere obscurantism. We know further of his struggle for technical precision in a mode dictated to him by his spirits:

> When this Verse was first dictated to me I consider'd a Monotonous Cadence like that used by Milton & Shakspeare & all writers of English Blank Verse, derived from

6. *Selected Poems of Blake*, p. ix. However, I cannot accept Morton Irving Seiden, who sees Blake as "quite overwhelmed" by his symbolism to the extent that in the later years he wrote "almost unintelligibly." *William Butler Yeats: The Poet as Mythmaker, 1865–1939* (East Lansing: Michigan State Univ. Press, 1962), p. 20.

the modern bondage of Rhyming; to be a necessary and
indispensible part of Verse. But I soon found that in the
mouth of a true Orator such monotony was not only
awkward, but as much a bondage as rhyme itself. I therefore have produced a variety in every line, both of ca-
dences & number of syllables. Every word and every letter
is studied and put into its fit place: the terrific numbers
are reserved for the terrific parts—the mild & gentle, for
the mild & gentle parts, and the prosaic, for inferior parts:
all are necessary to each other.

                                                             (*J*, 3)

Graves' view that "Blake began as a poet; later he lost
heart and turned prophet" is thus too glib.[7]
To read Blake is an education in Revelation; it is
to be similarly inspired and led back to the Edenic state
where all things concentre; to see the Many as One.
Likewise, what takes place on an epistemological level
has ramifications on the moral and aesthetic and political levels. Blake's universe is indeed organic and vital,
and the multiplicity of levels are to be experienced
finally as one—Vision. In the same way, to use Blake's
image, all things humanize and are seen as members
of the Divine Family. Any multiplicity, therefore, is
a separation, something the reader becomes aware of
only when he dissects or analyses. Like Wordsworth
in "The Tables Turned," Blake believed that "We murder to dissect." In itself, analysis is reading in an un-
mythical way and limiting one's vision; one might
object, with Tharmas in *The Four Zoas*, against this
process whatever form it might take: "Why wilt thou
Examine every little fibre of my soul / Spreading them
out before the Sun like Stalks of flax to dry" (I,
4: 28–29). The difficulty of multiple meaning, however,
is that it strives to express the noumenon at the level
of the phenomenon, the age-old problem of articulating

7. *Crowning Privilege*, p. 81.

the inarticulate. Yet the marvellous sense of discovery to which Blake can lead his reader is to experience vicariously that same thrilling, vibrant universe which echoes throughout his work, from *Poetical Sketches* (1783) to *Jerusalem* (1804–15) and *The Everlasting Gospel* (c. 1818). Blake's world is always noisy; even in *Songs of Experience* there are howls and shrieks and groans. That same organicism which gives rise to the multiplicity of meaning finds definite expression in the reverberating world the poet portrays and lives in. His organicism or vitalism is also the source of his violent rejection of the eighteenth-century philosophy of death. Eliot was wrong in believing Blake concentrated excessively on philosophy; Blake's rejection of empiricism was related precisely to "the problems of the poet" to which Eliot refers. The inspired man defies abstraction with vision and its correlative, vitalism.

1

Blake's vitalism, with its centre in the self's creative power, is antithetical to the predominantly mechanical philosophy, based on empirical epistemology and offered by the eighteenth century as a scientific description of reality. As we have seen, that empiricism accepted the mind's passivity in the processes of perception while asserting the intellect as the supreme instrument to truth. The universe, similarly structured, fixed and rationally comprehensible, was like a finely constructed mechanism—in Paley's image, a superb watch, to which the Creator remained suitably external, as an absentee watchmaker.[8] However, while the Augustan concept of a Great Chain of Being underwent

8. *The Works of William Paley, D.D., Archdeacon of Carlisle* (Edinburgh: Brown and Nelson, 1828), pp. 435–39. Cf. Blake's annotations to Swedenborg's *Divine Love and Divine Wisdom* (1788): "Heaven would upon this plan be but a Clock" (E, p. 593).

scrutiny even in the Age of the Augustans itself, David
Hume, the latest in the line of British empiricists, concluded in utter scepticism, the *reductio ad absurdum*
of that particular school. His relativism in *A Treatise
of Human Nature* (1739–40) was so thorough as to
preclude even a self to experience those isolated sense-
impressions about which one could be certain only
that they exist. In answer to such scepticism, Blake,
like Coleridge, Kant, and others following in the nineteenth century, restated an idealist philosophy, in
Blake's case resolving the empiricist dichotomy of subject and object in a theory of the Imagination. For him,
Locke and Newton became scapegoats for the present
state of mankind. What was called the Enlightenment
was for him Darkness visible.

Empiricism, or "Natural Religion," imposes a limitation upon man's self in its insistence upon the senses
as the origin of knowledge. If knowledge is acquired
only by operation of "ratio" upon material obtained
from sense-perception, a bound is drawn around the
self, its desires, its whole organic nature, so creating
those same Satanic mills Blake saw in industrial Britain, symbols of tyranny and restraint. "The bounded
is loathed by its possessor. The same dull round even
of a universe would soon become a mill with complicated wheels" (*NNR*, b, iv). The same imagery is present in Wordsworth's superb description of the monstrous anarchy and spiritual wasteland of London,
composed of "A Parliament of Monsters," in *The Prelude*, VII, 718–21:

>   Tents and Booths
>   Meanwhile, as if the whole were one vast mill,
>   Are vomiting, receiving, on all sides,
>   Men, Women, three-years' Children, Babes in arms.

In Carlyle too there is a similar sense of sham, of people
participating in a fearful and spiritually deadening

charade, disguising their true selves behind the façades of clothes and appearances, until nothing is left but the disguise. That vast parade of unreality often takes the more ominous form of mills. And Carlyle's creaking machinery, endlessly and monotonously repeating its fixed pattern, corresponds to Blake's objections to empiricism. For, Blake says, "the ratio of all things" would soon be known; the self would "stand still unable to do other than repeat the same dull round over again" (*NNR*, a, conclusion). Instead, he offers a vision of the Infinite, made possible to all men by virtue of their "Poetic Genius" which is "the true Man," in turn sustained by "an universal Poetic Genius," in the manner of Yeats's *Anima Mundi* (*All Religions are One*). From a Humean scepticism in which man is denied knowledge in any real sense, we move to a theory of the Divine Imagination in which man knows not nothing but all.

In themselves the senses are not to be disregarded but, rather, used correctly. Man is deceived when he sees "with not thro the Eye" (*EG*, 52–54, l. 104). For Blake there was no dichotomy of body and soul, subject and object, since the body was simply a part of the more vital soul. The object's existence depends upon the subject. Consequently, in *A Vision of the Last Judgment* he asserts a Berkeleyan idealism: "Mental Things are alone Real what is Calld Corporeal Nobody Knows of its dwelling Place it is in Fallacy & its Existence an Imposture Where is the Existence Out of Mind or Thought Where is it but in the Mind of a Fool" (94). Nor does he hold back from the logical conclusion: to renounce the vegetable world, in much the manner of Swedenborg, as "the Dirt upon my feet No part of Me" (95). Blake is not promoting an ascetic self-denial; rather than renunciation, he seeks the transformation of the physical world. His transcendentalism is not other-worldly but directs us to the kingdom of God which is within us all at all times, a

potentiality to be divine which we must learn to culti-
vate. "What it will be Questiond When the Sun rises
do you not see a round Disk of fire somewhat like a
Guinea O no no I see an Innumerable company of the
Heavenly host crying Holy Holy Holy is the Lord God
Almighty I question not my Corporeal or Vegetative
Eye any more than I would Question a Window con-
cerning a Sight I look thro it & not with it" (95).

In looking through the eye, Blake's vision blossoms
in such a way as to enable the self to perceive a radically different world, no longer bounded by the physical nature but in its true essence, infinite and holy.
The expanding world works at the same time in the
opposite direction: it enables the self to recognize the
Minute Particular, the unique individuality, the *quid-
ditas* of things. Blake had little time for Nature,
whether landscape, material reality, or Earth Mother.
A true city-dweller, he asserted, "Where man is not
nature is barren" (*MHH*, 10: 68). Commenting in
marginalia on Wordsworth's *Poems* (1815), Blake
wrote, "Natural Objects always did & now do Weaken
deaden & obliterate Imagination in Me" (E, p. 655).
And in the light of the intrinsically social nature of
his myth, it is characteristic and appropriate that the
myth centres on the building of the cities of Golgonooza and Jerusalem.

However, when the creative mind is brought to bear
on the Minute Particular (the infant child, grain of
sand, thistle, worm, or clod of clay), the Particular
expands to include all eternity. Hence, in *Milton* Blake
proclaims gleefully the timeless moment, or what
might conceivably be called a temporal particular:
"There is a Moment in each Day that Satan cannot
find" (35: 42), a moment of inspiration when the poet's
work is done (29: 1–3), when all time is coexistent in
"the Eternal Now" (E, p. 581). Similarly, he speaks of
a spatial moment, a paradoxical term since space, like
time, is illusory (Ulro). Such a space "opens / Into

Eternity of which this vegetable Earth is but a shadow" (*M*, 29: 21-22). In a note on Berkeley's *Siris*, Blake commented thus upon both the visionary and the particular character of the world: "Harmony [and] Proportion are Qualities & Not Things The Harmony & Proportion of a Horse are not the same with those of a Bull Every Thing has its own Harmony & Proportion Two Inferior Qualities in it For its Reality is Its Imaginative Form" (E, p. 653). Again, "deduct from a rose its redness, from a lilly its whiteness from a diamond its hardness from a spunge its softness from an oak its heighth from a daisy its lowness & rectify every thing in Nature as the Philosophers do. & then we shall return to Chaos & God will be compelld to be Excentric if he Creates O happy Philosopher" (E, pp. 584–85). "General Knowledge is Remote Knowledge it is in Particulars that Wisdom consists & Happiness too" (*VLJ*, 82). The eighteenth century, however, with its elevation of the worst abstractions (God, Man, and Nature), relied heavily upon generalization. In answer to Burke's praise of Sir Joshua Reynolds as a great generalizer and his elevation of "this disposition to abstractions" as "the great glory of the human mind," Blake retorted, "To Generalize is to be an Idiot To Particularize is the Alone Distinction of Merit—General Knowledges are those Knowledges that Idiots possess" (E, p. 630).

At times Blake's position takes on an extreme subjectivism: "Every Mans Wisdom is peculiar to his own Individuality" (*M*, 4: 8). In fact, the object and its qualities are dependent upon the degree of integration attained by the perceiving self; the greater the integration, the more complete is our knowledge of the object. "Every Eye Sees differently As the Eye—Such the Object" (E, p. 634); "The Suns Light when he unfolds it / Depends on the Organ that beholds it" (*GP*, frontis.). All knowledge then derives from mental experience, a conclusion which does not preclude sense experience, since the senses are merely organs of the mind. "Man has no Body distinct from his Soul for that calld Body is a portion of Soul discernd by the five Senses, the chief inlets of Soul in this age" (*MHH*, 4). Such Berkeleyan-Spinozan idealism reconciles the dichotomies of subject and object and of mind and body in a way Locke failed to do. For vision depends upon the self's integration, in turn achieved by way of vision or imagination. Such a mind, enlightened by imagination, will realize that perception involves self-development, that knowledge of objects alters the nature of the self in a movement of progression. As much as Wordsworth, Coleridge, or Keats, Blake stresses the interaction of subject and object and the subsequent effects upon both agents. The process is equally crucial to Carlyle, whose Teufelsdröckh learns "that this so solid-seeming World . . . were but an air-image, our ME the only reality: and Nature, with its thousandfold production and destruction, but the reflex of our own inward Force, the 'phantasy of our Dream'" (*SR*, 43). Like Blake, Carlyle could learn from the creative self and the dialectical nature of the world and Force that what we see depends upon what we are. Similarly, Lawrence in his essay "On Being a Man" (1924) offered a subjectivism derived from Berkeleyan epistemology: "To this known me, everything exists as a term of knowledge. A man is what I know he is. England is what I know it to be. I am what I know I am. And Bishop Berkeley is absolutely right: things only exist in our own consciousness."[9]

While Blake rejected the Age of Analysis and the corresponding faith in the externality of the world, his antagonism to Locke and Newton, though very real, was not negative. His position indeed is again close to that of Carlyle, Lawrence, and Yeats. He attacked not

9. D. H. Lawrence, *Phoenix II: Uncollected, Unpublished, and Other Prose Works*, ed. Warren Roberts and Harry T. Moore (New York: Viking, 1968), p. 617; hereafter cited in the text as *Ph. II*, followed by the page reference.

reason, science, or the senses per se, but their misuse. The scientist and empiricist elevated reason and memory to undeserved positions of authority and, to a corresponding degree, excluded the imagination. Blake may pray to be kept "From Single vision & Newtons sleep" (E, p. 693), but total exclusion of the intellect would bring as radical a disintegration as that of the scientist. Blake is no more an anti-intellectual than he is a Luddite, for imagination is not necessarily antithetical to intellect. Integration went further, to include all four faculties—the Four Zoas of intellect, feeling, senses, and imagination—working in harmony. Blake may describe empirical modes in terms of mechanism, but on the other hand he did not oppose machines in themselves. There are wheels in Eden too, but they differ in operation from those of Newton and Locke which move by "compulsion" (*J*, 15: 17–20). They move "in harmony & peace," Blake's positive virtues.

2

Blake's conception of the eighteenth-century universe of death takes in his poems the form of the fearful, cranking mechanism which is Ulro. But with the restoration of the Golden Age comes the defeat of the Gods of Priam, and the instruments of war are converted into instruments of peace and agricultural pursuits. The world reverberates with "The noise of rural work" (*FZ*, IX, 124: 14), with loaded wagons, ploughing, harvesting, and the sports of children. The regenerated society finds its simplest expression, as foreshadowed in the *Songs of Innocence* (1789), in that recurrent Romantic archetypal image, the resonant landscape.

Just as Wordsworth has his boy hallooing to the hills or mimicking hootings to the midnight owls, so Blake places his innocent children on the echoing green:

The Sun does arise,
And make happy the skies.
The merry bells ring
To welcome the Spring.
The sky-lark and thrush,
The birds of the bush,
Sing louder around,
To the bells chearful sound.
While our sports shall be seen
On the Ecchoing Green.

("The Ecchoing Green")

The jubilation is shared by the entire universe known to the children: from the sunrise and the sky's happiness to the church bells pealing in the spring and the birds' joyful response. The limits of day are filled with innocent delight and careless rapture, in which one element corresponds with another, heaven and earth in divine harmony. Out of such harmony comes the music with which the world echoes.

But such responsiveness is not limited to the non-human or the infantile levels of existence; the aged too, in a considerable leap of faith and love, can understand empathically the participation of all things (sun, sky, bird, child, and green) in this jubilee. Even "Old John with white hair / Does laugh away care," sitting under an oak which Experience will pervert into a Druidic emblem. The old folk congregate and commune more than communicate, not only among themselves and certainly not in divisive envy, but at a level in which they become as children once more—a preparation indeed for entrance into heaven. Such a world is not unnaturally idyllic—Tennyson's Lotus-land in which it was always afternoon—but subject to the temptations of the temporal cycle. The sun will descend and a natural self-imposed discipline will indicate to the children that they need to rest and seek protection. "Excess of joy weeps," Blake says in *The*

Marriage of Heaven and Hell (8: 26); here the little
ones merely tire and "No more can be merry." But
their world does not cease to be founded upon the
relationship or reverberation of another kind. Even the
womblike images of maternal laps and nest continue
the sensation of concentricity:

> Round the laps of their mothers,
> Many sisters and brothers,
> Like birds in their nest,
> Are ready for rest;
> And sport no more seen,
> On the darkening Green.

The encroaching night—another image of feminine
embrace—is only a temporary respite, a necessary
breathing space, to proceed with more "sport" and
further experience and celebration of this universe of
joy. In a less responsive environment, night would be
dreaded and baulked at; here it is accepted as necessary for rest and sleep. Besides, the innocent child is
almost as aware of the divine reality while asleep as
when awake: in both cases it exists on a subconscious
or thoughtless level of existence. At nighttime comes
the protection of the child by its mother ("A Cradle
Song") and the reciprocal relationship extends, as always, from child and mother to God. For the principle
of reciprocity is captured in the very descent of Christ
into the world, becoming a child as we are that we
might be like him. In dreams too the child learns of
the nature of that relationship, whether he be the
enslaved chimney sweep "lock'd up in coffins of black"
and released by the Angel to "wash in a river and shine
in the Sun" ("The Chimney Sweeper"), or the infant
dreamer (also in an "Angel-guarded bed") who learns
of the need for pity and love, as well as of the protec-
tiveness of God and mother, in the allegory of the
emmet and glowworm ("A Dream").

Precisely these characteristics or elements—the nighttime situation, the angelic guard, the mother-God protection of the infant joy, and the all-embracing concentricity of selves transforming or humanizing all things—are present in "Night," a song of Innocence. Over the entire situation presides not the burning fiery sun of "The Ecchoing Green" but the soft bosomy moon, an embryonic Beulah state which is the penultimate stage in the soul's ascent to God. In the course of this six-stanza lyric the point of view shifts from that of the "I" (presumably a child), who recognizes the necessity on his part to correspond to the natural cycle of day-night, sun-moon, to that of the lion, symbol of destructiveness and wrath. As the sun sets and birds return to their nests for the necessary rest and peace of Beulah, so too must the child. Again, the lack of any childlike reluctance is the result not only of the self-imposed discipline but of the speaker's awareness that the correspondence of God and child will not cease with the advent of darkness, and that nighttime, while restful, can still effect change or spiritual regeneration. The moon is "like a flower"; the skies are imaged in an equally organic state ("heavens high bower"); while "The feet of angels bright" continue to move, though silently and unseen, through the world.

> Unseen they pour blessing,
> And joy without ceasing,
> On each bud and blossom,
> And each sleeping bosom.

Blake's technique—the metrical change from the iambic to the anapaestic in lines 5–8 of each stanza, the reduction in accented syllables, and the shift from a masculine to a feminine rhyme—supports the impression of continued movement. Night, at the level of innocence, does not bring stasis, petrification, or stonification.

Not only is innocence a state through which the self must pass—as Thel and Oothoon to varying degrees learn—but within the very world of the child are the threats and temptations of experience. For this is what is indicated by "The Chimney Sweeper," "The Little Boy Lost" and "Little Boy Found," "A Dream," "On Another's Sorrow," and "Holy Thursday." And it is this which distinguishes the vicariousness (or "Negative Capability," as Keats called it) of the several adults (Old John, the mother, the nurse, the shepherd). Likewise, in "Night" the angels protect, first by visiting bird, beast, and child and offering love and comfort where needed, changing weeping to sleeping; but second by adopting various tactics in the face of destructive wild animals. The destructive element is manipulated so as to become a benevolent force, and angelic intervention receives the mild spirits of the sheep, which experience an apotheosis to a new and better world. Somewhat inevitably, the Edenic allows both lamb and lion to lie down together, while the lion's superior strength and force are applied now not to destruction but protection. Interestingly enough, the point of view shifts to the lion who proceeds to speak the last twelve lines of the poem. The shift is calculated and significant, for the lion has learnt love and practises it. It has learnt through the symbolic lamb of the Christ who effects the regeneration the poem itself expresses. And the all-embracing leonine view incorporates all—lamb, lion, Christ, and also the child with which the poem began—in what the lion calls "our immortal day." Night, significantly enough, has been transformed into eternal day.

The very fact that night can be beneficial in innocence, while on most other occasions belonging to the category of experience and evil, is evidence of other relevant aspects of Blake's vision: that we misread

Blake if we assume that certain images or states are intrinsically good or bad, for such intrinsicality denies change and organic growth; that we misread Blake also if we fail to appreciate point of view; that both change and point of view are the inevitable consequence of the principle of multiplicity; and finally, that in a sort of perversely logical way, even the interdependence of this argument evidences the interdependence of all things which the poem itself illustrates.

The vision of the innocent is as yet unaffected by the Fall. But Blake did not stop with the *Songs of Innocence*. He recognized the existence of the Fall, of the present disintegration of man and the strife between men. Moreover, he recognized the inadequacy of the state of innocence. It was impossible to remain a child; among the forces of experience it was difficult to retain the divine vision. Blake wanted no retreat into an idyllic world, no dreaming of an enchanted existence out of time and out of mind, protected from the ravages of existence, the nagging pains and frustrations of birth, copulation, and death. At no point does Blake withdraw or evade; his transcendentalism is always more real than the delusion we call existence within time and space. Not only was it impossible to remain a child, it was even undesirable. He wished for no Peter Pan escapism but saw the value in experience. Innocence untempered by experience is unorganized; experience divorced from innocence is evil and spiritual death; organized innocence is that perfection of self which resolves the antitheses of innocence and experience in a state superior to both and arrived at by that "Mental Fight" he later explored in more detail in the Prophetic Books.

The *Songs of Innocence* sing of the golden state of the child, where freedom and love, instinct and imagination, operate in a world of light and peace, gentleness and love. Hence the two-day-old infant in "Infant Joy" epitomizes a level of subconscious existence which denies, because it precedes, conflict. In antithesis to the Cartesian *cogito, ergo sum,* the child's essential self is of a different nature: "I happy am." Its name, Joy, is that inexplicable—because expansive and organic—power a child possesses inherently: it involves that sense of uniqueness and particularity denied by the mechanical and categorizing structure of the Newtonian universe. Consequently, the inarticulate new-born child is limited to statement of essentials and is played off against a well-meaning but more verbose adult. The adult's questioning and desire to categorize is enlightened, and eventually overcome, by his capacity to share in the child's joy and, like the little black boy, "be like him."[10]

There are poems in both *Innocence* and *Experience* which embrace or contain the contraries rather than precede or transcend them. "The Blossom" is Blake's version of the dual nature of love, which can be both energetic and humble, selfish and selfless, centripetal and centrifugal. Here we are given, by way of the sparrow and robin (appropriately imagery of the nursery) the two states of love—passion and compassion—in both of which is fulfilment. The blossom is happy, free from conflict, capable of growth and fruition, accepting both loves but preferring neither the one nor the other. The sparrow, traditionally a symbol of lechery, is aggressive, energetic in his search for satisfaction. Like an arrow of desire, Cupid's arrow, he seeks rest in the sexual as well as maternal "cradle narrow." The robin, on the other hand, reflects a passive love and is, in "Who Killed Cock Robin?," capable of being killed by the sparrow. When the north wind doth blow, he can only go live in a barn to keep himself warm, and hide himself under his wing, poor thing! An entire range

10. I am indebted in my interpretation of both "Infant Joy" and "The Blossom" to John F. Danby, *The Simple Wordsworth: Studies in the Poems, 1797–1807* (London: Routledge and Kegan Paul, 1960), pp. 21–22, 26–29.

of attitudes distinguishes merriment (sparrow) from prettiness (robin). And the robin's love suffers; he sobs in search of sympathy and compassion. Blake withholds any real show of preference; in both cases there are the means to fulfilment. Nor is it for the reader to choose, since choice would limit the inclusiveness of vision.

Similarly, in *Experience*, the companion piece is "The Clod & the Pebble." Love can consist of the humble, passive, unresisting selflessness of the lowly clod of clay, trodden incessantly by the cattle, taking its form from outside forces, or the antithetical pebble, hard and cold, self-sufficient, stony, active and resistant, a self-assertive and possessive love. Once more choice is withheld. Blake intends us to be more aware of the multiple nature of existence, of the war of contraries as the basis for continued existence and for any evolution.

While the *Songs of Experience* (1794) differ radically from those of *Innocence*, with bard replacing piper, old age substituted for childlike innocence, jealous and selfish paternalism with its petty tyrannies and authoritarianism instead of the humane liberalism of Innocence's adults, we would be wrong to conclude that Blake's dialectic is a simple either-or. Certainly, from the golden pastoralism of innocence, which is all freshness and joy, colour and growth, the self declines into experience, with its industrial imagery of mills, wheels, spindles and looms, nets of delusion and hatred, a state of bondage, misery, and repression, where love is lost and men are reduced to the status of things. Science and exclusive reliance upon intellect work hand in hand with authoritarianism and repressive religions to fashion existence in the new image—no longer the Divine Image but the Human Abstract. The state of experience, however, is not without its enlightenment. Not always are the parents so undiscerning as those in "A Little Boy Lost" or "A Little Girl Lost." Not always is the innocent vision unheeded. Innocence precedes conflict; the new synthesis Blake sought was one in which innocence comes to terms with experience. He prepares us for precisely this progression in a pair of poems, "The Little Girl Lost" and "The Little Girl Found." The child tames the tygers of experience and, in her superior organized innocence, leads her parents to a similar position. Blake later named this state Beulah, the threefold vision—often a trinity achieved through sexual love, the Sexual Threefold—which is the prelude to the final harmony, the fourfold Jerusalem. The parents are thus led along the same progression, from desert to garden, from woe to joy. However, their resting place is still only "a lonely dell," a long way from the golden city of Jerusalem. And, just as likely, the dialectic remains at work. As the child's innocence has been denied by its father, so too will the father be crucified by the child—an endless Heraclitean war of antinomies.

Blake's problem then was to point a way out of this dreadful cyclism. Once more experience offers the solution; once more we must admire Blake's terrifying honesty.[11] Just as he was capable of seeing the range and ambivalence of love—whether it be the humble clod of clay, the self-loving pebble, the aggressive sparrow, or the pretty robin—so too there is considerable ambiguity in the tyger. "The Tyger" is clearly the companion piece to "The Lamb," its antithesis. Yet to concentrate only on the delight of the lamb and to overlook the dynamic energy of the tyger is to fail to appreciate the inclusiveness of Blake's vision. Certainly the tyger is experience in its fearful and destructive essence. The industrial imagery of furnace, anvil, hammer, and chain also points in the direction of mecha-

11. T. S. Eliot, *Sacred Wood*, p. 151: Blake's poetry has "a peculiar honesty, which, in a world too frightened to be honest, is peculiarly terrifying."

nism rather than organic growth. Yet the dialectic, as Blake notes in *The Marriage of Heaven and Hell* (16–17), involves "the Devouring" as well as "the Prolific." To those who would associate God only with the Prolific he answered, "God only Acts & Is, in existing beings or Men"; these two forces are enemies and "whoever tries to reconcile them seeks to destroy existence." Blake's Christ came to announce "Mental Fight": "I came not to send Peace but a Sword." The point was not lost upon Yeats later and we find a similar position adopted by Carlyle in his estimate of Cromwell.[12] To concentrate upon one force alone is to take "portions of existence and [fancy] . . . that the whole." The tyger—Blake's spelling must be retained to capture the heightened ferocity and destructiveness inherent in the misspelling—possesses a "fearful symmetry." It is capable of "burning bright, / In the forests of the night." The question "Did he who made the Lamb make thee?" is not wholly incredulous. Blake directs us precisely to that energy and reliance upon impulse he associated with Christ: "no virtue can exist without breaking [the] . . . ten commandments" (*MHH*, 23). Likewise, in *The Everlasting Gospel*, one of the last poetic works, his Christ is one of energy as well as the New Testament forgiver of sins, a Christ who hates cant and hypocrisy, whose only humility is to God. And even this God denied him, since that humility humbled both God and man.

 Humility is only doubt
 And does the Sun & Moon blot out

12. Carlyle, *OC*, II, 63–64. The massacre at Drogheda was preferable to the "Rose-water" surgery which was the lesser alternative. Cromwell's Irish Campaign was directed against Satan, the Antichrist, Popery, and those forces which led to the 1641 massacre. Any Cromwellian massacre was thus just and fit retribution, while at the same time assuring that "there was no other storm or slaughter needed in that Country" (II, 64).

Rooting over with thorns & stems
The buried Soul & all its Gems.

(52–54, ll. 97–100)

The orthodox gentle Jesus, meek and mild—"Creeping Jesus"—Blake rejects scornfully, for such orthodoxy produces the laws of prudence and the snares of religious tyranny. Indeed, he denies Christ chastity and virgin birth. The two qualities, energy and forgiveness of sins, are not incompatible in his eyes. Christ is both Tyger and Lamb and, at times, like Milton, an unrestrained rebel against authority. Blake's own deliberate and ironic inversion of traditional values in *The Marriage of Heaven and Hell* emphasizes his break with orthodoxy. As such, "The tygers of wrath are wiser than the horses of instruction" (9: 44).

3

The vitalism central later to Carlyle, Yeats, and Lawrence is expressed most plainly in *The Marriage of Heaven and Hell* (1792–93). In its Swiftian irony and distinctive satiric mode, that work closely resembles Carlyle's *Sartor Resartus* and is as essential to its author's development as was *Sartor* to Carlyle. For both men satire became a vehicle of prophetic utterance. Likewise, the variety of concerns expressed in the *Marriage*—concepts like the infinite nature of existence, the creative self, the imagination, the rejection of materialism and rationalism, the divinity of man— all are central to Carlyle and *Sartor Resartus*. Above all, the unifying principle intrinsic to both works is a faith in energy, or Force. The source of those errors enshrouding man in doubt and darkness is the restraint, whatever its form, placed upon energy. The Voice of the Devil makes it abundantly clear that the codification of good into a religion or collection of moral laws results only in error—the division of man into body and soul; the evil nature of energy which is to be renounced; the source of good as reason, the soul; eternal damnation as the punishment reserved for the pursuers of energy. Blake's contraries assert the very opposite: "Energy is Eternal Delight" (4). The scapegoat once more is the rational faculty, the usurpation of the self lacking in energy:

> Those who restrain desire, do so because theirs is weak enough to be restrained; and the restrainer or reason usurps its place & governs the unwilling.
> And being restraind it by degrees becomes passive till it is only the shadow of desire.
>
>   (5)

The "Proverbs of Hell" expand this position: "The road of excess leads to the palace of wisdom"; "Prudence is a rich ugly old maid courted by Incapacity"; "He who desires but acts not, breeds pestilence"; "Prisons are built with stones of Law, Brothels with bricks of Religion." The instances are endless and sometimes deliberately shocking: "Sooner murder an infant in its cradle than nurse unacted desires." The conclusion is constant: repression whatever its form is spiritual death. "One Law for the Lion & Ox is Oppression" (24).

The *Marriage* ends with "A Song of Liberty" in which the political interpretation of man's Fall and Redemption is given fuller expression than hitherto in Blake's work. It was to the political sphere that he was tempted in *The French Revolution* (1791) and *America* (1793), though with the cancelled plates of *America* and the more private mythology of *Europe* (1794) and succeeding prophecies of 1794–95 (*The Song of Los, The [First] Book of Urizen, The Book of Ahania*, and *The Book of Los*) Blake turned increasingly away from the political to the cosmological interpretations of his myth. This is not to argue that Blake lost heart or became apolitical, though it may be he was responding to the particularly oppressive censorship in the England of the nineties. A more satisfying argument has recently been put forward: that Blake's position was untenable "while the poet-magician remained mystically harnessed to the actual revolutionary movements of his time. Los demands the apocalyptic: Pitt, Napoleon, and George III manifestly do not provide it. Even a magician has to show results."[13] But, in the last resort, Blake's myth with its multiple levels of interpretation retained always a political relevance, in the same way that his treatment of the French and American revolutions transcended the exclusively political.

It is precisely this supra-political relevance which is paralleled in Carlyle. Blake viewed the French Revolution in much the same light as Carlyle—as a transcendental phenomenon, a divine revelation, in which men broke out of their chains and walked freely once more in the light of day. Similarly, as expressed in *America*, if the American rebels ("Washington Franklin Paine & Warren Allen Gates & Lee," 14: 2) had failed, the eternal vision would have been diminished:

Then had America been lost, o'erwhelm'd by the Atlantic,
And Earth had lost another portion of the infinite,

(14: 17–18)

Carlyle, writing with one eye on the French Revolution and the other on the Chartists and Hungry Forties, could not allow himself such a thoroughgoing enthusiasm. Nevertheless, the Revolution did epitomize for Carlyle the emergence of the hero and the throwing off of sham ideals and values. Likewise, in Blake, the

13. Harold Fisch, "Blake's Miltonic Moment," in *William Blake: Essays for S. Foster Damon*, ed. Alvin H. Rosenfeld (Providence: Brown Univ. Press, 1969), p. 42.

revolutionary figures—whether Washington or Lafay-
ette, the Duke of Orleans or the mythological Orc—are
capable of greatness insofar as they express the eternal
vision or are members of the human form divine.

With these parallel views Blake and Carlyle share
other fundamental principles in their conception of
history. For both men history reveals a divine purpose,
a teleology most clearly evinced in great men and their
acts. Hence, biography and action are crucial elements
in any historical interpretation. Historical phenomena
are the energetic or vital expression of great men in
a world of action. For both Blake and Carlyle the physical action and the mental world were not divorced but
united in heroic man in the single expression. Yeats
takes up the argument later to justify his heroic figures—"A great man in his pride" ("Death") knows
what Yeats urges upon contemporary Ireland:

> . . . that when all words are said
> And a man is fighting mad,
> Something drops from eyes long blind,
> He completes his partial mind,
> For an instant stands at ease,
> Laughs aloud, his heart at peace.
>
> ("Under Ben Bulben," ll. 27–32)

One essential distinction must be drawn here: Yeats's
lines come precariously close to preferring action to
mere words. Despite his recurrent insistence upon the
power of words and the importance of the poet, there
was, as Dr. Bronowski has argued, an anti-intellectual
element and an anti-poetic stance in Yeats, to be found
earlier in Carlyle.[14] Like Yeats, Carlyle preferred the
doer, the heroic man capable of physical action, to an
extent unparalleled in Blake. Unlike either Carlyle or

14. J. Bronowski, *The Poet's Defence* (Cambridge: C.U.P., 1939),
    p. 252.

Yeats, Blake had no second thoughts about his occupation as poet-engraver, whereas both later writers express a constant re-examining of personal choice and see the aesthetic and the worldly physical as antinomies. Blake was, in Samuel Palmer's words, "a man without a mask."[15]

All three writers focus upon the dramatic aspects of their respective revolutions and manipulate the historical events to coincide with their preconceived notions or symbolic purposes. Just as Yeats prefers to concentrate upon the Easter martyrs' heroic indifference to their own safety or upon the individual action epitomizing the whole movement of events, so too Blake and Carlyle treat the events of the French Revolution with less than purely historical faithfulness. Blake telescopes the action of several months into the scope of one day and invents fictitious figures (the Duke of Burgundy, "Earl of Borgogne," "Bourbon's strong Duke," and "Duke of Bretagne"). Carlyle too saw the events as part of a cosmic drama, focusing upon the dramatis personae and providing a dramatic interpretation of the interplay of figures. Moreover, their essentially Hebraic tone, indebted to a common schooling in the Bible, and even their common imagery are remarkably similar. In just the same way that Carlyle seizes upon the decadent foppery of the French nobles under Louis XVI (like that of the English nobles under Charles I or of the tailored dandies of the 1830s and '40s), so too among his villains Blake includes the "curl'd veterans." The Orc figure is that characteristic Romantic phenomenon, "the new born fire" complete with "flaming hair," who sends dismay into the breasts of the French nobles and King. Hence, in "A Song of Liberty" at the conclusion of *The Marriage*, "the jealous king" is surrounded by "his grey brow'd councellors, thunderous

15. Alexander Gilchrist, *The Life of William Blake* (London and Cambridge, 1863), I, 319.

warriors, curl'd veterans" (25: 15). The moment, however, is ripe for the genuine and vital, those souls who
are far-seeing and just and invincible because their
vision and sincerity correspond with the Divine Truth.
Macrocosm and microcosm interact in such men and
the Word is made flesh once more. The Countenance
Divine shines forth upon these clouded hills, though
Blake never allows his essential optimism in the in-
vincibility of the Divine Imagination to decline into
the more simplistic identification of might and right.
Carlyle was less able to resist the temptation of that
logic. Darkness and tyranny are overthrown in an
apocalyptic emergence of the heroic and vital, and the
rhetoric of both Blake and Carlyle is used to convey
precisely this state. Blake shared Carlyle's desire to
purge the writing of history of its dry-as-dust myopia.
The Bible, after all, is history and "Antiquity preaches
the Gospel of Jesus." "The reasoning historian," on the
other hand, that "turner and twister of causes and
consequences," fails to recognize with Blake and
Carlyle that "Acts themselves alone are history" (*DC*,
p. 44). Both men have prepared themselves for the
historian's objections: in Blake's words, "His opinions,
who does not see spiritual agency, is not worth any
man's reading; he who rejects a fact because it is im-
probable, must reject all History and retain doubts
only" (*DC*, p. 45).

4

What *The French Revolution* and "A Song of Liberty"
express on a political level is the triumph of vitalism
or energy over Empire or tyrannical restraint. But political liberation coincides in Blake's myth with psychological liberation also. And two of his finest minor
prophecies, *The Book of Thel* (1789–91) and *Visions
of the Daughters of Albion* (1793), concentrate upon
the psychological aspect of energy and freedom from

restraint, and thus resemble more closely not the work of Carlyle, but more particularly certain principles of Yeats and especially of D. H. Lawrence.

Thel, for example, living in some pre-existential state, attempts to escape from the mortal life which is her destiny. Disturbed by the idea of impermanence even in her present life, "she in paleness sought the secret air" (1: 2). She prefers to live in a dream world, "Like a reflection in a glass. like shadows in the water" (1: 9), to evade responsibilities and the pains of existence. Her dream is of a Keatsian indolence and ease, a swooning into death—"And gentle sleep the sleep of death" (1: 13). At various stages in the poem, however, she is confronted with a superior wisdom, provided by lowly creatures—the lily of the field, the cloud, the worm, and the clod of clay. Each reveals the infinitude of existence and the need for selflessness. Annihilation of self takes the form of both compassion and passion: the giving of self in compassion for others, that others may live; or the offering of self in the sexual act. The cloud, like the other creatures, informs her: "every thing that lives, / Lives not alone, nor for itself" (3: 26–27). Eventually led to a position where she is capable of experiencing a vision of her future mortal state, she can do nothing but retreat, shrieking in horror from the knowledge of her own sexual and spiritual deaths. The prospect is too much for her and she flees back to her original state, one of selfish virginity, exclusive in her self-love and shameful fears.[16] The final lines devoted to the voice from Thel's grave are full of energy, or Force, depicting the dynamic strength of at least four senses—ear, eye, tongue, nostril—though the fifth, touch, which has most bearing upon sexu-

16. I cannot accept John Beer's interpretation of Thel as possessed of "full adventurousness" and a "desire to face the minute particulars of human existence as well as the sublimities of eternal life." *Blake's Visionary Universe* (Manchester: Manchester Univ. Press, 1969), p. 72.

ality, proves the most terrifying and distasteful to the
virgin Thel.

The poem describes the failure of self to move from
unenlightened innocence to experience, and in Thel's
selfish retention of virginity and her inability to give
herself, whether sexually or spiritually, to anyone or
anything else, she resembles those frequent Lawrence
females who exercise what Blake called "Female Will."
Like Miriam in *Sons and Lovers*, she wants only to
possess and not to give of herself. Thel is in what
Lawrence called "The State of Funk" (*Ph. II*, pp.
565–70). And he was as certain as Blake that such fear
(or funk), which represses the natural flow and vital
contact of one being with another, is not living but
is a living death, reduced like Thel to nonentity. In
his essay "We Need One Another," Lawrence argued:

> It is in relationship to one another that they [men and
> women] have their true individuality and their distinct
> being: in contact, not out of contact. This is sex, if you
> like. But it is no more sex than sunshine on the grass is
> sex. It is a living contact, give and take: the great and subtle
> relationship of men and women, man and woman. In this
> and through this we become real individuals, without it,
> without the real contact, we remain more or less non-
> entities.[17]

Thel fears such contact and individuality, fleeing from
the vision of give and take, which appears in her eyes
merely destructive.

The progression towards contact and relationship is
made, however, by Oothoon in *Visions of the Daughters of Albion*. Blake's imagery gains strength and complexity in this poem while also becoming increasingly

17. *Phoenix: The Posthumous Papers of D. H. Lawrence* (1936),
    ed. Edward D. McDonald (reissued New York: Viking, 1968),
    p. 191; hereafter cited in the text as *Ph*, followed by the page
    reference.

private. Oothoon, whose name may be derived from Ossian's heroine Oithona,[18] is "the soft soul of America" (1: 3), so indicating a political level increasingly reduced as the poem was finally formed. Moving out of the vales of Leutha—surely with overtones of Lethe—and capable of exercising her desire in the plucking of the nymph-flower, Oothoon loves Theotormon, whose name suggests Blake's fondness for playing upon names. For he is tormented by God or, more exactly, by theology or false gods. Meanwhile, Oothoon is raped by Bromion, a Urizenic figure representing Reason and, on the political level, George III. Thrust forth as a harlot upon her lover, Theotormon, she suffers considerably from his jealousy and rage. Theotormon retreats to Bromion's caves, divided within himself and divorced in hatred from Oothoon, who does not share his mental state. Retaining her innocence, now enlarged by experience, she calls on her lover to share her expanded vision:

> Arise my Theotormon I am pure.
> Because the night is gone that clos'd me in its deadly black.
> They told me that the night & day were all that I
>   could see;
> They told me that I had five senses to inclose me up.
> And they inclos'd my infinite brain into a narrow circle.
> And sunk my heart into the Abyss, a red round globe
>   hot burning
> Till all from life I was obliterated and erased.
>
>   (2: 28–34)

Her wisdom is that of the creatures in *The Book of Thel*: "How can I be defild when I reflect thy image pure? / Sweetest the fruit that the worm feeds on. and the soul prey'd on by woe" (3: 16–17). Bromion's in-

18. See S. Foster Damon, *A Blake Dictionary* (Providence: Brown Univ. Press, 1965), p. 309.

terruption points in the opposite direction, a deliberate
reversal of her position (4: 13–24). Instead, Oothoon in
her lamentation offers a vision of the Minute Particular
and its infinitude. She rightly condemns Bromion's
repressive philosophy as justifying tyranny, whether
sexual, political, or spiritual, and exclaims excitedly of
"happy copulation":

> The moment of desire! the moment of desire! The
>   virgin
> That pines for man; shall awaken her womb to enormous
>   joys
> In the secret shadows of her chamber; the youth shut
>   up from
> The lustful joy. shall forget to generate. & create an
>   amorous image
> In the shadows of his curtains and in the folds of his
>   silent pillow.
> Are not these the places of religion? the rewards of
>   continence?
> The self enjoyings of self denial? Why dost thou
>   seek religion?
> Is it because acts are not lovely, that thou seekest solitude,
> Where the horrible darkness is impressed with reflections
>   of desire.
>
> . . . .
>
> I cry, Love! Love! Love! happy happy Love! free as the
>   mountain wind!
>
> > (7: 3–11, 16)

Her vision of a sexual paradise "In lovely copulation
bliss on bliss" (7: 26) is reminiscent of Yeats's "News
for the Delphic Oracle," but Yeats's irony is not shared
by Blake. A closer parallel, even down to the condemnation of masturbation, is to be found in Lawrence,
the parallel extending also to biblical tone and language. For Lawrence, "the deepest of all communions,"

which gives rise to "the mystic marriage," is achieved through the sexual act, a truth shared by all religions. Like Blake, Lawrence would appreciate the fundamental oneness of all religions: "this Communion, this touching on one another of the two rivers, Euphrates and Tigris—to use old jargon—and the enclosing of the land of Mesopotamia, where Paradise was, or the Park of Eden, where man had his beginning. This is marriage, this circuit of the two rivers, this communion of the two blood-streams, this, and nothing else: as all the religions know" (*Ph. II*, p. 506).

However, Oothoon's "heaven of generous love," the "expansion" of which she sings, is rejected by the closed self Theotormon has made of himself. And the poem ends with Theotormon sitting beside a "margind ocean," suitably limited by the horizon (margin) in a diminished (marginal) world. There is nothing closer to Lawrence in the whole of Blake than *Visions of the Daughters of Albion*.

5

The fullest expression of Blake's vision is in his Prophetic Books, of which I shall consider only *Milton* (1804), the shortest, most compact, and most "finished" of the three major prophecies. It is also the most obviously autobiographical and seems to have been born out of Blake's three-year stay at Felpham (1800–1803); his relationship with William Hayley, his patron; his emergence from despair, and the throwing off of that spectre which had tormented him for some twenty years. Blake's letters over these years record the spiritual struggle dramatized in *Milton*.[19]

19. As Erdman argues in his textual notes, "In letters of April and July 1803 Blake declares that he has in the previous 'three years composed an immense number of verses' descriptive of his 'Spiritual Acts' during those years—an account that fits *Milton* better than *Vala* or *Jerusalem*" (E, p. 727).

To his friend Thomas Butts (22 November 1802) he confided:

> Tho I have been very unhappy I am so no longer I am again Emerged into the light of Day I still & shall to Eternity Embrace Christianity and Adore him who is the Express image of God but I have traveld thro Perils & Darkness not unlike a Champion I have Conquerd and shall still Go on Conquering Nothing can withstand the fury of my Course among the Stars of God & in the Abysses of the Accuser My Enthusiasm is still what it was only Enlarged and confirmd. (E, p. 691)

Five months later (25 April 1803) to Butts he was more explicit in his desire to move back to London, away from Hayley's well-meant interference:

> I can alone carry on my visionary studies in London unannoyd & . . . I may converse with my friends in Eternity. See Visions, Dream Dreams, & prophecy & speak Parables unobserv'd & at liberty from the Doubts of other Mortals. perhaps Doubts proceeding from Kindness. but Doubts are always pernicious Especially when we Doubt our Friends Christ is very decided on this Point. "He who is Not With Me is Against Me" There is no Medium or Middle state & if a Man is the Enemy of my Spiritual Life while he pretends to be the Friend of my Corporeal. he is a Real Enemy—but the Man may be the friend of my Spiritual Life while he seems the Enemy of my Corporeal but Not Vice Versa.

However, in characteristic fashion, even these largely difficult years of exile had a "Grand [that is, a divine] Reason." With his "heart . . . full of futurity," Blake continued:

> But none can know the Spiritual Acts of my three years Slumber on the banks of the Ocean unless he has seen them in the Spirit or unless he should read My long Poem descriptive of those Acts for I have in these three years composed an immense number of verses on One Grand

Theme Similar to Homers Iliad or Miltons Paradise Lost the Persons & Machinery intirely new to the Inhabitants of Earth (some of the Persons Excepted) I have written this Poem from immediate Dictation twelve or sometimes twenty or thirty lines at a time without Premeditation & even against my Will. the Time it has taken in writing was thus renderd Non Existent. & an immense Poem Exists which seems to be the Labour of a long Life all producd without Labour or Study. I mention this to shew you what I think the Grand Reason of my being brought down here. (E, p. 697)

Further tribulation followed in the trial for sedition to which he became subjected, a charge which, if proved, would have meant the death penalty. In this matter at least, Hayley proved indispensable. And certainly it was to Hayley Blake wrote exultantly (23 October 1804) of his emergence from twenty years of darkness and ascribing blame to the spiritual deficiences of both himself and Catherine.

For now! O Glory! and O Delight! I have entirely reduced that spectrous Fiend to his station, whose annoyance has been the ruin of my labours for the last passed twenty years of my life. He is the enemy of conjugal love and is the Jupiter of the Greeks, an iron-hearted tyrant, the ruiner of ancient Greece. I speak with perfect confidence and certainty of the fact which has passed upon me. Nebuchadnezzar had seven times passed over him; I have had twenty; thank God I was not altogether a beast as he was; but I was a slave bound in a mill among beasts and devils; these beasts and these devils are now, together with myself, become children of light and liberty, and my feet and my wife's feet are free from fetters. O lovely Felpham, parent of Immortal Friendship, to thee I am eternally indebted for my three years' rest from perturbation and the strength I now enjoy. (E, pp. 702–3)

Six weeks later (4 December 1804) Hayley was again informed of Blake's triumph over his "Confusion of

Thought" and "Divided Existence" (E, p. 704). The
result was *Milton,* a poem which parallels *The Prelude*
in being equally the tracing of "The Growth of a Poet's
Mind,"[20] as book II, 36: 21–25, indicates:

> For when Los joind with me he took me in his firy
>   whirlwind
> My Vegetated portion was hurried from Lambeths shades
> He set me down in Felphams Vale & prepard a beautiful
> Cottage for me that in three years I might write all
>   these Visions
> To display Natures cruel holiness: the deceits of Natural
>   Religion.

Intended "To Justify the Ways of God to Men," as
the title page indicates in its quotation from *Paradise
Lost,* the poem is prefaced with a declaration against
those forces "who would if they could, for ever depress
Mental & prolong Corporeal War." In that category
Blake places the classical writers of Greece and Rome
(Homer, Ovid, Plato, and Cicero) and those unduly
"curbd" (Shakespeare and Milton). The alternative is
the Bible and the Imagination—"the Daughters of Inspiration" rather than "the Daughters of Memory."

20. Those parallels are clearer since M. H. Abrams, *Natural Super-
    naturalism.* His description of *The Prelude* as "a fully devel-
    oped poetic equivalent" (p. 74) of the *Bildungsroman* and
    Künstlerroman is equally applicable to *Milton.* Both works are
    in the Christian tradition of *peregrinatio* (p. 194) or "the
    distinctive Romantic genre of the *Bildungsgeschichte"* (p. 96).
    Likewise, both poems evidence indebtedness to *Paradise Lost;*
    depend upon "spots of time" (*Prelude,* XII, 208), as Bloom has
    argued (E, p. 840); and trace the renovation of the Imagination.
    Moreover, Coleridge serves as the traditional epic guide figure
    as does Milton in Blake's poem. The fundamental differences,
    however, are crucial: Wordsworth's insistence upon Nature,
    memory, suffering, fortitude, and fear as factors in the spiritual
    and imaginative regeneration is totally antithetical to Blake,
    just as his community of dalesmen and elevation of solitude
    are near-solipsistic compared to the City of Jerusalem.

Insisting upon "Mental Fight," Blake emphasizes the proper perspective the reader must adopt to what follows. The drama of Milton's descent to Blake and their mutual transformation into Jesus, the Divine Imagination, describes Blake's particular spiritual pilgrimage, his conversion to a Christological aesthetic, together with the means to redemption for all mankind. Blake also provides for the purging of Milton of the several errors he promoted. The Poet as Mental Prince is engaged in a mental drama or war resolved in Redemption. We find a similar symbolic use of war or conflict in Carlyle and Yeats, while all these authors likewise thought of man in Lawrence's terms as "a thought-adventurer" (*Ph. II*, p. 616).

Blake's rejection in the Preface of both "Greek or Roman Models" needs closer examination. While the broad conception of the myth, the particularities of imagery or symbol, the culmination of the heroic in the figure of Jesus, and even the language and style, are more peculiarly Hebraic and derived from Blake's reading of the Bible, nevertheless, we would underestimate his intention and achievement if we failed to appreciate the *epic* quality of the poem. Blake's letter to Butts (25 April 1803), already noted, specifies explicitly the epic nature of his model: *Milton* consists of "an immense number of verses on One Grand Theme Similar to Homers Iliad or Miltons Paradise Lost." Only in "the Persons & Machinery intirely new to the Inhabitants of Earth" is Blake diverging radically from his epic models, and with the dictation of spirits Blake was not inclined to argue for greater conformity. Besides, in a satiric verse in his notebook he records his divergence from Homer:

I am no Homers Hero you all know
I profess not Generosity to a Foe
My Generosity is to my Friends
That for their Friendship I may make amends.

The Generous to Enemies promotes their Ends
And becomes the Enemy & Betrayer of his Friends

(E, p. 493)

Similarly, in two prose pieces written perhaps in 1820, "On Homers Poetry" and "On Virgil," Blake vehemently opposes the classical Greek as promoter of wars and perverter of arts and sciences; the "Gothic" is the "Living Form" preferable to the Grecian "Mathematic Form," which is the product of "the Reasoning Memory" (E, p. 267).[21] Blake's preference finds its parallel in Yeats, who substitutes his own antithesis of Greek culture and Babylonian mathematical starlight and chooses Homer as his "example" ("Vacillation").

Blake's original intention was to develop his tale within the epic convention of twelve books. Although this was drastically reduced to two, certain epic conventions remain. Like all Blake's work but particularly the prophecies, the poem is public poetry, with all the solemnity of purpose and ceremonial ritual that accompany the traditional public and epic poem. For such is the stature and profound spiritual concern of his theme that the grandiose form is as necessary to that purpose as are the solid-looking lines and long paragraphs—"the march of long resounding strong heroic Verse" (*FZ*, I, 3: 2). The scope is cosmic, ranging from Heaven to earth and down to Hell itself, with great "panning" shots in time and space, over a six-

21. Despite Blake's antipathy, however, we know that he and Hayley were reading the *Iliad* at Felpham and through Hayley he learnt Greek there; that he contributed a portrait of Homer for Hayley's planned Felpham library; and that he engraved three of Flaxman's designs for the *Iliad*, published by Longmans in 1805. See G. E. Bentley, *Blake Records* (Oxford: Clarendon Press, 1969), pp. 69, 86, 89, 616. Kathleen Raine, "A Note on Blake's 'Unfettered Verse,'" in *William Blake*, ed. Rosenfeld, pp. 383–92, notes also Blake's use of Chapman's Homer.

thousand-year span (though temporal divisions are at best symbolic) and frequent focusing upon minute particulars, individual dramas, situations, scenes, or perspectives. The epic form makes upon the reader demands which he did not confront in the Songs and only to a lesser extent in the minor prophecies. As C. S. Lewis has argued, the reader of an epic must not expect " 'good lines'—little ebullient patches of delight—such as he is accustomed to find in lyrics." Rather, he must learn to appreciate "the continuity of a long narrative poem, the subordination of the line to the paragraph and the paragraph to the Book and even of the Book to the whole," together with "the grand sweeping effects that take a quarter of an hour to develop themselves." "To look for single, 'good' lines is like looking for single 'good' stones in a cathedral."[22]

Blake's reliance upon the epic form extends further: book I opens with the epic convention of an apostrophe to the Muses (here the Daughters of Beulah) to inspire him to sing suitably of "the journey of immortal Milton" (2: 2), and proceeds with a bard's song, with banquets and assemblies of Eternals, counterlamentations, and finally climaxes with the biblical Divine Harvest and Vintage in a universal apocalypse. The fundamental epic framework is inherited but given new articulation and meaning: the heroic figure sets off on his wandering, voluntarily becoming the alien outcast who must undergo suffering to be reborn. In going to redeem his imperfect self "Lest the Last Judgment come & find [him] unannihilate" (14: 23), Milton also takes upon himself the fearful task of redeeming fallen mankind. The progression is a more cosmic version of the individual's growth from innocence through experience to a superior reorganized innocence.

22. This quotation and others in the rest of the paragraph are from C. S. Lewis, *A Preface to 'Paradise Lost'* (London: O.U.P., 1960), pp. 1–2, 21.

Why then should Blake choose the seventeenth-
century poet as his hero? The inclination among the
Romantics to mythologize Milton as the arch-rebel and
kindred revolutionary spirit is only part of the truth.
While Blake shared that admiration for Milton, echoed
in Wordsworth and Keats, he also recognized that
Milton was responsible for the promulgation of various
Urizenic errors now bedevilling mankind. Blake's
imagination thus transformed Milton into a symbolic
entity, with greater significance than a Locke or a
Newton. For Milton was indeed a great poet; his redemption from error was all the more crucial, since
his imaginative force and poetic influence were proving
the more fatal in their misdirection. Blake accepted
Milton's belief, expressed in *Areopagitica*, in "the ancient British History" (*DC*, p. 43), but with Milton's
faith in an Urizenic Jehovah, his elevation of Reason,
his views on love and subsequent treatment of his
wives and daughters, Blake could acknowledge only
their error and the need for Milton's redemption.
Moreover, as an admired poet and master-guide, in the
manner of Aeneas' Sybil or Dante's Virgil, Milton represented the Poet or Inspired Man. He becomes the
Blakean symbol for the Imagination, an historical figure
transformed into an Everyman Poet, and in the literal
meaning of Blake's myth unites finally not only with
Blake himself but with Albion and Jesus. There can
be nothing more literally inspired than such a merging
of identities, but that merging indicates also the spiritually deadening influence Milton has had upon
Blake's life. Hence Blake calls upon the Daughters of
Beulah to "Tell also of the False Tongue!" (2: 10).
While Bloom's explanation may be correct (that "the
'False Tongue' is the fallen Tharmas, become the Cov-
ering Cherub or accuser of sin, for the sense of taste
in Eden becomes the serpent's lying tongue in Beulah,"
E, p. 824), the Tongue is also the appropriate organ to

pervert the Word which Milton and Jesus need to redeem.

The epic is psychological as well as cosmological or aesthetic in relevance. In the most obvious of ways the poem depends upon autobiography: Blake and Catherine, his "sweet Shadow of Delight" (42: 28), take their place in the myth, while the climactic visionary experiences occur in their Felpham cottage garden. In the manner of the Romantic artist—Joyce and Yeats are perhaps the best parallels—Blake has transformed private life into public art and cosmic drama, making life into art in a more literal sense than usual. More than just a matter of details—Blake, Catherine, Hyle (Hayley), Hand (the Hunt brothers), Scofield—the total conception depends upon autobiography. The details of Blake's private life support and extend the larger vision or drama involving Albion and Jesus and universal redemption. Macrocosm and microcosm are for Blake synonymous; everything that lives is holy, infinite, and part of the Divine Imagination external-ized in the giant figure of Albion.

But because the epic is writ large in cosmic terms and because the drama, its settings, and its personae are so vivid and supposedly external, we must con-stantly remind ourselves that the arena is mental, the action internal; that Milton, the Four Zoas, Satan, and Jesus are all mental states, potentialities within the Eternal or Universal Man in whom we all participate and have our being. The epic struggle is a "Mental Fight" (1: 13), an "Intellectual Battle" (*FZ*, I, 3: 3), for the "Four Mighty Ones are in every Man" (*FZ*, I, 3: 4). Thus far has the Romantic subjectivism proceeded, that one becomes what one beholds.[23] This it was

23. The instances in Blake's works are many, indicating the con-stant interrelationship and transformation of self and object: *FZ*, IV, 53: 24; 55 (second portion): 22–23; *M*, 3: 29; *J*, 30: 50, 54; 32: 9, 14–15, 19; 65: 75, 79; 66: 36.

which enabled Blake to extricate himself from the in-
fernal abyss of the Angel in *The Marriage of Heaven
and Hell.* And the principle was central to all the major
English Romantics. Moreover, to write an epic which
would include the modern introspection with its ad-
vances into the workings of the human heart was a
fundamental concern for Keats as much as for Blake,
and to Milton also Keats turned. In a letter to J. H.
Reynolds (3 May 1818) Keats wrote of his study of
Milton and Wordsworth in the evolution of his modern
epic style: "—And here I have nothing but surmises,
from an uncertainty whether Miltons apparently less
anxiety for Humanity proceeds from his seeing further
or no than Wordsworth: And whether Wordsworth has
in truth epic passion, and martyrs himself to the
human heart, the main region of his song."[24] Blake
doubtless would have been of little practical help to
Keats had the younger poet known of his work. Nevertheless, Keats's problem of allying the Miltonic epic
with the new awareness of the workings of the psyche
and heart was precisely Blake's also.[25]

No doubt the poem makes fearful demands upon us,
and not always does Blake avoid the pitfalls of exces-

---

24. *The Letters of John Keats, 1814–1821,* ed. Hyder Edward
    Rollins (Cambridge, Mass.: Harvard Univ. Press, 1958), I,
    278–79.
25. Bernard Blackstone has expressed his conviction that Keats was
    aware of Blake's work, in *The Consecrated Urn* (London:
    Longmans, Green, 1959), p. xiv. Whether or not he is correct,
    Blackstone is right to stress affinities rather than sources or
    influences. However, the long poem proved hazardous for the
    Romantics and Victorians, as may be seen in Keats's two
    Hyperion poems, Browning's *Pauline, Paracelsus,* and *Sordello,*
    and, later, Yeats's *The Wanderings of Oisin* and *The Shadowy
    Waters.* The epic was indeed superseded as a form by the
    novel: Joyce's *Ulysses,* for example, marries the epic to intro-
    spection and Keats's "human heart." Cf. Damon who also
    compares *Milton* with Joyce's *Ulysses* as "a book whose subject
    is its own composition" (*Blake Dictionary,* p. 277).

sive didacticism, bewildering obscurity, pedantic anthropomorphism, even sheer bad rhetoric. Yet, as a
poem, *Milton* still remains impressive, its merits continually revealing themselves to the persistent and at-
tentive reader.

Appropriately enough, Milton's descent to Eternal
Death is the consequence not only of his seeing his
"Sixfold Emanation" still in need of redemption but
of his being inspired by "A Bards prophetic Song!"
Blake's conception of Art goes beyond mere didacticism to inspiration proper, and he was as aware as Yeats
later of the power of words. The broad framework of
the action then centres on Milton's voluntary descent
to Eternal Death to redeem his whole self. Milton confronts this choice when he becomes aware of the torment of his Sixfold Emanation, which Bloom rightly
identifies as "Milton's three wives and three daughters
or even . . . Milton's literary works, or . . . the English
society he sought to create" (E, p. 824). Such an identification of personal life, aesthetic achievement, and
politico-spiritual goals parallels the constant identification of these three aspects in Blake's work generally
and especially in *Milton.* In just the same way, Blake
himself constantly scrutinized his own imperfections
and saw the need for that kind of spiritual death which
the poem traces.

As we follow Milton's descent, we are provided with
an account of the Fall and Creation of the temporal-
spatial universe—Blake reverses the Judaeo-Christian
account by postponing the Creation until after the
Fall, since the fallen world is the creation not of the
Elohim but of the fallen Eternals. While Blake is busy
filling in the reader with the various necessary details
concerning the nature of eternity and time, Milton
falls to receive, with the exception always of Los (Imagination), a less than enthusiastic welcome from the
fallen Zoas. His struggle with Urizen especially begins
at this stage and will not cease until the glorious rebirth

at the poem's conclusion. However, in Los, "The Watchman of Eternity" (24: 9), he has a considerable ally and, through his aid, the Harvest and Vintage and the subsequent awakening of Albion from his slumbers begin. Before Milton's final confrontation with Satan and his casting Satan into annihilation, the female Ololon descends from Beulah to join Milton in annihilation—a necessary sacrifice if Milton is to succeed. With Milton's struggle in Ulro with Satan and the subsequent sacrifice of Ololon, the poet successfully rouses Albion, merges with Jesus and Albion in turn, and the apocalyptic moment preluding Eternal Day is born.

The epic begins then with the bard's song and at once we are confronted with certain fundamental principles of Blake's aesthetic. The artist is conceived as inspired and capable of inspiring. Through his power of words he can communicate between God and man and effect liberation of self from the contingencies of fallen space and time, to the extent that individual man attains the fullest integration, his assumption of his divinity, and his participation once more in the Divine Vision or Being.

> The Bard replied. I am Inspired! I know it is Truth! for I Sing
> According to the inspiration of the Poetic Genius
> Who is the eternal all-protecting Divine Humanity
> To whom be Glory & Power & Dominion Evermore Amen

> (13: 51–14: 3)

With such faith in imagination as vision or inspiration, Blake chooses the poet Milton as his hero and characterizes the heroic journey as one of Self-Annihilation.

While it may be argued that this progression is essentially Christological, maybe even more peculiarly

Christian, in the offering up of oneself as an atonement, nevertheless it is also derived from that Romantic doctrine of the creative self which achieves
fulfilment only through sacrifice and abnegation (as
epitomized in "The Ancient Mariner") or which per-
ceives most fully and precisely only when capable of
merging with external nature (as in Coleridge, Shelley,
and Keats). Confronting Satan in a crucial exchange
preluding the awakening of Albion, Milton distinguishes between the self-abnegation he knows is divine
and the selfishly egotistical narcissism of the Satanic
myopia:

> I come to Self Annihilation
> Such are the Laws of Eternity that each shall mutually
> Annihilate himself for others good, as I for thee.

> (38: 34–36)

Satan's reply, however, imposes inevitable limits and
constrictions, and is egocentric in attitude and crude
in its bullying:

> I am God the judge of all, the living & the dead
> Fall therefore down & worship me. submit thy supreme
> Dictate, to my eternal Will & to my dictate bow
> I hold the Balances of Right & Just & mine the Sword
> Seven Angels bear my Name & in those Seven I appear
> But I alone am God & I alone in Heavn & Earth
> Of all that live dare utter this, others tremble & bow
> Till All Things become One Great Satan, in Holiness
> Oppos'd to Mercy, and the Divine Delusion Jesus be
>   no more

> (38: 51–39: 2)

Satan comes close to a Carlylean identification of
might and right, and it is characteristic of Blake that

he should reject that identification as Satanic, authoritarian, and part of the Urizenic stony law his revolutionary heroes stamp into dust. It might be argued that Blake's prophetic utterances are themselves not free of the arrogance and self-righteous insistence which sometimes mar Yeats and Lawrence as well as Carlyle. What distinguishes Blake, nevertheless, is his emphasis upon mercy and forgiveness, qualities in which the other authors are more peculiarly lacking.

Because Milton reaches self-annihilation and Satan's rejection is so forceful and terrible, we should not misconstrue the "fearful symmetry" of Milton's stature. He may offer himself as a sacrificial Christ figure while recognizing his own imperfections, but he is no creeping Jesus, and it is for others like Urizen, or Ololon, or even Blake himself, to faint and tremble (39: 53; 41: 29; 42: 25). Milton himself is a suitably heroic and magnificent figure, inspiring awe and love in the humble reprobate, fear and rage in the incorrigibly damned:

> Then Milton rose up from the heavens of Albion ardorous!
>
> (14: 10)

> And Milton collecting all his fibres into impregnable
>   strength
> Descended
>
> (38: 5–6)

and finally,

> . . . turning toward Ololon in terrible majesty Milton
> Replied.
>
> (40: 28–29)

Hence, while *Milton* may reflect Blake's conversion to

an unorthodox Christianity (dated usually at about 1800) and thus indicates a shift in emphasis from the self-assertion of the earlier Orc revolutionary figure, his hero preaches self-annihilation without any diminution of energy or revolutionary zeal. The Lamb and the Tyger are both contained in his being.

The dynamism of Milton and of the eternal life is contrasted vividly with the constricting, limited, fallen world. The bard's song tells of the succession of ages, echoing the petrification of the Divine Vision in *The Book of Urizen*, as Los works at his anvil in the creation of time and space (3: 7–27). Similarly, Albion's sons lament the diminished world they now inhabit:

> Ah weak & wide astray! Ah shut in narrow doleful
> form
> Creeping in reptile flesh upon the bosom of the ground
> The Eye of Man a little narrow orb closd up & dark
> Scarcely beholding the great light conversing with
> the Void
>
> (5: 19–22)

And so with the other four senses. Although such passages are frequent and familiar in Blake's account of the Fall,[26] we should not underestimate the savage indignation and ironic precision of the lines. Blake has focused properly and deliberately on the fearful shrivelling up of the Divine Vision. That Vision is available to all men but, in willingly refusing to acknowledge it, we continually re-create the Fall in ourselves in each perception. For our lamplike imagination we have substituted a mere reflecting mirror, uncreative, static, passive, limited, and limiting. For the Divine we have substituted the "Opake" (9: 31). The Divine Mercy, however, set limits to our fallen world, that we might

26. *Europe,* 10: 10–15; *The Song of Los,* 4: 7–12; *Urizen,* 10: 31–13: 19; *J,* 43: 67–70; 49: 32–41; *FZ,* III, 42: 1–5; IV, 54: 8–55: 9.

indeed be saved; such a marking out of the limits was the first in a series of obligations imposed upon Los, the fallen imagination, in the creation of the fallen world.

While fallen man persists in remaining an inhabitant of the Mundane Shell, bounded by time and space, his imagination retains, though in a limited way, its potential visionary force and can still provide him with perceptions of the real and eternally existing. Infinity does not cease to exist despite man's wilful myopia; the dialectic continues even in eternity. The famous passage defining infinity (15: 21–35), while providing us with essential information, captures in its image of the vortex the vital and organic nature of the real—an ironic accomplishment since Blake's "vortexes" derive from Descartes' vortices, while at the same time answering the Cartesian mathematical cosmology. Descartes had seized a truth but, under his myopic Urizenic vision, had failed to grasp the truth in its fullness and proceeded to pervert it into a "negation."

> The nature of infinity is this: That every thing has its
> Own Vortex; and when once a traveller thro' Eternity
> Has passd that Vortex, he percieves it roll backward
>   behind
> His path, into a globe itself infolding; like a sun:
> Or like a moon, or like a universe of starry majesty,
> While he keeps onwards in his wondrous journey on
>   the earth
> Or like a human form, a friend with whom he
>   livd benevolent.
> As the eye of man views both the east & west
>   encompassing
> Its vortex; and the north & south, with all their
>   starry host;
> Also the rising sun & setting moon he views
>   surrounding
> His corn-fields and his valleys of five hundred
>   acres square.

Thus is the earth one infinite plane, and not
   as apparent
To the weak traveller confin'd beneath the moony
   shade.
Thus is the heaven a vortex passd already, and
   the earth
A vortex not yet pass'd by the traveller thro' Eternity.

(15: 21–35)

In a vivid and concrete image Blake establishes the distinctive nature of infinity and accounts for Milton's passage from eternity to time. From the outset of his career Blake had insisted upon the holiness of all things—rather in the manner of Keats's assertion of "the holiness of the Heart's affections"[27]—and argued that "If the doors of perception were cleansed every thing would appear to man as it is, infinite. / For man has closed himself up, till he sees all things thro' narrow chinks of his cavern" (*MHH*, 14). At the heart of Blake's epistemology and theory of perception is this awareness of the One, made ambivalent and oblique by wilful individual shortsightedness. What the marvellously precise and concrete image of the vortex manages to capture is the nature of infinity—its dynamic and dialectical character; its continued existence, despite the lack of vision on the part of men moving increasingly further from the vortex point; its omnipresence, even on earth, which presents to the mental traveller, man, a vortex through which he must proceed if he is to be reborn into Jerusalem. In passing through his vortex Milton moves from the oneness of eternity to the multiples of time and space. Eternity does not cease to exist, any more than his eternal self which suffers a temporary sleep "on a couch / Of gold" (15: 12–13). But in travelling through the vortex, the journeying self "percieves it roll backward behind / His

27. *Letters of John Keats*, I, 184.

path." He may see it as a globe, a sun or moon, or "universe of starry majesty"; but the "infinite plane" will be most truly known if it remains to be seen "like a human form, a friend with whom he livd benevolent."

In another superbly descriptive analysis (25: 66–26: 12), Blake captures precisely this ambivalence or vortex existing in all things. Having made Los call his sons together to participate in the apocalyptic Harvest and Vintage, Blake proceeds to define Los's sons. Inevitably, they are no more sons in the literal fashion than Los is a human being. The "sons" of the imaginative faculty appear to the Newtonian intellect as "Constellations" singing in the heavens, or trees blowing in the wind, or—in a memorable recollection of his previous song of Experience—flies:

> These are the Sons of Los, & these the Labourers of
> the Vintage
> Thou seest the gorgeous clothed Flies that dance & sport
> in summer
> Upon the sunny brooks & meadows: every one
> the dance
> Knows in its intricate mazes of delight artful to weave:
> Each one to sound his instruments of music in
> the dance,
> To touch each other & recede; to cross & change
> & return
> These are the Children of Los; thou seest the Trees
> on mountains
> The wind blows heavy, loud they thunder thro' the
> darksom sky
> Uttering prophecies & speaking instructive words to
> the sons
> Of men: These are the Sons of Los! These the Visions
> of Eternity
> But we see only as it were the hem of their garments
> When with our vegetable eyes we view these wond'rous
> Visions

(26: 1–12)

Damon rightly argues that Blake's flies are butter-flies; certainly in the original version of "The Fly" the reference is more explicitly to a butterfly; while else-where Blake uses the Greek myth and iconography of Psyche as having butterfly wings in association with the soul of man and spiritual rebirth.[28] That associa-tion is strengthened here by the biblical reference in the last lines to the story in Matthew 9 of the woman made whole by her touching the hem of Jesus' gar-ment. To see the butterflies as only butterflies is to see with vegetable eyes, but although such a vision is to see only a part (the hem) and not the whole (the garment), we can be made whole, nevertheless, as was the woman in Matthew by touch. The problem is one of perception, as Blake had made clear six plates earlier:

Seest thou the little winged fly, smaller than a grain
   of sand?
It has a heart like thee; a brain open to heaven & hell,
Withinside wondrous & expansive; its gates are not
   clos'd,
I hope thine are not:

(20: 27–30)

Indeed, Blake may be answering Pope who, in *An Essay on Man*, thus insisted upon man's limited vision:

Why has not Man a microscopic eye?
For this plain reason, Man is not a Fly.

(Epistle I, 193–94)

The passage is important for still other reasons. Not only is all the vibrancy and reverberation of Blake's universe caught in this natural description, but in seeing imaginatively we are led to interpret the very

28. *Blake Dictionary*, pp. 139–40; Jean Hagstrum, "The Fly," in *William Blake*, ed. Rosenfeld, p. 371.

criss-cross touching and receding movement of flies—a more lowly example than the music of the stars or the thunderous chorus of windblown trees—as an instance of the vortex vision. For at the heart of the image and vision is the principle of touch or contact, made reverent later by D. H. Lawrence;[29] the passage also prepares us for the equally thrilling and lyrical images of the lark and wild thyme. The lamentation of Beulah (plate 31), which follows Ololon's descent into Beulah's pleasant shadow, offers similarly lyrical descriptions of the lark and wild thyme.[30] These "natural objects" are Los's messengers, as Blake makes clear later (plate 35). Just as the flies' action images the vortex vision, so too the lark's song and the thyme's odour evidence the revival to life. The lark's song, "Reecchoing against the lovely blue & shining heavenly Shell" (31: 33), like the thyme's odour, mingling with that of the "Meadow-sweet," to "lead the sweet Dance" (31: 53), offers moments of vision when centres expand and the world is transformed. The lark particularly plays a more dramatic role later in plate 36 when, flying from his nest at Los's gate in Golgonooza, he is met by another, the

29. Instances abound throughout Lawrence's work, but one of the most explicit is in *Etruscan Places*, Phoenix ed. (London: Heinemann, 1956), pp. 45–46. Morton D. Paley, "Blake's *Night Thoughts:* An Exploration of the Fallen World," in *William Blake*, ed. Rosenfeld, p. 151, has argued for parallels between Blake and Lawrence's "democracy of touch."

30. Fisch, in *William Blake*, ed. Rosenfeld, p. 55, sees the lark and wild thyme derived from Milton; Raine, *Blake and Tradition*, II, 161, traces the lark to Shakespeare's "Hark, hark, the lark at heaven's gate sings" in *Cymbeline*, II, iii. Likewise, the wild thyme may be indebted to Oberon's "I know a bank where the wild thyme blows" in *Midsummer Night's Dream*, II, i, 249, particularly since Miss Raine has indicated Blake's fondness for the play (I, 265–66). Blake's lines impressed Yeats, as his review of *The Life of William Carleton* (*The Bookman*, Mar. 1896) indicates. See *Uncollected Prose by W. B. Yeats*, ed. John P. Frayne (London: Macmillan, 1970), I, 394.

twenty-eighth, lark. Their touching of wings preludes the grand climax of the poem when Ololon descends to be annihilated, Milton confronts and defeats Satan, and finally merges with Jesus.

> When on the highest lift of his light pinions he arrives
> At that bright Gate, another Lark meets him & back
>   to back
> They touch their pinions tip tip: and each descend
> To their respective Earths & there all night consult
>   with Angels
> Of Providence & with the Eyes of God all night in
>   slumbers
> Inspired: & at the dawn of day send out another Lark
> Into another Heaven to carry news upon his wings
> Thus are the Messengers dispatchd till they reach
>   the Earth again
> In the East Gate of Golgonooza, & the Twenty-eighth
>   bright
> Lark. met the Female Ololon descending into
>   my Garden
> Thus it appears to Mortal eyes & those of the Ulro
>   Heavens
> But not thus to Immortals, the Lark is a mighty Angel
>
>   (36: 1–12)

Likewise, Blake's own vision in the final plates is accompanied by both messengers:

> Immediately the Lark mounted with a loud trill
>   from Felphams Vale
> And the Wild Thyme from Wimbletons green &
>   impurpled Hills
>
>   (42: 29–30)

There is thus a spatial and a temporal Minute Particular, a visionary instance when time and the timeless intersect (or touch), and the dance of existence reaches

a climax which is both movement and change but also
eternity. Blake's eternity is not known for its stasis. The
parallel with T. S. Eliot in *Four Quartets* is obvious,
but the imagery Blake uses inspired Yeats more than
it did Eliot.

> For every Space larger than a red Globule of Mans
>   blood
> Is visionary: and is created by the Hammer of Los
> And every Space smaller than a Globule of Mans blood.
>   opens
> Into Eternity of which this vegetable Earth is but a
>   shadow:
>
> (29: 19–22)

The sons of Los are thus employed in creating temporal
Minute Particulars:

> Moments & Minutes & Hours
> And Days & Months & Years & Ages & Periods;
>   wondrous buildings
> And every Moment has a Couch of gold for soft repose,
> (A Moment equals a pulsation of the artery)
> And between every two Moments stands a Daughter
>   of Beulah
> To feed the Sleepers on their Couches with maternal
>   care.
>
> (28: 44–49)

Yeats was to learn and be moved by Blake's insistence
that in such a moment "the Poets Work is Done"
(29: 1), a moment which equals "A Pulsation of the
Artery." Even the image of the artery, with its parallel
in Keats's dictum that "axioms in philosophy are not
axioms until they are proved upon our pulses,"[31] captures precisely the thrilling vibrancy of the visionary

31. *Letters of John Keats*, I, 279.

experience. Descartes' mechanistic analogy in his *Treatise on Man* (noted in my Introduction) is characteristically turned inside out.

Even in his didactic passages, then, Blake can surpass mere didacticism and write poetry which delights and moves the reader. But the poem is exciting and dramatic in yet other ways—whether in the various conflicts between Milton, the Zoas, and Satan; in the appearance to Blake himself of the various personae; in cameolike pictures (Milton modelling clay on Urizen in the manner of God's creating Adam, 19: 10–14); or in gothic grotesque on a cosmic scale (the vast Polypus, 34: 24–30). Perhaps the most astonishing are the ultra-personal references: more markedly than elsewhere in his work, Blake and Catherine become personae in this poem. Hence, in following Milton's descent Blake offers a magical moment: entering his foot, Milton appears to Blake "As a bright sandal formd immortal of precious stones & gold: / I stooped down & bound it on to walk forward thro' Eternity" (21: 13–14).[32] With obvious enlightenment and inspiration being granted him, Blake is visited further by Los:

> And Los behind me stood; a terrible flaming Sun:
>   just close
> Behind my back; I turned round in terror, and behold.
> Los stood in that fierce glowing fire; & he also stoop'd
>   down
> And bound my sandals on in Udan-Adan; trembling I
>   stood
> Exceedingly with fear & terror, standing in the Vale
> Of Lambeth: but he kissed me, and wishd me health.
> And I became One Man with him arising in my
>   strength:
> Twas too late now to recede. Los had enterd into
>   my soul:

32. The incident reveals another Keatsian parallel: "Sandals more interwoven and complete / To fit the naked foot of Poesy" (Keats, "On the Sonnet").

His terrors now posses'd me whole! I arose in fury
    & strength.

                                 (22: 6–14)

    The passage is impressive for a variety of reasons: the dramatic nature of the visionary experience captures in a vivid and convincing manner both Los's significance and Blake's terror; there is the distinctive fusion of biblical-Miltonic myth (Udan-Adan) with Blake's personal life (Lambeth); the kissing and merging of selves is perhaps less striking than the marvellously commonplace transformed into symbolic statement ("and wishd me health"); even the use of the caesuras in the final lines and of the internal rhyme (soul-whole) contributes to a new sense of balance and equilibrium, now possessed by Blake and taking the form of "fury and strength."

    There are other occasions yet again when the poem is strikingly alive and impressive: as in the appearance before Blake of Ololon in the figure of a twelve-year-old virgin and of Milton in his Felpham cottage garden (36: 16–20; 39: 3–5); or Blake standing, in unforgettable fashion, "in Satans bosom" (38: 15); or Blake hearing the Four Trumpets proclaiming death to the temporal world while "Jesus wept & walked forth / From Felphams Vale clothed in Clouds of blood" (42: 19–20). Moreover, with an immediacy and a delightful sense of irony often present in his work, Blake incorporates into his myth his former London address, 13 Hercules Buildings, near the Asylum, the house where he saw the fearful vision of the "Ancient of Days":[33] Los proclaims the Harvest and Vintage "Begin[n]ing at Jerusalems Inner Court, Lambeth ruin'd & given / To the detestable Gods of Priam, to Apollo: and at the

---

33. Bentley, *Blake Records*, pp. 54, 64. When the Blakes returned from Felpham they lived first at 17 South Molton Street.

Asylum / Given to Hercules" (25: 48–50). In the same
way, like Urthona in *The Four Zoas*, Night the Ninth,
137: 8, "limping from his fall," Albion, awakening from
his couch in Beulah and, lacking sufficient strength and
insight, sinks back momentarily (39: 50–52). These are
all moments of superb drama and excitement as well
as moments of illumination, and their total effect is
conversion of the reader to Blake's myth and intention.
It would be misleading to suggest that Blake is always
successful: the lists and catalogues of names and places
(37: 20–38: 4) are stultifying in their exposition. But
Blake can pick up the narrative again with astonishing
vividness unequalled in his prophecies (38: 5 ff.).

The climax to the epic comes with Milton's resounding declaration to the despairing Ololon. There is no
finer piece of oratory in the Prophetic Books, and to
fail to respond to its peculiar force is a limitation in
critical sensibility. For parallels one needs to look to
the Bible and to the Hebraism in both Carlyle and
Lawrence:

But turning toward Ololon in terrible majesty Milton
Replied. Obey thou the Words of the Inspired Man
All that can be annihilated must be annihilated
That the Children of Jerusalem may be saved from
    slavery
There is a Negation, & there is a Contrary
The Negation must be destroyd to redeem
    the Contraries
The Negation is the Spectre; the Reasoning Power
    in Man
This is a false Body: an Incrustation over my Immortal
Spirit; a Selfhood, which must be put off & annihilated
    alway
To cleanse the Face of my Spirit by Self-examination.
To bathe in the Waters of Life; to wash off the
    Not Human
I come in Self-annihilation & the grandeur
    of Inspiration

To cast off Rational Demonstration by Faith in
    the Saviour
To cast off the rotten rags of Memory by Inspiration
To cast off Bacon, Locke & Newton from Albions
    covering
To take off his filthy garments, & clothe him
    with Imagination
To cast aside from Poetry, all that is not Inspiration
That it no longer shall dare to mock with the aspersion
    of Madness
Cast on the Inspired, by the tame high finisher of
    paltry Blots,
Indefinite, or paltry Rhymes; or paltry Harmonies.
Who creeps into State Government like a catterpiller
    to destroy
To cast off the idiot Questioner who is always
    questioning,
But never capable of answering; who sits with a sly grin
Silent plotting when to question, like a thief in a cave;
Who publishes doubt & calls it knowledge; whose
    Science is Despair,
Whose pretence to knowledge is Envy, whose whole
    Science is
To destroy the wisdom of ages to gratify ravenous Envy;
That rages round him like a Wolf day & night
    without rest
He smiles with condescension; he talks of Benevolence
    & Virtue
And those who act with Benevolence & Virtue, they
    murder time on time
These are the destroyers of Jerusalem, these are
    the murderers
Of Jesus, who deny the Faith & mock at Eternal Life!
Who pretend to Poetry that they may destroy
    Imagination;
By imitation of Natures Images drawn from
    Remembrance
These are the Sexual Garments, the Abomination
    of Desolation
Hiding the Human Lineaments as with an Ark
    & Curtains

Which Jesus rent: & now shall wholly purge away
  with Fire
Till Generation is swallowd up in Regeneration.

(40: 28–41: 28)

The peculiar force of this speech depends upon the
various rhetorical devices employed. Milton must now
speak with all the authority of the Inspired Man, and
the sentence structures have an appropriate solidity
and impressive force. One notes the great collection
of infinitives cataloguing those actions necessary to
salvation; the blank statement ("There is a Negation,
& there is a Contrary") with the caesura falling heavily
and most definitely in distinguishing between the two;
and the long extended sentences which pile up evidence after evidence of both "Negations" and "Contraries." But there is also the inevitable thrust at the
bungling, blotting artist or poet, and the *saeva indignatio* which acquires full expression in the force of argument accumulating from the inversions of truth
(doubt/knowledge, science/despair, knowledge/envy).
Or there is the familiar Blakean imagery of caterpillar,
thief, and wolf contradicted by the traditional, biblical,
and neoplatonic imagery of bathing, washing, rags,
and garments. None of this is poetry in the lyrical
sense, but as prophecy or revelation its force would be
considerably diminished in a less formidable mode.
This is not to argue that Blake is totally successful. The
climax is effective in its assertiveness and in its laying
bare, for a moment, those abstractions which Blake's
vision is destined to counteract. But it contains also
a heavy preponderance of those abstractions, while
lacking the concreteness characteristic of the greater
proportion of this prophetic poem.

Milton ends in noise and exultation and a quickening of existence as all things participate in "the Great
Harvest & Vintage of the Nations" (43: 1). The last
plates resound with the grand declaration of Milton

but also with the shrieks of Ololon dividing to eternal
death, the compassionate weeping of Jesus, the clarion
calls to apocalypse of the Four Trumpets, and the loud
trill of the lark ascending above Felpham. Both man
and the universe have been shown to be what they
truly are—infinite—and the limits of contraction and
expansion have been experienced and transcended.
Through Blake's entire work—from the margined
shrivelled limit of Ulro, through the divided existence
of Generation and the Beulah trinities of man, woman,
and child, to the Edenic Oneness of all things—the
visionary poet has explored those limits of contraction
and expansion. The marvellous irony or paradox is that
an awareness of the individual, the Minute Particular,
the truly singular, is also the necessary first step to
recognition not only of the plurality but also the
oneness of all existence. Similarly, in the quest for
self-fulfilment there lies the paradox of expansion
through contraction: that only by losing one's self,
through the necessary progression from Innocence to
Experience, or on a more cosmic scale, the voluntary
descent of a Milton to Eternal Death, can the self truly
be found. Only through paradox can one find that
freedom from paradox which is Eden.

6

Blake's relevance to the Romantic vitalist tradition, and
therefore to Carlyle, Yeats, and Lawrence, is out of all
proportion to the influence he exerted over taste in his
own day. His posthumous relevance derives from his
embracing those fundamental Romantic principles
which are explored and rearticulated at various stages
throughout the subsequent hundred and fifty years. At
the heart of these principles is an awareness of the
dialectical nature of existence which finds expression
in an organicism or perception of the quickening life,
in a focusing upon energy or force or revolution, and

to varying degrees in a symbolist faith, with its "corre-
spondences," its imagery of music, and its revelation
of the constant interaction of macrocosm and microcosm. Resolving the Cartesian mind-body dualism,
revealing the inadequacy of eighteenth-century empiricism, and warring persistently against the tyranny of
restraint, whether political, psychological, or aesthetic,
Blake reasserted a belief in the human form divine.
Man's intrinsic divinity and the holiness of all things
were made known only when the individual self was
itself most creative. The poet thus becomes in Blake's
description of himself, in *Public Address*, "a Mental
Prince," battling against those "Guilty of Mental High
Treason" (p. 18).

Blake's achievement, however, as distinct from his
relevance to the vitalist tradition, lies in the profundity
and scope of his vision, in the complexity and precision
of his insights, and in his capacity as a poet to capture
the true outline of that vision through his technical
accomplishment. His present stature is evidence of the
extent to which he can still speak to us, illuminating
our lives, our awareness of ourselves and the world.
Yet amidst the ramifications of his cosmological myth,
we sometimes lose sight of what was an overriding
concern on his part: his attention to the quality of
everyday life and the ways in which the poet can contribute to its betterment. Among the inscriptions on
his engraving "The Laocoön," Blake included this insistence: "The whole Business of Man Is The Arts &
All Things Common," adding "Jesus & his Apostles &
Disciples were all Artists" (E, p. 271). Carlyle, Yeats,
and Lawrence, while not adopting Blake's distinctive
synthesis of Art and Christianity, nevertheless shared
his concern with the interrelationship of art and life.
They continued the war against abstraction, mechanism, and mammonism, against the loss of the individual and of the sense of community, against the industrial squalor which debilitates both spirit and body, and

the substitution of mass production for craftsmanship. The disease, whatever form it might take, must be eradicated if men are to grow into the fullness of their true selves. In the hands of Thomas Carlyle, the creative self may be seen operating in a variety of heroic figures, but the figure of the artist-hero, like Blake's "Mental Prince," is central.

CHAPTER TWO

The Fictive World of Thomas Carlyle

Carlyle's influence upon his own society was profound and extensive; his relevance to the Victorian era and ours is considerable. Standing like one of his own titanic figures, he dominates the mid-Victorian scene, straddling the violent revolutionary world of the Romantics and the emerging world of empire builders and captains of industry. The various elements of Romanticism converge in him, to be scrutinized, transformed, and given new inflexions. He may be seen as the mid-Victorian climax to Coleridge in his contribution to the Coleridgean critical tradition and to the Broad Church Movement;[1] as such, his successors are Matthew Arnold and F. R. Leavis. Belonging also to the vitalist tradition, stressing energy, organicism, and passion, he provides an essential link between Blake and D. H.

1. See C. R. Sanders, *Coleridge and the Broad Church Movement* (Durham, N.C.: Duke Univ. Press, 1942).

Lawrence.[2] In another way yet again, Carlyle's faith in the heroic man of action and his interest in personae indicate the sharing of certain fundamental principles with Byron, Browning, Yeats, and Pound, figures who are not as disparate as they might at first seem. Above all, the adoption by the Victorian artist of a prophetic role and by the critic of the principle of "commitment" is to a large extent Carlyle's responsibility. Taken as a whole, it is an odd achievement for one regarding himself primarily as a historian and whose excursions into literature aroused within him the gravest misgivings.

It is precisely Carlyle's titanic stature, with his subsequent rearticulation of the Romantic quest for self-fulfilment, his rendering of history (past, present, and future) in epic terms, and his fusion of various concerns into a more popular symbolist and social aesthetic, which makes him crucial to our account. Carlyle was a necessary figure in the evolution of the vitalist tradition and, despite their antagonism towards him, essential to Yeats and Lawrence. As in his own day, Carlyle still provokes, even alienates, his readers, and he has suffered, like Yeats and Lawrence, from the

2. Despite F. R. Leavis, *D. H. Lawrence: Novelist* (London: Chatto and Windus, 1955), who denies Lawrence's affinity with Carlyle, I agree with Edward Alexander, "Thomas Carlyle and D. H. Lawrence: A Parallel," *University of Toronto Quarterly*, 37, no. 3 (1968), 248–67, who, with other critics, argues for such affinity and rejects Leavis. Certainly Lawrence read Carlyle's works, admitting at one time to "Carlyliophobia" from having been "bitten" by "that rabid philosopher." Lawrence to Blanche Jennings, 4 May 1908, in *The Collected Letters of D. H. Lawrence*, ed. Harry T. Moore, 2 vols. (New York: Viking, 1962), I, 8. As for affinity with Blake, at least one of Carlyle's disciples, Alexander Gilchrist, was, as Blake's biographer, closely connected with the mid-Victorian revival of interest in Blake. There seems no validity, however, in the thesis that Carlyle was the anonymous author of the essay "The Last of the Supernaturalists," *Fraser's Magazine* (Mar. 1830). See Bentley, *Blake Records*, pp. 386–93, 393 n.2.

charge of fascism. The charge, however, like that of insanity against Blake, is a mistaken one. Certainly, the overwhelming sense of his own rightness leads to an arrogance of perception and interpretation: in the absence of shading, his is a black and white world with no chiaroscuro. And while he has been described as "The Rembrandt of English Prose,"[3] in attitude and thought he more closely resembles the "sharp wirey outline" of Blake. Consequently, all the forces he wished to condemn were grouped together as the forces of darkness—Satan, the Antichrist—which reflect society as it is, given voice in the Everlasting No. Society as it was, should, and will be—for Carlyle is essentially optimistic—is that of light, the Everlasting Yea, pronouncing the reunion of the faithful with God, the Ultimate Reality. The two extremes bear some comparison to Blake's contrary states of the human soul, for it is between these polar opposites of spiritual life and death that man moves.

My own purpose is to show the distinctively *fictive* character of Carlyle's work, as it appears not only in his delineation of the forces of darkness and light but also in his style and technical accomplishment. For the latter I have concentrated upon *Past and Present*. However, wherever one looks, Carlyle's position will be seen to depend ultimately upon a faith in the creativity of the self, upon a vitalist metaphysics and description of the world, and upon a prophetic role expressed through essentially fictional techniques. More than a

3. Logan Pearsall Smith, "Thomas Carlyle: The Rembrandt of English Prose," in *Victorian Literature: Modern Essays in Criticism*, ed. Austin Wright (New York: O.U.P., 1961), pp. 113–27. Cf. Mark Roberts, "Carlyle and the Rhetoric of Unreason," *Essays in Criticism*, 18, no. 4 (1968), 397–419, who argues rightly that Carlylese "is not a style rich in nuances, the shades and subtleties of meaning: it suggests a mind less aware of distinctions and exceptions than of broad, if sometimes rather cloudy, generalities" (405).

quirky kind of Victorian Hebraism, Carlyle's style
might best be appreciated as a necessary mask, paralleling, extending, and making concrete the vision which
it seeks to communicate.

1

The epitome of the power of darkness in contemporary
society, as Carlyle saw early in his career, in *Sartor
Resartus* (1831), was the Dandy. For the Dandy represented the essence of sham, artificiality, cant, and
quackery; in his antithesis to the Life Force and the
individual spirit, he symbolized the inadequacy of the
nineteenth-century hero. The decline of the heroic
ideal could be seen in the transference of worship from
the real and true to the unreal and false. At once
Carlyle had gained a weapon barbed for his satire and
denunciation of Victorian England. It served him for
his entire career. More important, Carlyle's campaign
against darkness was waged with a persistence and faith
that contribute greatly to his total significance and
worth. We may disagree with him, dislike the turns
of argument, the arrogance and booming rhetoric, the
heavy weight of his likes and dislikes. Through it all,
however, comes his overwhelming sincerity, in itself
the mark of his hero.

    Like many seekers after truth, then, Carlyle became
increasingly sickened by the inability in others to distinguish the real from the appearance of things.
Through the clothes imagery of *Sartor* and the unfolding of the autobiography or spiritual pilgrimage of Pro-
fessor Teufelsdröckh, we are led to see with Carlyle
that "there is something great in the moment when
a man first strips himself of adventitious wrappages;
and sees indeed that he is naked" (45). The progression
towards naked truth is clearly a central preoccupation
of Blake, Yeats, and Lawrence, as it has been of many
others outside the vitalist tradition. What makes the
preoccupation more particularly vitalist in the case of

Blake, Yeats, and Carlyle at least, is their common use of the neoplatonic view which images the world as a garment, the individual body as a vesture upon the soul, and mortality as appearance or disguise. And in the history of ideas one can see the interaction and cross-fertilization from time to time of traditions like the vitalist and neoplatonist. For Carlyle, the breakthrough marks "the beginning of all Wisdom" (52), when man, seeing through the fictitious unreal, squarely confronts the actual. The progression of Teufelsdröckh—that of Carlyle himself—is finally "to look through the Shows of things into Things themselves" (164),[4] where alone is peace. Carlyle could say, with Wallace Stevens, that he strove after "Not Ideas About the Thing But the Thing Itself," in a process Stevens also called one of "reification." For Carlyle, however, as for Blake and Lawrence, the process is visionary or mystical, one of coming through.

At the heart of Carlyle's social criticism are these optimistic premises: that "quackery gives birth to nothing; gives death to all things" (*HHW*, 4); that there is a divine justice in Nature which predestines the eventual final victory of good over evil; and that "man everywhere is the born enemy of lies" (5). That which is false cannot, by definition, possess any seeds of growth; the two states are simply and naturally contradictory. No other had proclaimed that faith with equivalent fervour since Shelley in his *Revolt of Islam* or Blake in his prophetic works. In all three cases, that faith was founded upon an organicism which upheld the natural, vital, and energetic as indicative of the dialectical Life Force, while the artificial, mechanical, and restrained imaged death and inertness. Consequently, Carlyle's disgust with sham and the dandy standards of existence is founded on a rejection of

4. This is the insight of the hero; the phrase is repeated almost verbatim in *HHW*, 55: "He looks through the shows of things into *things*."

artificiality as such. His Non-Conformist upbringing
confirmed his Romantic preference for the natural; he
died before seeing his aristocratic ideals, undergoing
further mutation in the nineties, lead to an aestheti-
cism at the centre of which was a worship of artifice.
It was, nevertheless, an aesthetic which profoundly
affected the early Yeats and which, in at least *The
Symbolist Movement in Literature* (1899) by Yeats's
friend Arthur Symons, formally acknowledged its debt
to Carlyle.[5] Brummelism, however, of which Oscar
Wilde was a later variant, Carlyle abhorred.

For Carlyle, Nature's laws are just, eternal, and divine. The Dandy, on the other hand, is antithetical to
the natural and true; as "a Clothes-wearing Man," his
whole life is "heroically consecrated to this one object,
the wearing of Clothes wisely and well," wanting
merely to be noticed (*SR*, 217). Since the hero is distin-
guishable by his sincerity (*HHW*, 45), the dandy hero
is a contradiction in terms. A false ideal disqualifies
itself by reason of its own falseness, and any success
will be temporary only. The final victory will always
be with the good and true (56–57, 62). Carlyle could
thus ask safely, "Are not all true men that live, or that
ever lived, soldiers of the same army, enlisted, under
Heaven's captaincy, to do battle against the same
enemy, the empire of Darkness and Wrong?" (120). A
similar spiritual militancy is recognizable in Blake's
Mental Fight, Yeats's principle of conflict, and

5. Arthur Symons began his introductory chapter with a quotation
   from Carlyle acknowledging the worth and significance of symbol: "It is in and through symbols that man, consciously or
   unconsciously, lives, works, and has his being: those ages, moreover, are accounted the noblest which can the best recognise
   symbolical worth, and prize it highest." This view is close to
   that which Yeats himself was promoting at this time, acknowledging Blake and Shelley as his models, though it may be here,
   as in other places, Yeats's debt to Carlyle was more considerable
   than he would wish to admit.

Lawrence's crusade against philistinism, sexual, literary, or otherwise. The battle, for Carlyle, was a serious business in which dilettantism, the contrary state to heroic sincerity, had no place: "Dilettantism, hypothesis, speculation, a kind of amateur-search for Truth, toying and coquetting with Truth: this is the sorest sin" (73).

The exposure of such sin within the present remained a constant concern throughout Carlyle's work. The confusion of "the Outer Sham-true" for "the right Inner True" (*PP*, 8) takes many forms, and from the deceit of the Dandy, with his obscuring the truth from himself, it is not far to the political sham, the obscuring the truth from others. Nor is the confusion confined to any one period in history: while no society or age is wholly perfect and untainted, some centuries are more afflicted with myopia than others. Nevertheless, through a Romantic medievalism, inherited largely from Scott, Carlyle claimed a near-perfection for the Middle Ages with arguments analogous to those of Eliot, Pound, and Yeats in their conception of the dissociation of the sensibility.[6]

> Religion was everywhere; Philosophy lay hid under it, peaceably included in it. Herein, as in the life-centre of all, lay the true health and oneness. Only at a later era must Religion split itself into Philosophies; and thereby, the vital union of Thought being lost, disunion and mutual collision in all provinces of Speech and Action more and more prevail. For if the Poet, or Priest, or by whatever title the inspired thinker may be named, is the sign of vigour and well-being; so likewise is the Logician, or uninspired thinker, the sign of disease, probably of decrepitude and decay. (*CME*, III, 15–16)

Carlyle's argument bears certain striking parallels to Blake's conception of the Fall and man's loss of vision

6. Cf. *CME*, II, 73; III, 30; *PP*, 48.

and dependence upon Urizenic logic—in itself a myth
of the dissociated sensibility. With increasing zeal and
resounding denunciations, Carlyle proceeded throughout his work to purge Victorian England of its adherence to the Devil, who remained, as for Blake, a fearful
potentiality within all men. One major distinction between Blake and Carlyle, however, is Carlyle's profound, characteristically Victorian fear that new and
more horrible forces of darkness will soon be unleashed. As acutely as Yeats, Carlyle saw that the centre
could not hold and that subsequent chaos threatened
total calamity.

Consequently, Carlyle was capable of admiring the
release of dynamic energy in the 1789 Revolution while
at the same time being deeply fearful of the transference of such revolutionary feelings to the England
of the thirties and Hungry Forties. He watched with
apprehension the People's Charter, the troubles in Ireland, and the succession of European revolutions. But
the 1789 Revolution remained glorious in its initial
rejection of sham and the not-Real—"a stripping bare
of the human soul: a fearful bursting out of the Infinite
thro' the thin rinds of Habit."[7] Worship is founded on
worth—a favourite Carlyle maxim—whereas the
French monarchy throughout the eighteenth century
showed only decline and disease. "A long ugly Slough
of Despond" was how in 1854 he saw the previous
century, redeemed only by being "Frederick's Century"
and by cutting its own throat in the French Revolution.[8] France as a whole had been afflicted and the

7. Journal entry, dated 28 Dec. 1832, quoted by D. A. Wilson, *The
   Life of Carlyle*, 6 vols. (London: Kegan Paul, 1923–34), II, 311.
   The Life consists of vol. I, *Carlyle Till Marriage*; II, *Carlyle To
   "The French Revolution"*; III, *Carlyle On Cromwell and
   Others*; IV, *Carlyle At His Zenith*; V, *Carlyle To Threescore-
   and-Ten*; VI, *Carlyle In Old Age* (completed by D. Wilson
   MacArthur). Hereafter cited as Wilson, *Life*, with volume and
   page numbers.
8. Carlyle to Joseph Neuberg, 8 Oct. 1854, in Wilson, *Life*, V, 121.

relationship between governor and governed had become unreal, unworthy, and unjust. Obedience to the heroic ideal lapsed into "*Mumbo-Jumbo*" (*FR*, I, 6). Decadence had hollowed out the ideal, the sovereign becoming "the Supreme Quack" (11). Experiencing a spiritual as well as an economic bankruptcy, France ceased to be an organic unit and creeping paralysis set in. To Carlyle writing in the thirties, the lessons for England were only too obvious.

No matter how destructive the revolutionary forces became or how horrendous might be the Terror, Carlyle was fascinated by the explosion of dynamic energy in the Sansculottes and the emergence of modern heroes like Mirabeau and Danton. For here was a "*transcendental*" phenomenon, "the crowning Phenomenon of our Modern Time" (212) warring against formulas and the decaying inorganic order. In a magnificent and characteristic paragraph Carlyle expresses "the miraculous Thing":

Whence it cometh? Whither it goeth? These are questions! When the age of Miracles lay faded into the distance as an incredible tradition, and even the age of Conventionalities was now old; and Man's Existence had for long generations rested on mere formulas which were grown hollow by course of time; and it seemed as if no Reality any longer existed, but only Phantasms of realities, and God's Universe were the work of the Tailor and Upholsterer mainly, and men were buckram masks that went about becking and grimacing there,—on a sudden, the Earth yawns asunder, and amid Tartarean smoke, and glare of fierce brightness, rises SANSCULOTTISM, many-headed, fire-breathing, and asks: What think ye of *me*? . . . The age of Miracles has come back! "Behold the World-Phoenix, in fire-consummation and fire-creation: wide are her fanning wings; loud is her death-melody, of battle-thunders and falling towns; skyward lashes the funeral flame, enveloping all things: it is the Death-Birth of a World!" (212–13)

The rhetoric of the passage indicates the inter-dependence of style and thought peculiar to Carlyle. It is not merely that he stage-manages the emergence of the Sansculottes in a dramatic fashion, so that from the midst of his rambling clauses the revolutionaries suddenly make their appearance—though this too is Carlyle's intention. The drama of the paragraph must indeed contribute to the sense of miracle he wishes to convey. But, more significantly, the inorganic mass of the first sentences is rendered organic, shaped, and made clear by the vision presented in the conclusion. In the manner in which the anarchic confusion and fearful meaninglessness of men's lives are at once swept away by the revolutionaries, who provide new forms and purposes, so too the paragraph corresponds in its style. The great and mysterious, whether cosmic and eternal or individually finite and human, is scaled down by mere formulas: the Creator is reduced to the status of a tailor or upholsterer; men become mere masks. But with the cataclysmic intrusion of the Sansculottes, rising like freed Titans from Tartarus, the passage changes direction, and before the newly emerging dynamic principle can be imaged as "the World-Phoenix" comes the monosyllabic question: "What think ye of *me?*" The vortex point is reached and the rest of the paragraph fans out from the question, spiralling out in circles of ever-increasing scope, to catch in a strangely physical manner the sense of universal apocalypse and the purifying fire. For an equivalent vision, dynamism, rhetoric, even imagery, we must look to Blake and D. H. Lawrence. All three writers manipulate the biblical epic manner to strengthen their particular social purpose and vision.

Carlyle did not admire the Revolution for its demo-cratic spirit or political radicalism. Rather, he saw it as a wonderful expression, on a national scale, of man's refusal to live with sham ideals. What saved the an-archic radicalism of the Sansculottes was the evolution of the heroic ideal, which restored a hierarchical unity

to that which was democratic and chaotic. A Napoleon
was needed to redeem what, through Robespierre, had
become anarchic and negative.[9] For similar reasons he
admired Cromwell and England's revolution in the
mid-seventeenth century. The fight for parliamentary
democracy was directed against a faith by that time
decayed into sham, quackery, and (in Laud's contro-
versy over surplices) a concern for clothes. He justifies
Charles I's execution as the death of "Flunkyism," or
cant, or clothes-worship, at the hands of those seeking
a "a new genuine Hero-worship" (*OC*, I, 414). Likewise,
Oliver's campaigns against the Irish were aimed against
Satan and Papism, those same destructive elements
which provoked the 1641 massacre. Any massacre by
Oliver, on the other hand, is just. One does not handle
the Devil with kid gloves. "If you are impious enough
to tolerate darkness, you will get ever more darkness
to tolerate" (*LDP*, 129), an argument satisfying enough
only if one is as certain as Carlyle in his perception
of right and wrong. Carlyle's own task was to restore
due honour to Cromwell's name and thus enable England to return to her heroic past and move away from
her canting present.[10]

9. Carlyle's admiration for Napoleon began early and may be
   compared with Byron's esteem for him as well (Wilson, *Life*,
   I, 256; II, 277). However, such admiration became more qualified and critical in *HHW* (1840), until, by 1856, at least, Carlyle
   was able to be downright derogatory. To a young woman who
   had asked about material for studies of Mirabeau and Napoleon,
   he wrote (28 Nov. 1856): Napoleon "has a great deal of the
   Play-actor-turned-Pirate in his character and history, an immense Gambler à la Dick Turpin; who, after all his huge reckless
   bettings, and enormous temporary successes (more astonishing
   to the foolish than to the wise), ended by losing his last guinea,
   and by being flung out of the room head foremost" (Wilson,
   Life, V, 257).
10. Like his admiration for Napoleon, Carlyle's admiration for
   Cromwell began early—at least by 1822 (Wilson, *Life*, I, 233,
   239–40) and was paralleled in Macaulay (I, 395). In his 1822
   notebook he even envisaged a history of Cromwell (II, 6).

Accompanying the loss of the heroic ideal is the democratic "leveller," the Chartist or radical who wishes to dilute the sum total of wisdom among the ruling class by enabling all men to vote, all men to rule. The blind cannot lead the blind; the fool, knowing only folly, will never choose wisdom. Government requires an awareness of the eternal virtues, recognizable only by the wise and enlightened few. Democracy "abrogates the old arrangement of things; and leaves, as we say, *zero* and vacuity for the institution of a new arrangement. It is the consummation of No-government and *Laissez-faire*" (*CME*, IV, 159).

By 1850 the condition-of-England question remained unsolved, and, remembering the most recent French revolution, Carlyle described the present as a time of democracy and chaos (*LDP*, 1–47). However, much as Yeats looked towards the Second Coming as a cataclysmic purgative, so Carlyle welcomed the Latter Day, or Niagara, as presaging a future regenerated society rising phoenixlike from the flames like Blake's Jerusalem or Lawrence's Rananim. The present revolutionary fervour discloses the imposture of the existing order, while democracy merely extends the falsity and folly among the governing class. Parliamentary democracy is "Constituted Anarchy" (29), while a true Parliament is "an eminently human, veracious, and indispensable entity" (218). The authentic organic unit meeting to discover God's Law has become that sham "National Palaver" filled with "Stump-Orators" (220). Counting of heads is substituted for "the revelation of God's eternal Law" (274). No believer in the *vox populi* as the *vox dei*, Carlyle felt indeed that the universe itself was rapidly being turned into one enormously loud and blathering *Vox*.

Carlyle's views, clearly related closely to his organicism, should not be written off as blindly authoritarian, foolishly paternalistic, or, worse, plainly fascist. We should not forget that for the working population he possessed a very real and lasting sympathy, sharpened by his sense of impending disaster and bloodshed. A sympathy, as well as an awareness of crisis, informs not only his famous essay "Chartism" (1839) but his first major distinctively "social" essay, "Signs of the Times" (1829). The delirium, thuggery, rioting, and incendiarism stemmed from deep-rooted grievances, not to be eradicated by the wave of a few reforms. In this "*our* French Revolution" (*CME*, IV, 149–50), the workers are rising up against a phantom aristocracy and reacting against the bond broken between master and worker. While he cannot accept the People's Charter, especially the insistence upon universal male suffrage, Carlyle interprets their protest as a weary articulation of their desire for real government by the wisest and best, a heroic hierarchy, and not for a democratic and artificial equality.

This distinctive diagnosis of the Chartist movement contradicted that of the parliamentary reformers, especially the Benthamite party, whom he savages in "Chartism." They offer either extension of voting rights and thus a greater diffusion of folly, or argue *laissez-faire* economics, which is finally a cloak for do-nothingism. Their rejection of state control and planning as infringing upon individual liberty ignores the *Sans-potato*, Carlyle's brilliant title for the famine-stricken Irish. *Laissez-faire* indicates "an *abdication* on the part of governors; an admission that they are henceforth incompetent to govern, that they are not there to govern at all, but to do—one knows not what!" (156). Carlyle answers sternly, "Not misgovernment, nor yet no-government; only government will now serve" (157).

We should also recognize that behind Carlyle's arguments is his belief that all men desire to be led: that provided it is wise and, therefore, virtuous and not repressive, a strong government is always desirable to all men. They may temporarily forget this law of Nature, but it returns to haunt them and dictates their obedience to a true governor or master. That same faith in organicism which stressed the community of men led Blake to affirm freedom from restraint and tyranni- cal bonds. It led Carlyle likewise to stress the need for community, but for him the relationship between men was founded on obedience and freedom from mis- placed philanthropy. The distinction is crucial and indicates the extent to which the two men are in this respect antithetical. Discussing slavery, for example, or what he insisted on calling the Nigger question,[11] Carlyle offers a chilling ridicule reminiscent of Swift or, more recently, George Orwell. While not opposed to philanthropy nor favouring slavery, he wants the first directed by wiser men and the second abolished in a more virtuous way. Modern philanthropy has de- generated into what he savagely calls "the UNIVERSAL ABOLITION-OF-PAIN ASSOCIATION," which can only become "a universal 'Sluggard-and-Scoundrel Pro- tection Society'" (349). He took exception to the free- ing of black slaves, who will misuse their freedom in indolence, when the payment of their ransom could more effectively free the millions of honest workers in England, reduced to virtual slavery through poverty and disease.

While Blake could recognize that pity is occasionally misplaced and the voice of honest indignation is then to be preferred, Carlyle's arguments are closer to the negative position Blake fervently opposed: that pain and suffering, rather than requiring eradication, can temper the self and thus prove beneficial. The funda- mental difference between Blake and Carlyle derives from their differing conceptions of man: while Blake

11. "Occasional Discourse on the Nigger Question," in *CME*, IV, 348–83. When first published in *Fraser's Magazine* (Dec. 1849), it was called the "Negro Question." To answer its hostile reception Carlyle changed it to "Nigger" (Wilson, *Life*, IV, 215). It was later reprinted as a separate pamphlet (London, 1853).

believed man to be naturally good, Carlyle argued that
only through discipline and obedience can man arrive
at virtue and wisdom.[12] While neither man believed
in repression, Carlyle's arguments can more easily be
misused to justify that authoritarianism Blake labelled
Satanic and strove constantly to defeat. Ultimately,
their difference lies in their belonging to distinct and
antithetical political traditions, radical and conservative; and it is the conservative Yeats who echoed
Carlyle's position when he sang of the soldier's pride
in obedience to his captain in "Three Songs to the
Same Tune" (III). A similar authoritarianism is shared
by D. H. Lawrence, who, in writing of Dana's *Two
Years Before the Mast*, offers a peculiarly Carlylean
objection to Dana's repulsion towards whipping. "As
long as man has a bottom, he must surely be whipped.
It is as if the Lord intended it so." Moreover, in the
captain's whipping of the sailor Sam, "a new equilibrium" is established in the "polarised flow" between
master and servant, a flow "like love" which is de-
stroyed when "once you *abstract* both master and man,
and make them both serve an *idea:* production, wage,
efficiency, and so on. . . . you have changed the vital,
quivering circuit of master and man into a mechanical
machine unison. Just another way of life: or anti-
life."[13]

12. Carlyle would have disagreed with Blake for the same reasons
he rejected Dickens, as one whose "theory of life was entirely
wrong. He [Dickens] thought men ought to be buttered up,
and the world made soft and accommodating for them, and
all sorts of fellows have turkey for their Christmas dinner.
Commanding and controlling and punishing them he would
give up without any misgivings in order to coax and soothe
and delude them into doing right. But it was not in this manner the eternal laws operated, but quite otherwise." Sir Charles
Gavan Duffy, *Conversations With Carlyle* (New York: Scribner's, 1892), p. 75.
13. *Studies in Classic American Literature*, Phoenix ed. (London:
Heinemann, 1964), pp. 109–10.

Likewise, dismissing "rosepink Sentimentalism," Carlyle scourges that radicalism which is "sunk in deep froth-oceans of 'Benevolence', 'Fraternity', 'Emancipation-principle', 'Christian Philanthropy', and other most amiable-looking, but most baseless, and in the end baleful and all bewildering jargon" (*CME*, IV, 351). Lack of guidance will only make a *"Black Ireland"* (353) of the West Indies, encouraging laziness, refusal to work, a state of sin, and a rejection of a primary law of Nature. "Do I, then, hate the Negro? No; except when the soul is killed out of him" (357). "Am I gratified in my mind by the ill-usage of any two- or four-legged thing; of any horse or any dog? Not so, I assure you" (358). Nevertheless, any sympathy stated here is tempered considerably by the scornful comparison to a horse or dog or by the dehumanized noun "thing." Carlyle was determined not only to avoid a sentimentalism but to provide arguments, terminology, and illustration which he knew would grate on the liberal ear. In his eyes abolitionists had got rid of "Slavery to Men" and substituted "Slavery to the Devil," "the slavery of Wisdom to Folly" (359-60).

Carlyle's position, whether or not we accept his definition of man and the world, is clear and consistent: "*Except* by Mastership and Servantship, there is no conceivable deliverance from Tyranny and Slavery. Cosmos is not Chaos, simply by this one quality, That it is governed" (362). Such a relationship involves an interaction of responsibilities and duties between governor and governed, which must be saved when slavery is abolished. He labels this the principle of *"permanency"* as opposed to *"nomadism"* (367). Moreover, such a relationship will be just, whereas justice is impossible in a state of slavery (371). Nevertheless, Carlyle insisted that the white is "born *wiser*" than the black man (379); the irony of Blake's poem "The Little Black Boy" would be lost on him, just as Blake would find unpardonable Carlyle's justification of Governor Eyre's brutality in Jamaica.[14]

Carlyle's objections to democracy, radicalism, and other forces of darkness remained firm to the end, and one of his finest last works, "Shooting Niagara: And After?" (1867), stands in relation to his entire work much as *On the Boiler* (1939) does to Yeats's—as a final, desperate, ruthless, and dangerously simplistic attempt to convert an obtuse world. Writing at a time of material prosperity and "universal self-congratulation" (*CME*, V, 1), Carlyle saw three events as disastrous but inevitable: democracy, dissolution of religion, and free trade. It was as if the country were being drawn relentlessly towards a state of great peril (Niagara) which she might pass over, only after having taken the proper precautions. The final expression of democracy was that terrible, because disordered, freedom by which all men's judgements were of equal worth; the hierarchy of the wise and foolish had succumbed and the anarchy of "the Bottomless" (1) was looming before us. True religion had evaporated into meaningless beliefs, while free trade, the height of eco-

14. To put down an insurrection of negroes in Jamaica in Oct. 1865 in which eighteen white men were murdered, Governor Eyre instituted martial law resulting in the execution of 354 black people. Tennyson, Ruskin, Kingsley joined with Carlyle on the Eyre Defence Committee in answer to the Jamaica Committee, chaired by J. S. Mill and supported by T. H. Huxley, Herbert Spencer, and Thomas Hughes, which sought Eyre's prosecution for murder. Eyre was successfully defended in this and another suit, was even paid for his expenses by the British government and awarded a pension (Wilson, *Life*, VI, 99–105). Cf. Walter E. Houghton, *The Victorian Frame of Mind, 1830–1870* (New Haven: Yale Univ. Press, 1957), p. 213, who sees, especially in Kingsley, a pathological source of sadistic brutality in the Victorians. J. S. Mill, *Autobiography*, World's Classics (London: O.U.P., 1955), pp. 251–54, offers his version of the proceedings.

nomic liberalism, represented only the same lack of discipline. Seeing only "'Free racing, ere long with unlimited speed, in the career of *Cheap and Nasty'"* (2), he predicted that vulgarization of taste and culture which proved of such concern in his own time to Matthew Arnold, to F. R. Leavis later, and also to Lawrence and Yeats. The cheap and nasty became identified in Yeats's mind with a commercialism peculiarly English, while Lawrence's diatribes against mass taste and mass production are in direct descendance from those of Carlyle.

> Certain it is, there is nothing but vulgarity in our People's expectations, resolutions or desires, in this Epoch. It is all a peaceable mouldering or tumbling down from mere rottenness and decay; whether slowly mouldering or rapidly tumbling, there will be nothing found of real or true in the rubbish-heap, but a most true desire of making money easily, and of eating it pleasantly. (19)

Since approximately 1660, when Carlyle dates the beginning of England's spiritual decline, our method has been *"varnish,* instead of actual repair by honest *carpentry"* (20), so that men in turn have become varnish only, liars in word and deed. Or, with another homely example, the fact that modern London brick becomes brittle after sixty years, compared with the survival of three-thousand-year-old Etruscan pottery, he finds a sad comment on our civilization (33). The ultimate source of the disease lies in man's rejection of discipline, order, and harmony—a curious misunderstanding not only of urban London's pollution problem but of an ancient culture which, as Lawrence rejoiced, included phallic worship. However, the instances are used to image the debilitating influence of liberalism, sentimentalism, or radicalism, which have led only to the confusion of the real and the sham in their preference for anarchy and so-called freedom from responsibilities and Law. Yet, in Carlyle's eyes, Law was neither restrictive nor discipline inorganic and mechanical. Progression towards real harmony and freedom was possible only through obedience.

Liberalism was only part of a broader movement of mind to which Carlyle took strong exception. Byronism or Wertherism he identified with a self-consciousness essentially egocentric, weakly introspective, and selfish. Subjective, flashy, artificial, and mannered, its social manifestation was the Dandy. The life philosophies of the decadent present he grouped together as "Dilettantism, Pococurantism, Beau-Brummelism, with perhaps an occasional, half-mad, protesting burst of Byronism" (*PP*, 219). Despite his early reading of Byron and Goethe's *Werther*, he rejects such Romantic self-consciousness as one more instance of the Everlasting No. In *Sartor Resartus* it reaches its height in the famous imperative: "Close thy *Byron*; open thy *Goethe*" (153), though his rejection can be seen in his earliest essays. In "Goethe" (1828), for example, accounting for the German's supremacy among other authors of his age, Carlyle admits Goethe's evil influence. Whereas now we are "satisfied, nay, sated to nausea . . . with the doctrines of Sentimentality" (*CME*, I, 212), *Werther* gave voice to the unrest and agony many were experiencing, while in Britain Byron appeared with his "life-weariness, his moody melancholy, and mad stormful indignation, borne on the tones of a wild and quite artless melody" (218). The objections again prelude those of Matthew Arnold in berating the modern dialogue of the mind with itself. Goethe's superiority, however, is founded on what Carlyle designates as the "great change" in Goethe's "moral disposition": "a change from inward imprisonment, doubt and discontent, into freedom, belief and clear activity: such a change . . . must take place, more or less consciously, in every character that, especially in these times, attains to spiritual manhood" (242–43).

Self-consciousness leads to egoism, whereas true awareness of self can remain only mysterious; the final mystery of existence is a fundamental Carlyle principle. Knowledge is a matter of faith and belief; truth is not to be found by analysis but by nonanalytical and unconscious means. Indeed, Carlyle's prophetic insight depends upon the vitalist influx of divine truth. And although Blake would doubtless take exception to this predilection for mystery, his own "Vision" depends upon a similar supra-rational, intuitive leap. However, there remains a distinctive difference in the certainty and clarity of their respective faiths: what for Carlyle was an act of faith was more definitely asserted by Blake. No matter how insistent Carlyle's tirades, there exists an element of Victorian doubt and uncertainty which colours his discussions of faith. He does not convince us as Blake does; the intellectual climate has changed and, like Yeats, Carlyle strives for the eternal vision from without, standing on the darkling plain surrounded by Victorian pessimism.

For Carlyle the conscious is the mechanical and artificial, and thus spiritually impotent: as he argued in "Characteristics" (1831), "everywhere the grand vital energy . . . is an unseen unconscious one" (*CME*, III, 10). The excessively introspective leads to denial, dejection, and atheism rather than affirmation, hope, faith, and joy. This inorganic process applies as much to a society as to an individual: religion gives way to unbelief, and literature—"but a branch of Religion" (23)—to sentimental Wertherism. Too great a concern with the self leads in metaphysics to excessive emphasis upon thought as opposed to action.

For placing too great an emphasis upon happiness, Carlyle rejected another contemporary solution, utilitarianism. Happiness is *not* man's natural right nor should it be his greatest concern. To think so is to confuse the stomach for the soul, as Carlyle derisively described the Benthamite formula.[15] Yet happiness should not be any man's end—a point John Stuart Mill, with the help of Coleridge and perhaps also Carlyle, came to appreciate.[16] While he could distinguish between the man and the party, nevertheless, Carlyle's most cutting and ironic attacks were in the early years reserved for the utilitarians. The height of his opposition may be seen in *Sartor*, though he never ceased to oppose "the monster UTILITARIA" (188) as the most considerable force leading to the Everlasting No. For the utilitarians represented all the "isms" he most sought to defeat: materialism, scepticism, atheism, mechanism, formulism, *laissez-faire* liberalism, sentimentalism, and egoism. "The Philosopher of this age," he wrote in "Signs of the Times," "is not a Socrates, a Plato, a Hooker, or Taylor, who inculcates on men the necessity and infinite worth of moral goodness, the great truth that our happiness depends on the mind which is within us, and not on the circumstances which are without us; but a Smith, a De Lolme, a

15. A recurrent dictum in Carlyle's satire (*SR*, 94, 129; *PP*, 154).
16. "The experiences of this period [1826–27] had two very marked effects on my opinions and character. In the first place, they led me to adopt a theory of life, very unlike that on which I had before acted, and having much in common with what at that time I certainly had never heard of, the anti-self-consciousness theory of Carlyle. I never, indeed, wavered in the conviction that happiness is the test of all rules of conduct, and the end of life. But I now thought that this end was only to be attained by not making it the direct end. Those only are happy (I thought) who have their minds fixed on some object other than their own happiness; on the happiness of others, on the improvement of mankind, even on some art or pursuit, followed not as a means, but as itself an ideal end." The second change was to give greater importance to another Carlylean principle, "the internal culture of the individual," as opposed to the "almost exclusive importance [previously given] to the ordering of outward circumstances" (Mill, *Autobiography*, pp. 120–21).

Bentham, who chiefly inculcates the reverse of this"
(*CME*, II, 67).

Utilitarianism is to be rejected not only for its excessive and selfish preoccupation with pleasure or happiness; the principle of utility, confusing stomach and
soul, also reduces morality, with its insights into the
eternal laws of Nature and God, to an arithmetical
sum. Such "profit and loss calculations" further evidenced the worship of mammon and machine inherent
in Victorian England. Both *Sartor* and *Past and Present*
contain lengthy tirades against this "universal Social
Gangrene, threatening all modern things with frightful
death" (*PP*, 137). Or, with another satirical barb, morality and cookery have become confused (*SR*, 130).
The most frequent and effective instance of Carlyle's
satire depends upon his pun in *Sartor*, using imagery
already employed effectively by Blake: utilitarianism
reduces men's minds to "an Arithmetical Mill" (53).
The Romantic and idealist doctrine of the creativity
of the self is at once superseded: that which is organic
and at best unconscious is reduced to a bundle of
motives open to calculation. Carlyle has little mercy
for "Logic-choppers" (54). Their stress on environment
contradicted his conception of the heroic genius, while
their fundamental empiricism not only opposed his
transcendental faith but was responsible for the modern materialism and scepticism. The world had lost its
wonder before the empirical eye. In his state of blindness, Teufelsdröckh asks, "Where is the Godhead; our
eyes never saw him?" (131).

Arguing from the Romantic vitalist position, Carlyle
recognizes the loss of the universe's symbolic nature
before the myopic, analytical intellect: "Not our Logical, Mensurative faculty, but our Imaginative one is
King over us" (176). The "Motive-Millwrights" offer
a dead mechanism for a healthy organism. Elsewhere
Carlyle described Mill's *Autobiography* as that of "a

Steam-Engine."[17] Blake likewise saw the conjunction
of the analytical mind and repressive economic conditions: "Bring out number weight & measure in a year
of dearth" (*MHH*, 7: 14). For the mensurative emphasis
reduces the imaginative faculty to that familiar
Urizenic level of Ulro; in our everyday life it takes the
form of mammonism. And although Carlyle's indictment of the present worship of money is paralleled in
Lawrence and Yeats too, it is Blake again who comes
closest to the Victorian. "Money," Blake argued," . . .
is The Great Satan or Reason the Root of Good & Evil
In the Accusation of Sin"; "Where any view of Money
exists Art cannot be carried on, but War only" (E, p.
272). While admitting "I seldom carry money in my
pockets they are generally full of paper" (E, p. 588),
Blake warred against that deflation of art and the artist
which kept him, or any other person, enslaved in poverty. Exposing the viciousness of contemporary society
which reduces men to the status of things to be bought,
and not even at a fair price, Blake's indignation
matches the savageness of Carlyle. Both recognize that
money worship and metaphysics are not distinct:
"Bacon has no notion of any thing but Mammon,"
Blake commented in a marginal annotation (E,
p. 614).

   No less than Blake, Carlyle read among the signs of

17. Carlyle was considerably saddened by the publication of Mill's
    autobiography. To his brother he declared: "You have lost
    nothing by missing it. I have never read a more uninteresting
    book, nor I should say a sillier, by a man of sense, integrity,
    and seriousness of mind . . . little more of human in it than
    if it had been done by a thing of mechanical iron: 'Auto-
    biography of a Steam-Engine'. . . . The thought of poor Mill
    . . . gives me real pain and sorrow" (Wilson, *Life*, VI, 294).
    Cf. Alexander, "Carlyle and Lawrence," 263, who compares
    Carlyle's relations with Mill to Lawrence's relations with
    Bertrand Russell.

the times in 1829 that "the infinite, absolute character of Virtue has passed into a finite, conditional one; it is no longer a worship of the Beautiful and Good; but a calculation of the Profitable" (*CME*, II, 74). Both contact and contrast between men rest primarily upon cash payment; reduced to "hands" or "things," men have lost the sense of relationship and brotherhood in a world rendered competitive and capitalist. The loss of relationship results in a diminished sense of the interaction of duties and responsibilities. Expediency, economics, or utility are no substitutes for morality and eternal truth.

While Carlyle's arguments against mammonism, scepticism, materialism, empiricism, and utilitarianism derive from his participation in the Romantic vitalist tradition, his rejection of science, like that of Blake, applied only to those mechanical scientific methods and concerns attempting to explain away the magical nature of things. To such a "scientist" "the Creation of a World is little more mysterious than the cooking of a dumpling" (*SR*, 2), a satirical scorn which is matched in Lawrence's description of the universe made dead by science: "'Knowledge' has killed the sun, making it a ball of gas, with spots; 'knowledge' has killed the moon, it is a dead little earth fretted with extinct craters as with smallpox" (*Ph. II*, p. 511). Similarly, for Carlyle, who befriended Darwin and Tyndall, admired Franklin, Newton, and Brindley, and was trained in mathematics, "Nature is more than some boundless Volume of . . . Recipes, or huge, well-nigh inexhaustible Domestic-Cookery Book" (*SR*, 206). The "trivial chemical name" is no substitute for the pagan worship of Fire (*HHW*, 17). The old pagan myth of the Tree Igdrasil (20–21), favoured also by Lawrence, is a truer conception of existence than that World-Machine the clankings of which Carlyle attacks with a ferocity previously unmatched, excepting Blake.

Likewise, the period is one of formulism, substituting a formula for the genuine, intuitive perception of truth. Formulas are too precise; wisdom is mysterious and unconscious.

Early in his career Carlyle wrote of the mechanical nature of the age. "Signs of the Times," for example, is a fervent plea for vitalism in metaphysics, education, religion, politics, science, art, and literature. Instead, "the Age of Machinery" (*CME*, II, 59) has provided machines for all these areas of human activity, and the natural, eternal, and divine is increasingly forgotten amid this neat "Codification" (68). Man retains "his celestial birthright" by means of his "Dynamical nature" (70–71). The highest achievements in the arts and sciences are derived naturally and spontaneously. No more anti-scientific or anti-intellectual than Blake, Carlyle is likewise not a Luddite nor opposed to industrialism.[18] Total integration in the last resort is required, neither half of the self preponderating, in Carlyle's definition of the central Romantic preoccupation—the integration of the self in its dynamic and mechanical aspects:

> Only in the right coördination of the two, and the vigorous forwarding of *both*, does our true line of action lie. Undue cultivation of the inward or Dynamical province leads to idle, visionary, impracticable courses, and, especially in rude eras, to Superstition and Fanaticism, with their long train of baleful and well-known evils. Undue cultivation of the outward, again, though less immediately prejudicial, and even for the time productive of many palpable benefits, must, in the long-run, by destroying Moral Force, which is the parent of all other Force, prove not less cer-

18. Cf. Herbert L. Sussmann, *Victorians and the Machine: The Literary Response to Technology* (Cambridge, Mass.: Harvard Univ. Press, 1968), pp. 12–40.

tainly, and perhaps still more hopelessly, pernicious. This, we take it, is the grand characteristic of our age. (73)[19]

The Everlasting No, Carlyle's label for the life-denial or scepticism, the sum total of evil forces at work in nineteenth-century society, is evident in the spiritual disintegration described here. It was this which Carlyle dramatized in Teufelsdröckh's experiences. Proceeding through a kind of dark night of the soul, which Carlyle himself compares to the Faustian situation, his protagonist, in total isolation from God, man, and Nature, exclaims: "A feeble unit in the middle of a threatening Infinitude, I seemed to have nothing given me but eyes, whereby to discern my own wretchedness. Invisible yet impenetrable walls, as of Enchantment, divided me from all living: was there, in the wide world, any true bosom I could press trustfully to mine? O Heaven, No, there was none!" (*SR,* 132). The parallel with John Stuart Mill's mental crisis in the autumn of 1826 is immediately apparent,[20] made all the more striking by the terrible vision that Teufelsdröckh is finally granted:

To me the Universe was all void of Life, of Purpose, of Volition, even of Hostility: it was one huge, dead, immeasurable Steam-engine, rolling on, in its dead indifference, to grind me limb from limb. O, the vast, gloomy, solitary Golgotha, and Mill of Death! Why was the Living banished

19. Cf. Carlyle's inaugural address as rector of Edinburgh University, 2 Apr. 1866, in *CME,* IV, 449–83. There he spoke of the need for the *whole* man, who is also the holy and healthy man: "A man all lucid, and in equilibrium. His intellect a clear mirror geometrically plane, brilliantly sensitive to all objects and impressions made on it, and imaging all things in their correct proportions; not twisted up into convex or concave, and distorting everything, so that he cannot see the truth of the matter without endless groping and manipulation: healthy, clear and free, and discerning truly all round him. We can never attain that at all" (479).

20. Mill, *Autobiography,* chap. 5.

> thither companionless, conscious? Why, if there is no
> Devil; nay, unless the Devil is your God? (133)

At this point Carlyle was unable to proceed with the
startling inversion of God and Satan which illuminates
The Marriage of Heaven and Hell. He was, however,
able to recognize, like Blake wrestling with his Angel,
that "All that we saw was owing to your metaphysics"
(*MHH*, 19).

2

Man by nature strives towards the light; the forces of
darkness are unnatural and restricting; and in a world
of Becoming, characterized by the dialectical process,
man struggles to attain completeness. The integrated
self is granted the luminous moment, beatific vision,
and eventual reunion with God. For Carlyle, the representative figure is the hero, the man of action, capable
in the fullest sense of governing. Even in the darkest
days of Chartism or Benthamism, the hero is never
wholly gone from the earth, though, in elevating his
ideal man, Carlyle points to past glory and future bliss.
The present age is one of darkness; the future will
provide the heroic.

Carlyle ruled at the opening of his second lecture
of *Heroes and Hero-Worship* (1841): "The most significant feature in the history of an epoch is the manner it has of welcoming a Great Man" (42). Today,
Carlyle says, he is almost an embarrassment; we do not
know how to behave before him. Since different epochs
react in different ways, he provides a quasi-historical
survey of the evolution of the heroic ideal. From the
beginnings of Western civilization (the Scandinavian
myths of Odin and Thor), the Islamic culture and
religion of Mahomet, down to the Renaissance phenomenon of the hero-poet and the Reformation's
hero-priest, the modern hero of the man of letters has

evolved. Moreover, the way in which the heroic has evolved reveals its very essence. Carlyle's account bears some resemblance to Blake's version of the priesthood (*MHH*, 11). Blake's account begins with paganism—the attributing of divine powers to "woods, rivers, mountains, lakes, cities, nations"—and the evolution of an enslaving system and attendant priesthood. The process declines further from the divine reality until "men forgot that All deities reside in the human breast." Not only is Carlyle unprepared to proceed towards such a full-scale fusion of God and man but, it must be remembered, Blake is tracing the evolution of the negative, fallen, Urizenic dichotomy of God and man, an inevitable consequence of which is that perverse class of men, the priesthood. Hence, although there is a superficial resemblance here between Carlyle and Blake, the two men are in fact working from opposite poles. Similarly, while Blake uses the divinity resting in every human breast to impress upon the Urizenic profiteer, employer, parent, priest, or king the need for mercy, pity, peace, and love, Carlyle finds a different purpose. Stressing those principles Blake found Satanic—obedience and submission—Carlyle uses man's near-divinity to justify exploitation and repression in the name of government by the best and wisest. He chose to stress worship and obedience as manifesting man's reverence of God in his earthly image, the Great Man.

Primitive man first expressed his faith in and humble submission to the heroic principle by conceiving the hero as divine. The early heroes were mythical gods, the oldest form of heroism. Despite Carlyle's objections to paganism, he saw that man had seized upon an important, true, and eternal principle: the worship of God in man and nature. All religions, faith, loyalty, obedience, law, and order are founded on this fundamental truth: that the Great Man is a purer reflection of the divinity in all men. The hero is the finite image of that One, "the greatest of all Heroes," whose name is unutterable (*HHW*, 11). Consequently, the hero derives his strength from God and is "the lightning" (13) that kindles the dead fuel of a declining society. The argument had been preceded by that of Blake: "those who envy or calumniate great men hate God, for there is no other God" (*MHH*, 23).

The hero as prophet, the second manifestation of the heroic ideal, is of a similar nature; now, however, the distinction between man and God has occurred. Instead of the hero as divine, he is now only divinely inspired. Nevertheless, he derives his strength and essential heroism from God: "A messenger he, sent from the Infinite Unknown with tidings to us" (*HHW*, 45). Coming "direct from the Inner Fact of things," the hero is a "portion of the primal reality" (45, 46). Likewise, Carlyle wrote of Cromwell: "He is projected with a terrible force out of the Eternities, and in the Times and their arenas there is nothing that can withstand him" (*OC*, II, 174–75). Our present difficulties stem from our inability to distinguish the true from the sham, while our modern heroes (Johnson, Burns, Rousseau) are characteristically "not heroic bringers of the light, but heroic seekers of it" (*HHW*, 158). The true hero, however, is literally a divine force and intended to lead men to reunion with God. "I do not want cheaper cotton, swifter railways," Carlyle exclaimed bitterly; "I want what Novalis calls 'God, Freedom, Immortality': will swift railways, and sacrifices to Hudson, help me towards that?" (*LDP*, 277).

The hero is also a transcendentalist, capable of discerning the interaction of the two existences, appearance and real, temporal and eternal. The finite is but an inadequate semblance of the infinite reality, while the hero sees the world as the symbolic expression of God Himself. Capable of reading the eternal laws of Nature, the hero is the divine messenger and interpreter. Government can become holy and spiritual,

then, only if the wise or heroic govern, an argument
which colours Carlyle's objections to universal suffrage
and his definition of slavery as alliance with the
Satanic forces of darkness. The responsibility of governing can be properly borne only by him "who is *loyal*
to the Laws of this Universe; who in his heart sees and
knows, across all contradictions, that injustice *cannot*
befall him here; that except by sloth and cowardly
falsity evil is not possible here" (251).

The hero is therefore the supremely good as well as
the supremely wise man, for wisdom includes goodness. The fact of integration entails the interrelationship of values, a fundamental step in Carlyle's arguments. Early in his lectures on *Heroes* he expressed the
view that "the right good fighter was oftenest also the
right good forest-feller,—the right good improver, dis-
cerner, doer and worker in every kind; for true valour,
different enough from ferocity, is the basis of all" (33).
At first this seems a questionable step, a part of that
doubtful side to Carlyle often labelled fascist. However,
his distinction between true valour and mere ferocity,
a distinction applied later to Luther (140), is of the
kind made previously between freedom and slavery.
The brutal, violent man fails to provide the proper
spiritual leadership. A hero is courageous; the brute
merely ferocious. Courage implies a sense of right and
wrong, of justice, pity, sympathy, and love. Carlyle's
assertion that "Valour is the fountain of Pity" (35)
tempers very considerably the popular tendency to
dismiss him as unfeeling or unsympathetic. Rather, he
was warmly passionate and profoundly concerned with
mankind. He shared that "savage sincerity" he saw also
in Burns: "not cruel, far from that; but wild, wrestling
naked with the truth of things. In that sense, there is
something of the savage in all great men" (192–93).

The heroic, integrated man evidences both the syntheses of valour and love, courage and morality, and
further syntheses yet again: of love and knowledge, and
of might and right. Of Carlyle's arguments the last is

usually the least understood and the most abused. Yet he is not worshipping the display of mere muscle and attributing to it justice and virtue. Rather, like bravery and heroism, might can be said to exist only when it is allied with right. When separate, it becomes brutality or savagery, of which he rightly disapproves. Although he is not without sin (which no man is completely), the hero is yet the most perfect representative we have. As the man of intellect, he is thus also "the noble-hearted man withal, the true, just, humane and valiant man" (169). For, arguing in the manner of Blake as well as of Coleridge or Keats, Carlyle insists that knowledge involves participation, almost empathy: "To know a thing, what we can call knowing, a man must first *love* the thing, sympathize with it: that is, be *virtuously* related to it" (107). Similarly, in *Past and Present*, true aristocracy or nobility requires "a valiant suffering for others, not . . . a slothful making others suffer for us" (180). Selflessness is one mark of the hero: "the brave man has to give his Life away" (204), and is distinguished from the enlightened egoist (33), Carlyle's derogatory label for utilitarianism and any other philosophy of self-interest. Likewise, in *Sartor* the first step towards the Everlasting Yea is the annihilation of the self. This discipline he admired in feudal society. Indeed, in some senses the hero is the archetypal sacrificial hero, the scapegoat who takes on others' sufferings in a Christ-like atonement. Hence, when Carlyle argues for the need for suffering, he is arguing less like Malthus than like Keats or Yeats with their emphasis upon a "Vision of Evil," to use Yeats's terms. Indeed, like Yeats, Carlyle elevates Dante for his suffering and also concentrates upon the face as imaging the spiritual conflict within.

To me it is a most touching face; perhaps of all faces that I know, the most so. Lonely there, painted as on vacancy, with the simple laurel wound round it; the deathless sorrow and pain, the known victory which is also deathless;—

significant of the whole history of Dante! I think it is the
mournfulest face that ever was painted from reality; an
altogether tragic, heart-affecting face. There is in it, as
foundation of it, the softness, tenderness, gentle affection
as of a child; but all this is as if congealed into sharp
contradiction, into abnegation, isolation, proud hopeless
pain. (*HHW*, 86)

All the tragedy, proud isolation, and solitariness of the
Yeatsian hero is caught in the face, reflecting the consumption of heart that for Yeats is the means to consummation: "The lip is curled in a kind of godlike
disdain of the thing that is eating-out his heart,—as
if it were withal a mean insignificant thing, as if he
whom it had power to torture and strangle were greater
than it. The face of one wholly in protest, and life-long
unsurrendering battle, against the world" (86). This it
is which makes Yeats celebrate Dante in "Ego Dominus
Tuus" as "The chief imagination of Christendom," and
place him as *"Daimonic Man"* in Phase 17 of *A Vision*.

The heroic, then, is more than mere morality; it is
a state of blessedness. Hero-worship is "the summary,
ultimate essence, and supreme practical perfection of
all manner of 'worship', and true worthships and noble-
nesses whatsoever" (*PP*, 34). So Carlyle looks towards
a "blessed Parliament and, were it once in perfection,
blessed Aristocracy of the Wisest, god-honoured and
man-honoured . . . the topmost blessed practical apex
of a whole world reformed from sham-worship, informed anew with worship, with truth and blessedness!" (34).[21]

The direction of Carlyle's arguments is not neces-

---

21. In the light of these views, it is hard to accept Osbert Burdett's
final view of Carlyle's hero-worship as worship of selfishness,
in *The Two Carlyles* (London: Faber, 1930), p. 291. There is
a certain truth, however, in Burdett's further claim that it is
a worship of success, but only because Carlyle has faith in
that law of Nature which dictates the success of the truly
worthwhile. It is not worship of success in the usual sense of
the word. Hence, Carlyle justified Mahomet's propagation of
the gospel by the sword (*HHW*, 61).

sarily away from the man of action as towards the
identification of the active hero with the contemplative
seer or prophet, who "lives in the inward sphere of
things, in the True, Divine and Eternal" (*HHW*, 155).
Hence Carlyle admired the 1789 French revolutionaries
for contributing to a renewal of faith (*FR*, III, 119) and
sympathized with the Saint-Simonians.[22] The moral
strength of Goethe likewise stemmed from his upholding faith in an age of unbelief (*CME*, II, 379–82). A
similar strength he admired and defined in his essay
"Chartism." Compulsion and brute force are never
sufficient to conquer a nation; the law of Nature provides for the lasting success only of the good and wise.
Tyranny is never lasting and must be distinguished
from true strength. Who then is the strong man? Carlyle's answer is of profound significance to our proper
appreciation: the strong man is

> the wise man; the man with the gift of method, of faithful-
> ness and valour, all of which are of the basis of wisdom;
> who has insight into what is what, into what will follow
> out of what, the eye to see and the hand to do; who is
> *fit* to administer, to direct, and guidingly command: he
> is the strong man. His muscles and bones are no stronger
> than ours; but his soul is stronger, his soul is wiser,
> clearer,—is better and nobler. (IV, 147)

Both Carlyle and Yeats tend to confuse spiritual and
physical strength, mental and physical battle. Both men
give the (not always mistaken) impression that their
elevation of the strong man is derived from an awareness of their own physical inadequacy. Blake's conflict,
on the other hand, was always spiritual or psychological, and he never mistook physical war for that mental
fight he perpetually conducted. Although both Carlyle
and Yeats also prefer to distinguish between spiritual
and physical strength, and thus avoid worshipping

22. Wilson, *Life*, II, 158, 162–64, 206–9.

mere brute force,[23] neither is as successful as Blake in convincing us of the clarity of his distinction. Carlyle's definition here of the strong man is an important exception. However, the organicism and dialectical faith upheld by all three writers lead inevitably to the principle of Force, or energy, with which Carlyle associates heroism. The entire universe, of which the hero is almost a microcosmic expression, is one of energy, or Force. All we can know of the universe is

> that it is a Force, and thousandfold Complexity of Forces; a Force which is *not we*. . . . Force, Force, everywhere Force; we ourselves a mysterious Force in the centre of that. "There is not a leaf rotting on the highway but has Force in it: how else could it rot?" . . . this huge illimitable whirlwind of Force, which envelops us here; never-resting whirlwind, high as Immensity, old as Eternity. (*HHW*, 8–9)

The term "force" has unfortunate connotations of coercion, physical violence, and brutality which have proved damaging to Carlyle. Yet, as a consequence of his dialectic, any tension of opposites requires, indeed evinces, the vital force, or energy. And as an important figure in the history of ideas, he unites the newly emerging German dialecticism with the older, more esoteric vitalist tradition of the cabbalists and neoplatonists. From the beginning Carlyle preferred the Romantic organicist description of existence to that of mechanism. However, that organicism or dialecticism also enabled him to see the existential process, whether in the external world or the internal self, as a plant incorporating the opposite poles or antinomies in that process, in the manner of Yeats's winding stair, dancer, or chestnut tree. Consequently, he saw the vitality in Shakespeare or Goethe balanced with a "majestic

23. Cf. Letter 36, *OC*, I, 246, where Cromwell indicates his lack of faith in "anger" or violence as a "cure" for "difference of opinion."

Calmness" (*CME*, II, 438), and, while upholding conflict as a winnowing of "the imperishable, the true and exact" (*PP*, 191), he disapproved of war, killing, and violence.

Carlyle's position is clarified by his own regeneration myth of the Phoenix, which recurs frequently in his work and which becomes, as it did for Lawrence, a symbol imaging in a very personal way his life, purpose, and achievement.[24] Destruction leads inevitably to new creation; life is a battle the discordant forces of which the hero reconciles. While the natural is cyclical, society too goes through various cyclical transformations, a concept inherited from his brief flirtation with Saint-Simonism,[25] though it is also to be seen in Blake and Yeats. With a faith verging upon fatalism, he insists, as does Blake, on the final victory coming only to the good and true. It is this which establishes the relationship between might and right. However, from his secret admiration of the forces unleashed by the Terror, it is easy enough to see how Carlyle and other vitalists lapsed into admiration of mere violence. The parallel with Yeats in *On the Boiler* is again close. Indeed, the concept of the superman, from Byron to Nietzsche and Yeats, would have been seriously weakened without the contribution of Carlyle.[26]

Similarly, while the hero engages in a process of

24. *SR*, 189, 194; cf. the inevitability of destruction and warfare, *HHW*, 119; *PP*, 291; and of cyclism, *PP*, 57–58.
25. *SR*, 237; Houghton, *Victorian Frame of Mind*, p. 31, notes a cyclical view held by Herder, Novalis, Goethe, and the Saint-Simonians. However, both René Wellek, "Carlyle and the Philosophy of History," *Philological Quarterly*, 23 (1944), 55–76, and G. B. Tennyson, *Sartor Called Resartus* (Princeton: Princeton Univ. Press, 1965), p. 143 n.24, have argued firmly for distinctions between Carlyle's view and a cyclism.
26. The topic has recently been explored in Albert J. LaValley, *Carlyle and the Idea of the Modern: Studies in Carlyle's Prophetic Literature and Its Relation to Blake, Nietzsche, Marx, and Others* (New Haven: Yale Univ. Press, 1968).

self-annihilation, Carlyle was equally sure of the divinity of man: "What is man's whole terrestrial Life but
a Symbolic Representation, and making visible, of the
Celestial invisible Force that is in him?" (*FR*, II, 47).
Such divinity of selfhood may be fulfilled only by the
abnegation of that very self, a process which is "the
first law of our existence" (*HHW*, 225). Consequently,
during his spiritual pilgrimage Teufelsdröckh discovers
the creative nature of the self as the only reality. When
he asks "Who am I; the thing that can say 'I'?" (*SR*,
41), he finds, with the help of Kant and the idealist
school, that space and time are only appearances, and
"that this so solid-seeming World, after all, were but
an air-image, our ME the only reality: and Nature, with
its thousandfold production and destruction, but the
reflex of our own inward Force, the 'phantasy of our
Dream'" (43). The divinity of man thus led Carlyle
to an elevation of that self-consciousness he himself
attacked.[27] Likewise, it accounts for his conception of
history as biography or a succession of great men. With
his constant focusing on his mythological figures, Blake
contributes to such a view; it is present more explicitly
in Coleridge, Balzac, Ruskin, and Yeats. In the manner
of Blake and Yeats, Carlyle asserted also the holiness
of the body: he reminds us of Blake, that "God only
Acts & Is, in existing beings or Men" (*MHH*, 16), when
he recurrently quotes Novalis (*SR*, 190–91; *HHW*, 10;
PP, 124). Compared with ordinary men, the hero is
clearly superior and distinct. Teufelsdröckh early recognized his uniqueness, which elsewhere Carlyle associates with abnormality and suffering. He points to
Cromwell's spleen, Dr. Johnson's hypochondria, while
surely thinking also of his own dyspepsia. Believing

27. G. H. Mead, *Movements of Thought in the Nineteenth Cen-*
    tury (Chicago: Univ. of Chicago Press, 1936), p. 63, makes this
    point, relating Carlyle's views to Fichte, a relationship indi-
    cated also by René Wellek, *Immanuel Kant in England: 1793–*
    1838 (Princeton: Princeton Univ. Press, 1931), p. 201.

that "all great souls are apt" to experience "Temptations in the Wilderness, Choices of Hercules" (*OC*, I,
50), he argues after Byron that wisdom is sorrow. He
extended the argument to oppose those forms of charity he felt encouraged laziness and suppressed man's
capacity to suffer pain.

Carlyle's emphasis upon the heroic uniqueness does
not preclude either the hero or Carlyle from being
deeply concerned for men and society. Carlyle's élitism
never became anti-social or spiritually isolationist.
While Jeffrey might legitimately criticize him in 1830
for arrogance and disdain towards the ordinary man—
attitudes which erupt from time to time in his work
and behaviour—Harriet Martineau was surely equally
right to see Carlyle motivated by pity.[28] Certainly, the
regenerated Teufelsdröckh regards his fellowman "with
an infinite Love, an infinite Pity" (*SR*, 150). The same
feelings are present in the savage attack in *Sartor* on
"the Dandiacal Body" and the subsequent comparison
with the Irish sect of Poor Slaves or Drudges. Indeed,
the same feelings provoked his criticism throughout his
work. Just as knowledge includes love and virtue, so
the future society would need brotherhood as well as
hero-worship: "Man is *not* independent of his brother.
Twenty men united in love can accomplish much that
to two thousand isolated men were impossible."[29] His
walks around Chelsea and his visits to Merthyr Tydfil,
Birmingham, Liverpool, Manchester, and Ireland made
him all too aware of the actual state of the operatives.[30]
However, having no faith in that weak sentimentalism
which seeks the reform of criminals, he is led to up-

---

28. For Harriet Martineau, see Wilson, *Life*, I, 23; for Jeffrey, see
    II, 131, 138, 202–5. Cf. Grace J. Calder, who notes the fervour
    and intensity of Carlyle's pity, in *The Writing of 'Past and
    Present,'* Yale Studies in English, vol. 112 (New Haven: Yale
    Univ. Press, 1949), p. 2.
29. 1830 notebook, Wilson, *Life*, II, 141.
30. Wilson, *Life*, II, 254; III, 148–50, 182–88; IV, 306.

hold an authoritarianism too easily misconstrued—
"this universal syllabub of philanthropic twaddle!"
(*LDP*, 68). Though still concerned for man and
society, his own solution of whips and collars (59), like
Gurth's brass collar in *Past and Present*, would in fact
lead to further brutalization of the entire society, a
condition he most wished to avoid.

This misguided authoritarianism distinguishes him
from Blake who did not share his faith in Law and
Authority. Blake hated the Old Testament God of revenge, just as he hated the patriarchal parent clipping
the wings of Innocence. Carlyle, on the other hand,
regarded revenge as "intrinsically a correct, and even
a divine feeling in the mind of every man. Only the
excess of it is diabolic; the essence I say is manlike,
and even godlike,—a monition sent to poor man by
the Maker himself" (*LDP*, 78). However, both men saw
the inhumanity, misery, and degradation of what
Carlyle called "Workhouse Bastilles" or the "Ugolino
Hunger-cellars" of Stockport and Manchester (*PP*, 171).
And always proclaiming the necessity of love,[31] Carlyle
recognized the superiority of the feudal system, which,
though rigorous, was at least one of love and relationship. Owing much to Swift, he shares the same
saeva indignatio, the same seemingly paradoxical fusion of compassion and scorn, the same desire that
man should fulfil high ideals with the same detestation
of conditions thwarting that fulfilment. He even pro-
posed a Swiftian solution to the Irish problem—
improvement or extermination (*CME*, IV, 139).
Curiously enough, Yeats, a later admirer of Swift, allied
Swift and Blake as men of passion or frenzy, but remained disdainful of Carlyle's "ill-breeding."[32]

As further expression of Carlyle's moral concern, the

31. See *FR*, III, 315; *PP*, 272; *CME*, II, 381, 394.
32. "Certain Noble Plays of Japan" (1916), in *E & I*, p. 236. Cf. his
    placing Carlyle in Phase 7 in *A Vision*, p. 116, and also "Per
    Amica Silentia Lunae" (1917), in *Mythologies* (London:
    Macmillan, 1959), p. 365.

hero is of necessity honest, opposed to formulas, sham, and hypocrisy. Although Yeats was right in noting that there was a theatrical element in Carlyle (*E & I*, p. 236), Carlyle spurns insincerity, artifice, and posing. And, rather paradoxically in the light of his own constant rhetoric, Carlyle sees the strong man as also the silent man, unable to articulate, able only to evince, the mysterious intuitions of the Real and the True he experiences. Hence he admires in Cromwell's speeches the broken sentences, the archaisms and dialect, the struggle for self-expression, the tortuous style being the nearest Cromwell can come to uttering the heroic luminous truth within him. The source is surely Byron, who influenced Carlyle considerably. The Romanticism of both preferred the mysterious to the measurable, the inarticulate to the articulate, the unconscious and infinite to the conscious and finite. These for Blake were not always the necessary antitheses, though they persisted to affect later Romantics like Yeats and Lawrence. The preference for silence is paralleled by the further preference for action above thought. Thus Carlyle contrasts this essentially English quality for silence with "the noisy inanity of the world" (*HHW*, 224). The hero communes with the great Empire of Silence. The egoistic self-assertion is contradictory to the silent submission of the hero. "Deeds are greater than Words" (*PP*, 161). Yet one cannot help echoing the jibe of Lawrence, who owed much to Carlyle and who, like Carlyle, could never cease and desist from lengthy diatribes against man's folly: "I'm like Carlyle, who, they say, wrote 50 volumes on the value of silence."[33]

Behind all these expressions of the heroic ideal lies one central assumption deriving from Carlyle's hierarchical sense: that obedience and leadership are fun-

33. Lawrence to Ernest Collings, 17 Jan. 1913, in *The Letters of D. H. Lawrence*, ed. Aldous Huxley (London: Heinemann, 1956), p. 95.

damental to any spiritual society and that both are
dangerously lacking in Victorian England. The same
vitalism and organicism motivating Blake is now used
to justify a philosophy of authority he would find in-
sidious and offensive. While we might find Blake
agreeing that the eternal lodestars of right and wrong
have been lost in an overwhelming London fog (*LDP*,
51), Carlyle's diagnosis depends upon a reaffirmation
of a Calvinistic-Kantian emphasis upon Moral Law and
upon man's duty and need to submit in obedience and
obeisance. Self-abnegation is the first moral act and a
principle he found in diverse places—in Mahomet and
Job, but also in Prussian military drill and Cromwell's
Ironsides and Model Army. However, obedience must
be to the right man. Our most important duty then
is to find the right man to govern. The world for
Carlyle is hierarchical—"The Universe itself is a Monarchy and Hierarchy" (21)—with certain men destined
to govern and the vast mass to serve. This distinction
was supported by the claims of duty and justice, by
the laws of God and Nature. This alone gave man the
right and the might to govern over others. Without it
there would be chaos, whereas every man is destined
to create order out of disorder (*HHW*, 204). But it is
also God's law that the best must govern. The term
"lord," says Carlyle in one of his frequent etymological
excursions, means *"Law-ward,"* he who guards and
practises the law (*PP*, 193). Nothing can prevent the
eventual government of intellect; it is a law of Nature
overriding all objections and obstructions. By reverenc-
ing worth, however, we can all aid the evolution of
the heroic ideal.

With the arrogance of the prophet and the intoler-
ance of the evangelist, Carlyle bases his arguments
upon the unquestioning faith in his own perceptive
insight. Thus, in his final *Heroes* lecture, he declared
unhesitatingly, "I say, Find me the true *Könning*, King,
or Able-man, and he *has* a divine right over me" (199).
The statement is reminiscent of Yeats's 1938 claim that

with a hundred or so able men Ireland's revolution could be effected.[34] The discovery of Carlyle's ideal governor will not come through mechanical methods or mere extension of voting rights. The parallel with Yeats is again apparent: Yeats prided himself upon his elevation to the Irish Senate, an appointed position not requiring election. Carlyle, on the other hand, would have us pray for God's goodness, reverence wisdom wherever we meet it, and await the return of wisdom in a future fullness of time. Both Carlyle and Yeats assume that wisdom is readily recognizable and that government by the best justifies arbitrary means. Unlike Yeats, however, Carlyle does not argue in favour of the hereditary principle: his aristocracy is to be a Napoleonic one of the talents. While admiring Frederick the Great as "the *last* real *king* that we have had in Europe,"[35] he also proclaimed that England still possessed "many *kings*," "many men not needing 'election' to command, but eternally elected for it by the Maker Himself" (*LDP*, 32). Besides, the alternative to these undemocratic thoughts is anarchy, chaos, and descent into Hell (248). There are no doubts in Carlyle's mind which is to be preferred.

The parallels with Yeats extend even to Carlyle's feelings about literature. In at least one fundamental sense Yeats would reject Carlyle for the same reasons he rejected early in his career both Tennyson and Browning. The Victorian poets, Yeats argued, had filled their work with "'impurities.'"[36] Straining after a

---

34. *On the Boiler* (1939), in *Explorations* (New York: Macmillan, 1962), pp. 441–42.
35. Carlyle to Varnhagen von Ense, 29 Oct. 1851, in Wilson, *Life*, IV, 388.
36. *Autobiographies* (London: Macmillan, 1956), p. 167: "I saw . . . that Swinburne in one way, Browning in another, and Tennyson in a third, had filled their work with what I called 'impurities', curiosities about politics, about science, about history, about religion; and that we must create once more the pure work."

fusion of art and life, writers distorted that fusion to mere preoccupation with social, political, or theological problems. At the vital centre of art—revelation of eternal truths about the world and the human heart—lay instead the debilitating concern with finite moralizing and improvement. The symbolic nature of art was thus reduced to petty peddling of "ideas." Carlyle's contribution to such an aesthetic was profound. His artist is concerned with prophecy, vision, and deliverance and, disparaging literature of an exclusively aesthetic nature, he recognizes his responsibility to deliver society from the powers of darkness. No "idle singer of an empty day" (to use Morris' terms), Carlyle praises those artists who go beyond the mere lyricism of "pleasant singing" to "wise and earnest speaking" (*CME*, V, 24). Yeats himself was not entirely free from such evangelical zeal, which motivated Blake and Lawrence also.

More interestingly, however, both Yeats and Carlyle display a distinctive ambivalence in their attitudes towards art. Yeats vacillated throughout his life, upholding the superiority of either art or life at different stages in his writing. And although he offers a persistent defence of the artist, often elevating him to positions of supreme social and metaphysical importance, Yeats also experienced considerable internal conflict in the antithetical temptation of action, as imaged in his heroic masks. From *The Wanderings of Oisin* (1889) onwards, Yeats was tormented by such a choice. As he writes in the poem "Words" (1910), "I might have thrown poor words away / And been content to live."

Carlyle too regretted being denied fulfilment in the world of action, and his embarrassment with his own profession of writing, well documented in both published work and conversation, has long been recognized. In later life, with fame established, he frequently advised a young and promising writer to seek another more desirable and active profession.[37] In a similar vein, he offered the stricture, echoed by Edward Fitzgerald and others, that Tennyson would have been a less melancholy and hypochondriac man if he had been a Life-Guardsman.[38] Carlyle himself sought compensation in his heroic ideal. To the new men, the empire builders and modern industrial heroes—his "Captains of Industry"—he looked for the organic shaping and ordering of the increasingly anarchic and mechanistic world. But the writer too has a similar task, and a close examination of Carlyle's literary techniques in *Past and Present* will indicate not only that he chose to practise his art with considerable skill and effectiveness, but that his technical achievement evidences a process parallel to that of the industrial hero—a shaping and ordering of language and vision. His description of Tennyson to Emerson is peculiarly appropriate to himself: "a man solitary and sad, as certain men are, dwelling in an element of gloom, carrying a bit of Chaos about him, in short, which he

---

37. He advised Elizabeth Barrett to stick to prose; "used to say that to write a novel was 'on the whole, to screw one's-self up on one's big toe'"; praised Mrs. Gaskell's *Mary Barton* but dismissed Jane Austen's novels as "dish-washings" and Trollope's as "alum" (Wilson, *Life*, IV, 13; cf. IV, 10–16, 62, 399–400; VI, 265). On his first visit to Carlyle's house, 29 Nov. 1855, Alexander Gilchrist reports Carlyle's advice: "One might as well go on the stage and be a mountebank as take to literature" (V, 196). And in 1868 Carlyle advised one young man, "better die" than write novels (Gavan Duffy, *Conversations with Carlyle*, p. 232.)

38. Carlyle saw Tennyson as "a Life-Guardsman spoiled by making poetry." *Tennyson and His Friends*, ed. Hallam, Lord Tennyson (London: Macmillan, 1911), p. 133. Fitzgerald's comment on the MS *In Memoriam* was similarly Carlylean: "I felt that if Tennyson had got on a horse & ridden 20 miles, instead of moaning over his pipe, he would have been cured of his sorrows in half the time." F. L. Lucas, *Tennyson*, Writers and Their Work, no. 83 (London: Longmans, Green, 1957), pp. 22–23. Cf. Carlyle's elevation of the Life-Guardsman, in *PP*, 260–61.

is manufacturing into Cosmos."[39] And it is equally significant that Carlyle should apply the industrial image of "manufacturing" to the fictive process of the creative self, thus suggesting the parallel between the artist and the industrial hero. The force of Carlyle's argument, moreover, depends heavily upon his distinctive manipulation of style, and he emerges as a more conscious artist than he himself usually professed. His style reveals an interdependence of logic and language; his persuasiveness deriving as much, if not more, from his literary accomplishment as from his visionary perception. The lesson was not lost upon Lawrence, whose style resembles Carlyle's more closely than that of any other single influence or model.

3

While it has long been recognized that Carlyle's distinctiveness derives in part from his characteristic style and rhetoric, it comes as something of a shock to have to take Carlyle seriously as an artist, rather than as a historian, biographer, social critic, or simply man of letters. Yet it is precisely this shock that several recent studies have been administering to our estimate of Carlyle.[40] To take Carlyle seriously as a literary artist,

39. Quoted by Sir Harold Nicolson, *Tennyson* (London: Arrow Books, 1960), p. 139. Cf. *SR*, 157, and *CME*, IV, 362.
40. I am particularly indebted to the following: John Holloway, *The Victorian Sage* (London: Macmillan, 1953); George Levine, *The Boundaries of Fiction: Carlyle, Macaulay, Newman* (Princeton: Princeton Univ. Press, 1968); George Levine, "The Use and Abuse of Carlylese," in *The Art of Victorian Prose*, ed. George Levine and William Madden (New York: O.U.P., 1968), pp. 101–26; George Levine, "*Sartor Resartus* and the Balance of Fiction," *Victorian Studies*, 8 (1964), 131–60; G. B. Tennyson, *Sartor Called Resartus*; Paul West, "Carlyle's Creative Disregard," *Melbourne Critical Review*, no. 5 (1962), 16–26. This particular critical approach is also indebted to more pioneering efforts by Calder, *Writing of 'Past and Pres-*

however, is by no means so foreign to his way of looking at the world. His excursions into literature are one with his preoccupations with history and social criticism, activities upon which he looked more favourably. In this final section I intend to show, first, the extent to which Carlyle's achievement depends upon a vision of reality essentially creative or "fictive"; secondly, that that vision is in fact his version of the Romantic search for fulfilment or integration of the personality; and, lastly, that he is no less the conscious artist in his reliance upon certain recurrent literary devices, which so markedly distinguish his prose style.

Early in his history *The French Revolution*, Carlyle pronounced upon the contemporary state of affairs with that unfailing certainty which characterizes his vision and in terms which, in their stubborn awkwardness and unmusicality, are representative Carlylese: "For ours is a most fictile world; and man is the most fingent plastic of creatures. A world not fixable; not fathomable! An unfathomable Somewhat, which is *Not we*; which we can work with, and live amidst,— and model, miraculously in our miraculous Being, and name World" (I, 6). Since the world is indeed "fictile," something malleable and plastic, and man, reflecting his environment, "the most fingent plastic of creatures," Carlyle wants us to recognize not only the extent to which man is the microcosmic reflection of the larger unit or macrocosm, the world, but also the

---

ent'; and Carlisle Moore, "Thomas Carlyle and Fiction: 1822–1834," in *Nineteenth-Century Studies*, ed. Herbert Davis, William C. DeVane, and R. C. Bald (Ithaca: Cornell Univ. Press, 1940), pp. 131–77; and others. Interestingly enough, John Stuart Mill reviewed Carlyle's *French Revolution* as using the method of the artist rather than of the scientist, while John Morley criticized Carlyle's hero-worship for applying "the standards of art" to the "business of choosing political heroes." Quoted by B. H. Lehman, *Carlyle's Theory of the Hero* (Durham, N.C.: Duke Univ. Press, 1928), pp. 173, 175–76.

extent to which man creates the world in which he lives. Carlyle's principles enable him to conclude thus: that the world is essentially creative, dynamic, organic— in sum, a world of Force; that its creativity is paralleled in and is to some extent dependent upon individual men; and, consequently, that its plasticity is a condition leading to both good and evil. In other words, Carlyle is adopting the familiar Romantic position, paralleled best of all perhaps in Blake, that the way in which we see depends upon what we are. Adopting a subjectivism shared by both Blake and Yeats, Carlyle agreed: "A man in all 'times' makes his own world."[41] Or again, that given the plasticity of existence, of both man and the world, the freedom to choose an existential condition in which to live can lead to both good and evil, to both order and anarchy. The more desirable alternatives, goodness and order, are derived from the nature of the creative self, whether that self is capable of projecting as complete a vision of the world as is possible, or whether that self is to be moulded by forces from without, forces which will undermine its autonomy and impose the less desirable alternatives, evil and anarchy. The fictile nature of the world becomes fictive, or the world a fiction, by being shaped or organized by the creative self. Here Coleridge's terms can be used to clarify Carlyle even further—not surprisingly since Carlyle was much indebted to Coleridge and contributes, despite his personal antipathy to the Sage of Highgate, to the nineteenth-century Coleridgean tradition. We can distinguish the desirable and undesirable consequences which follow from the fictile nature of the world by categorizing the undesirable elements as *plastic* and the desirable, *esemplastic* (to mould into one).[42] The plastic elements lead men to

41. Gavan Duffy, *Conversations with Carlyle*, p. 29.
42. I find my argument coincides with that of G. B. Tennyson, *Sartor Called Resartus*, p. 227.

pursue those activities and adopt those mental states which Carlyle saw conclude only in darkness, while the esemplastic lead to light.

I would like to delineate briefly what specifically Carlyle saw as plastic and esemplastic, and to consider in what ways these dialectical forces are either creative—that is, the fictile made fictive—or uncreative and thus illusory, mechanistic, and dead. While almost any major work of Carlyle would show the same fundamental preoccupations, the same arguments, panaceas, even imagery, certain works reveal a more extensive dependence upon fictive techniques: *Sartor Resartus*, for example, has been examined with profitable closeness, and Carlyle's reliance upon techniques of the novel much commented upon.[43] Yet, as a consequence of such close literary analysis, we are inclined to believe—mistakenly—that Carlyle is nowhere so "literary" hereafter. Indeed, if we turn to the *Latter-Day Pamphlets* or "Shooting Niagara," for example, we find a much reduced reliance upon such fictive art, which seems to coincide with a greater emphasis in the later years not upon art (as in the early essays on Goethe) but upon action and the captains of industry. While there is some truth in such a view, it is essentially shortsighted, and I intend to show a recurrent faith in the creative vision retained and practised by Carlyle.

Past and Present (1843) is a suitable example of that marriage of history, vision, and art which Carlyle upheld as his alternative to the myopic present. The work is divided into four parts, entitled "Proem," "The Ancient Monk," "The Modern Worker," and "Horo-

---

43. Apart from Levine and West, see Daniel P. Deneau, "Relationship of Style and Device in *Sartor Resartus*," *Victorian Newsletter*, no. 17 (1960), 17–20; John Lindberg, "The Artistic Unity of *Sartor Resartus*," *Victorian Newsletter*, no. 17 (1960), 20–23.

scope."[44] Clearly Carlyle's eye is upon past, present,
and future, the numerous ways in which time past and
time present interact, and the subsequent or future
enlargement of man's experience and self. This is to
be no cold objective eye cast upon the historically
accurate fact; Carlyle's history is vivid, alive, essentially subjective but equally essentially epic in grandeur and scope. Indeed, he was perpetually writing his
nineteenth-century epic, despite his calling it history
or biography, literary or social criticism. In *Past and
Present* he even clarifies "our Epic" as no longer being
Virgil's "Arms and the Man" nor the Dandy's "Shirt-
frills and the Man," but as having now become "'Tools
and the Man'" (209). Some twelve years earlier, in a
notebook entry of February 1831, he had asked himself,
"Are the true Heroic Poems of these times to be written
with the *ink of Science?* Were a correct philosophic
Biography of a Man (meaning by philosophic *all* that
the name can include) the only method of celebrating
him? The true History (had we any such, or even generally any dream of such) the true Epic Poem?—I partly
begin to surmise so."[45] More recently, in *Heroes and
Hero-Worship*, he had described Luther as a quasi-poet:
"He had to *work* an Epic Poem, not write one" (139).

This is history seen against a background of Divine
Force, Eternal Melodies, and Infinities of Time and
Space; history as part of the Creation, Fall, and Redemption; history in the epic, biblical, and Miltonic
sense, involving divine as well as temporal participants,
but brought up to date and given Romantic and Vic-

44. I cannot accept G. B. Tennyson's distinction that whereas
Sartor is organized along "the three-part principle," *Past and
Present* practises "the two-part principle" (*Sartor Called
Resartus*, p. 39). The structure of *Past and Present* is as relevant
to Carlyle's meaning as is that of *Sartor*: we shuttle from
present to past and, finally, to anticipated future, in a way
which will synthesize all that is best in both past and present.
45. Quoted by G. B. Tennyson, *Sartor Called Resartus*, pp. 157–58.

torian bearings. We may see this plainly enough by comparing Carlyle's history of the French Revolution with Blake's poem on the same subject: in both works there is the same concentration upon the Revolution as a transcendental fact; the rising-up of the organic self no longer willing to submit to the static dead world of the *ancien régime;* the same vitalism with its apocalyptic imagery of thunder and fire, and its elemental imagery of earth, air, fire, and water; the same involvement of heaven and earth in violent catastrophe; the same concentration upon the heroic; even the same booming rhetoric and imagery of darkness, night, and sickness. What is so markedly different is Carlyle's especially Victorian fear that the release of dynamic energy will lead to anarchy in the Chartist England of the late thirties and Hungry Forties. Carlyle, as we have seen, was more of a conservative than Blake could ever be.

Just as this is history in an extraordinary sense, so too the writing goes beyond that mode we associate with history.[46] For Carlyle's arguments consist of a succession of principles, images, and examples which intermingle and persistently attack the reader whenever opportunity arises, and which eventually work in conjunction to bowl him over and convert him to Carlyle's position. Needless to say, the arguments are not noted for their logic, their reliance upon rationality, or their moderation. Indeed, to read Carlyle for logic is to misread him. Rather, like D. H. Lawrence in our century, Carlyle appeals to our intuitive sense, to that divine spark in all men which enables them

46. Recent claims have been made for parallels with the nonfiction novel of Norman Mailer (LaValley, *Carlyle and the Idea of the Modern,* p. 7) and also Truman Capote (Alfred Kazin, "The World as a Novel: From Capote to Mailer," *New York Review of Books,* 8 Apr. 1971, pp. 26–30). A parallel Carlyle himself might more likely have appreciated would be with Swift's *Drapier's Letters.*

to transcend the limitations of a rational intelligence
and grasp the eternal truth.

On turning to *Past and Present*, then, we are confronted with those targets we find elsewhere in
Carlyle—those evils we may call plastic and which are
conducive only to darkness. In shuttling back and fore
in time, from present to past, Carlyle became only too
aware of the spiritual decline of the modern world.
And at the heart of darkness is the quack, sham,
flunkey, valet, or phantasm: Carlyle uses a variety of
terms to pinpoint that evil in all its protean shapes.
The quack is synonymous with the cowardly and
insincere, antithetical not only to the heroic but to the
eternal nature of things upon which the heroic depends and with which it coincides.

For Nature and Fact, not Redtape and Semblance, are to
this hour the basis of man's life; and on those, through
never such strata of these, man and his life and all his
interests do, sooner or later, infallibly come to rest,—and
to be supported or be swallowed according as they agree
with those. The question is asked of them, not, How do
you agree with Downing Street and accredited Semblance?
but, How do you agree with God's Universe and the actual
Reality of things? This Universe *has* its Laws. If we walk
according to the Law, the Law-Maker will befriend us; if
not, not. Alas, by no Reform Bill, Ballot-box, Five-point
Charter, by no boxes or bills or charters, can you perform
this alchemy: "Given a world of Knaves, to produce an
Honesty from their united action!" It is a distillation, once
for all, not possible. You pass it through alembic after
alembic, it comes out still a Dishonesty, with a new dress
on it, a new colour to it. "While we ourselves continue
valets, how *can* any hero come to govern us?" We are
governed, very infallibly, by the "sham-hero,"—whose
name is Quack, whose work and governance is Plausibility,
and also is Falsity and Fatuity; to which Nature says, and
must say when it comes to *her* to speak, eternally No!
(25–26)

The appeals to Nature and Fact, as opposed to artifice and Semblance, are inevitable and central to Carlyle's thinking. But here also is that continuing dialogue carried on in his prose between himself and imaginary voices, personae whose purpose is solely to state the contemporary alternatives in all their weak stupidity, insensitivity, and absurdity. Here also is that same use of clothes imagery which proved so successful to his satire in *Sartor Resartus*. For what is a valet but a servant, a flunkey, no true hero, and whose prime duties involve the laying out of clothes and the dressing of his gentleman? The valet goes hand in hand with the Dandy whom Carlyle ridiculed and whose prominence in early nineteenth-century society he viewed with alarm. Given Carlyle's propensity to satire, he shares the satirist's awareness of the discrepancy between reality and appearance, between man as he is and man as he should be. And what better example of such discrepancy is there than the Dandy? Carlyle's logic was irrefutable: "A heroic people chooses heroes, and is happy; a valet or flunky people chooses sham-heroes, what are called quacks, thinking them heroes, and is not happy" (75).

So that when Carlyle transports us back to the feudal and medieval, he asserts roundly, "Coeur-de-Lion was not a theatrical popinjay with greaves and steel-cap on it, but a man living upon victuals,—*not* imported by Peel's Tariff" (44–45). The assertion moves from the theatricality of the Dandy to the economics of Peel's Corn Laws. The injustices and economic sufferings associated with the Corn Laws are thus unheroic and seen as part of that larger denial of the heroic which includes the theatrical. Similarly, when Carlyle escorts us to St. Edmundsbury, where his heroic monk, Samson, and a host of other medieval worthies are to be found, we are given certain directives which will enable us to perceive more clearly. For Carlyle's vision of history is not that of his contemporary pedant,

Dryasdust, a persona borrowed from Scott, nor that of
the dilettante. He is struck by the present ruins of the
abbey, a suitable comment upon our times, but is not
prevented from imaginatively reconstructing that
ruined world and seeing the essential life and vitality
it represented and still instructs us with.

> . . . O dilettante friend, let us know always that it *was*
> a world, and not a void infinite of gray haze with fantasms
> swimming in it. These old St. Edmundsbury walls, I say,
> were not peopled with fantasms; but with men of flesh
> and blood, made altogether as we are. Had thou and I then
> been, who knows but we ourselves had taken refuge from
> an evil Time, and fled to dwell here, and meditate on an
> Eternity, in such fashion as we could? Alas, how like an
> old osseous fragment, a broken blackened shin-bone of the
> old dead Ages, this black ruin looks out, not yet covered
> by the soil; still indicating what a once gigantic Life lies
> buried there! It is dead now, and dumb; but was alive
> once, and spake. For twenty generations, here was the
> earthly arena where painful living men worked out their
> life-wrestle,—looked at by Earth, by Heaven and Hell. Bells
> tolled to prayers; and men, of many humours, various
> thoughts, chanted vespers, matins;—and round the little
> islet of their life rolled forever (as round ours still rolls,
> though we are blind and deaf) the illimitable Ocean, tint-
> ing all things with *its* eternal hues and reflexes; making
> strange prophetic music! How silent now; all departed,
> clean gone. The World-Dramaturgist has written: *Exeunt.*
> (48–49)

The imagery is precisely appropriate, persuasive in
its concreteness: the shin-bone, decayed as it may be,
still evincing greater truth than the phantasms we
choose to see; the arena reflecting that struggle all men
either endure nobly or relinquish weakly; the abbey
seen as an island in the midst of the eternal ocean,
thus commenting upon man's smallness and his relationship to the Divine. And his last image, of God as

"The World-Dramaturgist," points to the cosmic character of Carlyle's conception of history, but also, what is equally relevant, to his concentration upon the significance of individual players in this Divine Comedy. Like Blake and Yeats, among others, Carlyle saw history as a procession of great men, rather than an interplay of social, economic, or political forces. The latter phenomena occur only because of the emergence or disappearance of the heroic man. To quote Novalis, admired not only by Carlyle but by Hardy later, "Character is Fate."[47]

When we turn to those images Carlyle uses to point out scornfully the inadequacy of the present, we find only death, mechanism, and hollow appearance of the real. There are two rightly famous examples to which he returns frequently in *Past and Present:* that of the dummy Pope in a Corpus Christi Day procession and that of a London hatter's advertisement. With obvious satirical relish and irreverence and that dramatic invention he uses continually, Carlyle describes the papal plight:

> The old Pope of Rome, finding it laborious to kneel so long while they cart him through the streets to bless the people on *Corpus-Christi* Day, complains of rheumatism; whereupon his Cardinals consult;—construct him, after some study, a stuffed cloaked figure, of iron and wood, with wool or baked hair; and place it in a kneeling posture. Stuffed figure, or rump of a figure; to this stuffed rump he, sitting at his ease on a lower level, joins, by the aid of cloaks and drapery, his living head and outspread hands: the rump with its cloaks kneels, the Pope looks, and holds his hands spread; and so the two in concert bless the Roman population on *Corpus-Christi* Day, as well as they can.

47. Thomas Hardy, *The Mayor of Casterbridge*, ed. Robert B. Heilman, Riverside ed. (Boston: Houghton Mifflin, 1962), p. 98.

> I have considered this amphibious Pope, with the
> wool-and-iron back, with the flesh head and hands; and en-
> deavoured to calculate his horoscope. I reckon him the
> remarkablest Pontiff that has darkened God's daylight,
> or painted himself in the human retina, for these sev-
> eral thousand years. Nay, since Chaos first shivered, and
> "sneezed," as the Arabs say, with the first shaft of sunlight
> shot through it, what stranger product was there of Nature
> and Art working together? Here is a Supreme Priest who
> believes God to be—What, in the name of God, *does* he
> believe God to be?—and discerns that all worship of God
> is a scenic phantasmagory of wax-candles, organ-blasts,
> Gregorian Chants, mass-brayings, purple monsignori,
> wool-and-iron rumps, artistically spread out,—to save the
> ignorant from worse. (138)

In the same way that the Augustan poet's effect depends upon the subtle balancing of paradox within the
couplet or the suspension of a line, so too does Carlyle's
satirical tone depend upon the movement of his sentences; upon the fearful piling up of unfavourable evidence; the precise placement of a word to obtain the
greatest ironic effect (as in the absurd clerical paraphernalia listed here and finally modified by the adverb
"artistically"); upon the scornful editorial interjection
("What, in the name of God, *does* he believe God to
be?"); and upon the sudden deflation of the conclusion
("to save the ignorant from worse"). However, as
Levine has argued,[48] Carlyle's mature prose is distin-

---

48. "Use and Abuse of Carlylese," p. 107. Likewise, Calder, *Writing
    of 'Past and Present,'* p. 155, in comparing the Printer's Copy
    with Carlyle's First Draft, describes the stylistic improvement
    thus: "There is hardly a paragraph in the book but develops
    into expression more clear and accurate, or more forceful
    rhetorically; more rich in detail, more concrete, more charged
    with feeling, more poetic. The fact that the Printer's Copy is
    pre-eminently more forceful and brilliant than the First Draft
    is one of the most important revelations made by an analysis
    of the manuscripts of *Past and Present.*"

guished from his early, more eighteenth-century style by its "drama" and "passion," relying for its effect upon a dramatic, rather than an intellectual, presentation and appeal.

But we need not go abroad for phantasms, as Carlyle quickly points out. Another image is seized upon to give vent to his *saeva indignatio:*

> The Hatter in the Strand of London, instead of making better felt-hats than another, mounts a huge lath-and-plaster Hat, seven-feet high, upon wheels; sends a man to drive it through the streets; hoping to be saved *thereby.* He has not attempted to *make* better hats, as he was appointed by the Universe to do, and as with this ingenuity of his he could very probably have done; but his whole industry is turned to *persuade* us that he has made such! He too knows that the Quack has become God. Laugh not at him, O reader; or do not laugh only. He has ceased to be comic; he is fast becoming tragic. (141–42)

The tragedy is more easily recognizable when we attend to other imagery Carlyle uses to define the present: images of sickness and disease, paralysis and disability. So that we find the condition of England, for example, imaged as a "chronic gangrene" (3) at the heart of which is the fact that man has lost his soul, lost all awareness of soul, abandoned the eternal principle of soul which should be the foundation of self and society. "This is verily the plague-spot; centre of the universal Social Gangrene, threatening all modern things with frightful death" (137).

Appropriately enough, Carlyle inherits the Romantic image of the upas tree, a mythical tree poisoning all things around it. And with that dialectic which for Carlyle runs through all things, the upas has its antithesis in another favourite Carlylean image, the Tree Igdrasil. The dialectic then is defined by way of a host of images, of sickness and evil as opposed to vitality, health, and goodness. The life-giving organic Force is in the present perverted into the inorganic stasis which is the death of the universe and self. The tree, like that of Matthew Arnold's Scholar-Gypsy and many another Romantic tree, evidences the eternal, is a suitable image for the eternal permeating the temporal— the only testimony of permanence, stability, and continuity in a world rapidly resembling a darkling plain. "I am for permanence in all things," Carlyle asserted (280). And since "the Life-tree Igdrasil, in all its new developments, is the selfsame world-old Life-tree" (250), it is this which enables Carlyle to write his history, to focus his eyes and ours upon that which is permanent in a shifting world. For it is his business as editor of "these confused Paper-Masses now intrusted to him"

> to select a thing or two; and from the Past, in a circuitous way, illustrate the Present and the Future. The Past is a dim indubitable fact: the Future too is one, only dimmer; nay properly it is the *same* fact in new dress and development. For the Present holds in it both the whole Past and the whole Future;—as the LIFE-TREE IGDRASIL, wide-waving, many-toned, has its roots down deep in the Death-kingdoms, among the oldest dead dust of men, and with its boughs reaches always beyond the stars; and in all times and places is one and the same Life-tree! (38)

Carlyle's sentences are correspondingly all-embracing, reaching out in all directions, and thrilling with the same expression of force and vitality. For a similar rhetorical effect we turn again to D. H. Lawrence, who shares the same panache, the same charismatic appeal, and whose sentences depend equally for their persuasiveness upon such a piling-up of phrases and biblical alliteration. Paul West has gone further, seeing in *Sartor Resartus* "the nearest thing to the verbal debauchery" of Joyce's *Ulysses*.[49] And certainly

---

49. "Carlyle's Creative Disregard," p. 20. Cf. G. B. Tennyson, *Sartor Called Resartus*, p. 272: "Not until Joyce is there a comparable inventiveness in English prose."

Carlyle is more conscious and precise than his blurring of vision and sound makes him appear. His is a calculated, if cantankerous, imprecision; a style in a state of flux, or Becoming. V. S. Pritchett has said Carlyle "used language as a forceps,"[50] and indeed it is birth pangs we associate with his creative style. Like an Old Testament Jehovah, he seeks to refashion the world after his own image, creating it anew and capturing its essence in the very concreteness of his style. At best such a stylistic achievement can only approximate that solidity he ascribed to action alone. Moreover, the prophetic voice has no time for the unwilling reader; we either embrace Carlyle or reject him violently. He answers affirmatively, as did Blake, to the question posed in *The Marriage of Heaven and Hell*, "does a firm perswasion that a thing is so, make it so?" (12). For, like Blake, he believed "firm perswasion" entailed the rising up of the self in all its fullness and grasping the transcendent Fact.

Devices like the dummy Pope and the hatter's advertisement serve to dramatize and make concrete Carlyle's satire and are reiterated frequently. Once established, they both hold the strands of his arguments together and convince us of his veracity. Having received the image once, and having had it hammered at us thereafter, we come finally to recognize the reference and with the recognition—a *déja connu*—comes eventual acceptance. For just as he has particular images and concrete instances which describe and define the abstract principle to be upheld or denied, so too Carlyle plies us with a long line of such images, instances, and personae which dramatize them. He populates a whole world, in fact, in the manner of the

50. *The New Statesman and Nation*, 45 (Jan. 1953), 96–97. A contemporary historian, Oxford don, and reader for Oxford University Press, C. R. L. Fletcher, likewise objected to the style of D. H. Lawrence's *Movements in European History* as "epileptic." See John Gross, "Viewpoint," *TLS*, 26 May 1972, p. 602.

satirist, a world which careers along a course he wishes us to reject absolutely.

The fictile nature of the world is such, therefore, as to give rise either to good or evil: good government, order, peace, and heroic aristocratic life; or bad government, disorder, war, and unheroic democratic life. The potentialities within existence, as within man, are infinite (*PP*, 204). For we have it in us to pursue light or darkness, follow the gleam or the sham. If the present world offers us only the wrong choices, we may reject them, to work for the more desirable and, in the end, only alternative, founded upon hero-worship. For the antithesis of the sham, the dandy, the external man, is the right inner-true man, the hero. What characterized the medieval past for Carlyle was precisely this willingness, on a mass scale, to recognize the eternal realities and choose the heroic man to govern. The present depends upon certain machinery—a suitably industrial and nonvital image—machinery of the ballot box, extended suffrage, the Workers' Charter; and the result is the chaos of the nineteenth century (83). Rid ourselves of reliance upon mechanical devices by which to choose our heroes and the essentially benevolent, interpenetrating organic Force will correct the balance. The true man will organically evolve, as Carlyle shows in the election of Samson as the new abbot of St. Edmundsbury. And he will prove the "very singular man and landlord" (52) that the original Edmund, later canonized, was seen to be. Of the latter, St. Edmund, Carlyle wrote:

> For his tenants, it would appear, did not in the least complain of him; his labourers did not think of burning his wheat-stacks, breaking into his game-preserves; very far the reverse of all that. Clear evidence, satisfactory even to my friend Dryasdust, exists that, on the contrary, they honoured, loved, admired this ancient Landlord to a quite astonishing degree,—and indeed at last to an immeas-

urable and inexpressible degree; for, finding no limits or utterable words for their sense of his worth, they took to beatifying and adoring him! . . . His Life has become a poetic, nay a religious *Mythus*; though, undeniably enough, it was once a prose Fact, as our poor lives are; and even a very rugged unmanageable one. (52)

"No man," Carlyle adds, "becomes a Saint in his sleep" (52).

Medieval society, founding its pattern of life upon the feudal system, was essentially one of relationship, of bonds of love and affection, loyalty, fidelity, and obedience. "The Feudal Baron had a Man's Soul in him," lived a "fruitful enlarged existence," had "men round him who in heart loved him; whose life he watched over with rigour yet with love; who were prepared to give their life for him, if need came. It was beautiful; it was human! Man lives not otherwise, nor can live contented, anywhere or anywhen. Isolation is the sum-total of wretchedness to man. To be cut off, to be left solitary: to have a world alien, not your world. . . . It is the frightfulest enchantment; too truly a work of the Evil One" (274). So far has plasticity led us, when we fail to organize or render organic that which lacks proper shape and order. Blake labelled this condition "Single vision & Newtons sleep" (E, p. 693), at the opposite pole to which was the reorganized self. And precisely this isolation, alienation, and enchantment Carlyle saw in the St. Ives Workhouse in Huntingdonshire, an experience which affected him so deeply that, with another visit, to St. Edmundsbury in Suffolk, it gave rise to *Past and Present*. To echo the particular persona he uses at the beginning of the work, the picturesque . tourist, "There was something that reminded me of Dante's Hell in the look of all this; and I rode swiftly away" (2).

It was indeed a Dantean Hell which Carlyle had stumbled upon: the hopeless, degrading state to which

England's poor were doomed, in the name of progress, efficiency, laws of economics, and charity. He rightly called them "Workhouse Bastilles" or "Poor-law Prisons" (1–2). Feudal society with its practice of the principle of relationship overcame such economic and spiritual alienation by recognizing that men could make legitimate demands upon their lords and their lords on them. Society was thus organized and unified, its plasticity rendered esemplastic: man one with man, with Nature, and with God. Latter-day society distorted that relationship into one of cash payment and substituted "nomadism" for permanence and reduced men to the level of things. Despite his tirades against "rose-pink Sentimentalism" and misplaced philanthropy, Carlyle remains vitally concerned with man as man.

In order to dramatize the mammonism of the present, Carlyle relies primarily upon three recurrent images, three dramatic and concrete instances that serve as metaphors for the cash-payment condition of contemporary society: that of the Workhouse Bastille; of the Stockport assize case he called also the Ugolino Hunger-tower, or -cellar; and, lastly, of the typhoid Irish widow. The Workhouse Bastille imposes a state of enchantment upon its inhabitants and upon England as a whole, a dreadful enchanted sleep from which Carlyle attempts to rouse us to an awareness of the unreality and hell of the present and the glorious eternal existence surrounding us. The parallel with Blake's sleeping figures is obvious. The Ugolino Hunger-tower, taken from Dante's *Inferno*, is seen in its present form as revealed by the case at the Stockport assizes:

A Mother and a Father are arraigned and found guilty of poisoning three of their children, to defraud a "burial-society" of some 3*l*.8*s*. due on the death of each child: they are arraigned, found guilty; and the official authorities, it is whispered, hint that perhaps the case is not solitary, that perhaps you had better not probe farther into that department of things. (4)

He concludes in sombre incredulity: "This is in the autumn of 1841. . . ." Or the third instance, of the typhoid Irish widow, again a historical fact which he read of in a contemporary account:[51]

> A poor Irish Widow, her husband having died in one of the Lanes of Edinburgh, went forth with her three children, bare of all resource, to solicit help from the Charitable Establishments of that City. At this Charitable Establishment and then at that she was refused; referred from one to the other, helped by none;—till she had exhausted them all; till her strength and heart failed her: she sank down in typhus-fever; died, and infected her Lane with fever, so that "seventeen other persons" died of fever there in consequence. The humane Physician asks thereupon, as with a heart too full for speaking, Would it not have been *economy* to help this poor Widow? She took typhus-fever, and killed seventeen of you!—Very curious. The forlorn Irish Widow applies to her fellow-creatures, as if saying "Behold I am sinking, bare of help: ye must help me! I am your sister, bone of your bone; one God made us: ye must help me!" They answer, "No; impossible; thou art no sister of ours." But she proves her sisterhood; her typhus-fever kills *them*: they actually were her brothers, though denying it! Had human creature ever to go lower for a proof? (149)

The irony here is clear and effective; and its effect upon the reader is heightened by Carlyle's refusal to give the facts in a purely historical way. The facts must be dramatized, people made to come to life, persona conflicting with persona, in order that we be moved out of our nineteenth-century indifference and misguidedness.

Once more the instance is played off against the medieval and feudal, in the figure (taken from Scott's

51. William Pulteney Alison, M.D., *Observations on the Management of the Poor in Scotland* (Edinburgh, 1840)—"the humane Physician" mentioned in the passage quoted.

Ivanhoe) of "Gurth, born thrall of Cedric the Saxon,
. . . greatly pitied by Dryasdust and others" (211).
Carlyle admits that "Gurth, with the brass collar round
his neck, tending Cedric's pigs in the glades of the
wood, is not what I call an exemplar of human felicity"
(211–12). Though he may idealize the medieval past,
Carlyle is not entirely blind to its limitations. Indeed,
in "Horoscope," the last section of *Past and Present*,
he turns from "the hard, organic, but limited Feudal
Ages," to "glance timidly [*sic*] into the immense Industrial Ages, as yet all inorganic, and in a quite pulpy
condition, requiring desperately to harden themselves
into some organism!" (249). But in weighing the condition of Gurth's thralldom with that of the Irish typhoid
widow, in comparing the extent to which Gurth's relationship with his master is one founded on obedience,
yet the present is still found wanting. "Gurth to me
seems happy, in comparison with many a Lancashire
and Buckinghamshire man of these days, not born
thrall of anybody!" (212). And he concludes scornfully: "Gurth is now 'emancipated' long since; has
what we call 'Liberty.' Liberty, I am told, is a divine
thing. Liberty when it becomes the 'Liberty to die by
starvation' is not so divine!" (212). The same tragic
absurdity of the situation we find in the shirtless millions in an age of cheap cotton (172), or in the Irish
Sans-potato in "Chartism."

Now it matters little to Carlyle that we might accuse
him of a gross idealization of the past, of focusing
strangely unhistorical eyes, of sharing, with Scott,
Tennyson, Morris, or the early Yeats, that same impulse to retreat into a romantic past. For although he
may proclaim that "this is not playhouse poetry; it is
sober fact" (272), Carlyle is neither sober nor in the
usual sense factual. Indeed, his method of arriving at
Fact bears considerable resemblance to the Romantic
imaginative process. What constitutes a Fact for Carlyle
is that which is recognized by the whole man rising

up in a creative oneness of self, to an intuition, in an essentially fictive moment, of the eternal realities. The moment is one in which past, present, and future fuse into a transcendent moment, in and out of time; a numinous moment when the self is confronted in its vortex vision with the transcendent Fact. Such a transcendence is possible in the first place because Carlyle's universe is essentially optimistic, a place where good will inevitably triumph over evil; and, in the second, only if the self is constituted in such a way as to correspond in its esemplastic unity to similar, though larger, unities which are Nature and God. This epiphany is perhaps clearest in Carlyle's several classifications of the hero in *Heroes and Hero-Worship:* of the hero as divine, as prophet, as possessing transcendental wisdom; in short, as the supremely good and supremely wise man. Its most concrete expression is in the quasi-mystical experience Teufelsdröckh undergoes in *Sartor Resartus.* Consequently, history is transformed into transcendental Fact and involves the working out of the redemptive process in the universe and in individual men. Those who are heroic in Carlyle's eyes have the greatest propensity to grasp such a Fact. All men, in essence, possess this ability; it is more completely possessed and practised by some to whom we should turn for leadership. For they glance from heaven to earth, follow the gleam, struggle to know it and communicate it to society at large. Again Carlyle's logic is (to him) irrefutable: to his critics he answered simply, in the manner of Blake and any other prophet, that they were unable to perceive as completely and transcendentally as he.

In attempting to enlarge upon the imaginative process by which men are to find themselves and the only true reality, again we find Carlyle depending not only upon certain Romantic principles and arguments but upon recurrent Romantic and traditional imagery. The most obvious and inevitable images are those of light,

darkness, and fire. The darkness is that of the myopic
present, the satanic principle pulling all things down
to one common level of mechanism and death: "dead
and dark,—all cold, eyeless, deaf" (*PP*, 11), a "thick
Egyptian darkness" (284) of materialism and the Flesh.
The fire is both phoenixlike and apocalyptic, and prepares for the light. As such, the fire corresponds to
Carlyle's elevation of war and violence, an elevation
which seems to accompany almost inevitably a philosophy of Force. The light is that which all men necessarily prefer and should strive to attain, the light of
the transcendent Fact. And one dominant image in the
section of *Past and Present* dealing with the medieval
past is that of the light burning in St. Edmund's shrine
(65). The imagery of light is extended further to include the heightened perceptions, particularly the superior eyesight, of Carlyle's medieval heroes: "these
clear eyes of neighbour Jocelin," "daily in the very
eyesight, palpable to the very fingers of our Jocelin"
(45); Samson with "those clear eyes" (73). Or again,
in that more sacramental tone he reveals on occasion,
Carlyle pronounces, with obvious relevance to his own
art, "It is not known that the Tongue of Man is a sacred
organ; that Man himself is definable in Philosophy as
an 'Incarnate *Word*'" (151).

We should not be misled by Carlyle's transcendentalism to believe that he thus depreciated the physical
and sensory. His transcendentalism goes hand in hand
with a sacramentalism. Quoting Novalis, for example,
to comment upon the dead St. Edmund, Carlyle clarifies the need for obedience: "'Bending before men,'
says Novalis, 'is a reverence done to this Revelation
in the Flesh. We touch Heaven when we lay our hand
on a human Body'" (124). For, like Blake, Carlyle could
conceive the Divine Image as the Human Form Divine—
"Go or stand, in what time, in what place we will, are
there not Immensities, Eternities over us, around us,
in us" (228)—though he is never as thoroughgoing as

Blake and considerably more élitist. Yet his concluding chapter to *Past and Present* is strongly reminiscent of Blake in its apocalyptic vision and tone:

> Gradually, assaulted from beneath and from above, the Stygian mud-deluge of Laissez-faire, Supply-and-demand, Cash-payment the one Duty, will abate on all hands; and the everlasting mountain-tops, and secure rock-foundations that reach to the centre of the world, and rest on Nature's self, will again emerge, to found on, and to build on. When Mammon-worshippers here and there begin to be God-worshippers, and bipeds-of-prey become men, and there is a Soul felt once more in the huge-pulsing elephantine mechanic Animalism of this Earth, it will be again a blessed Earth. (294–95)

The hero is characterized not only by his superior eyesight but by his silence, his denial of cant and noise, and his struggling to articulate the inarticulate. Samson is the silent strong man, whose "*ineloquence*" is "his great invaluable 'talent of silence'!" (96). Carlyle prefers "silent practice" to "talking theory" (115), a practical sense he saw in the Romans, English, and Russians as opposed to the "ever-talking, ever-gesticulating French" (158). For the capacity for silence involves also the recognition of the Eternal Silence.

Hence the modern man of letters, as distinguished from Carlyle's literary hero, is a "twangling, jangling, vain, acrid, scrannel-piping man," whose sole purpose is to soothe the reader's soul "with visions of new, still wider Eldorados, Houri Paradises, richer Lands of Cockaigne" (293). The literary hero, on the other hand, offers poetry which is *"musical Thought"* (*HHW*, 83), work which is discernible from a mere "Daub of Artifice" (*SR*, 178) by its revelation of the Infinite. One sees "Eternity looking through Time; the Godlike rendered visible" (178). Carlyle's objections to fiction, then, in *Past and Present*, are directed against the ultra-sentimental novels of the Minerva Presses and not against fiction per se. The imagination proper, with its insight into the *natura naturans*, by way of symbols, remains the best means to truth. Nor is it restricted to the aesthetic mode but extended to include the metaphysical and practical modes also. Carlyle in fact is not far from the orthodox Romantic position as evidenced in Coleridge's distinctions between Imagination and Fancy, Reason and Understanding. Indeed, Carlyle described Shakespeare and Goethe in an early essay, "Goethe's Works" (1832), as melting down reality to create it anew—the esemplastic action of the secondary imagination. Carlyle's term was *"fusible"*: "For Goethe, as for Shakspeare, the world lies all translucent, all *fusible* we might call it, encircled with WONDER" (*CME*, II, 437). A similar task in the practical world he envisaged for the industrial hero in his later works.

Carlyle is indeed as much concerned with the integration of the personality as the major Romantics; in the final analysis, this is his overall concern. Despite his attacks upon the Byronic self-consciousness, which he saw, with utilitarianism, as responsible for modern egotism, subjectivism, and sentimentalism, Carlyle is no less preoccupied with the self and its potential fullness of experience. More, in certain respects we can see him working with characteristically Romantic principles, though perhaps using them in an individual way. Above all, he does so in a way we may term "literary." Not always is he as persistently fictive, as in *Sartor Resartus*, but he demands critical literary attention. With all his disregard for literature, his faulty ear, his limited critical opinions, Carlyle remains the self-conscious, creative artist, using an armoury of satirical techniques which we do not always credit him with being capable of using.

There remain still other fictive elements in Carlyle's style. The great weight of his truth, for example, is achieved partly by his own attempts at conversion and partly by persistent reference to and dependence upon a large number of sources or authorities. My list is not meant to be complete, but amongst those cited in *Past and Present* include not only Jocelin of Brakelond but also Homer, Virgil, Horace, Seneca, Ovid, the Bible, Dante, Shakespeare, Ben Jonson, Milton, Cromwell, Dryden, Addison, Dr. Johnson, Sterne, Goldsmith, Voltaire, Novalis, Richter, Maria Edgeworth, Burns, Scott, Tennyson (it helped his reputation), and, for good measure, Carlyle himself. We might note the number of epic poets included; indeed, Carlyle's authorities are almost exclusively literary. He is not engaged in name-dropping nor literary snobbery, attempting to display the nature and extent of his reading. The many literary and topical allusions with which his work abounds derive in part from the editorial role he was fond of playing, a role which was in varying degrees a defence against personal ridicule. Like Eliot in *The Waste Land*, he is also attempting to suggest the eternal nature of the problems facing mankind and to indicate the inadequacy of the present in confronting these problems and providing the kinds of answers men have always had to rely upon. In another way, too, he shows by his extensive cross-references that kind of enlightenment which awareness of the past, in literature as well as history, can provide us with. In this respect for the past and man's particular attempts at answering the riddles of the universe, he shows himself the historian but also, and eminently, the artist.

But Carlyle does not stop here. *Past and Present* is not only laced with the authority of those who are truly great but populated with a whole dramatis personae, either of Carlyle's own invention or taken from contemporary society or from his reading. So that the work comes alive in a more dynamic way yet again, with a glorious gallery of personae worthy of Thomas

Love Peacock or Byron in *Don Juan*. Another contemporary parallel, as Levine has noted,[52] is Browning, who, like Carlyle, is preoccupied with the revelation of personality in all its complexities in a transcendent and numinous moment. However, Carlyle's insights are limited by his satirical intent: his personae remain two-dimensional in a way Browning's almost never do. Indeed, Carlyle fails to recapture that "solidity" he recognized in action—"Narrative is *linear*, Action is *solid*" (*CME*, II, 89)—and his personae remain pale, inadequate versions of the real. Whatever solidity or fuller expression of the real which Carlyle's prose communicates is achieved not by his personae but by that kind of saturation or "plethora" Paul West has described.[53] The style blurs and absorbs rather than makes more precise, for Carlyle seeks to convulse as well as convert.

Apart from the obvious characters in Carlyle's epic—St. Edmund, Abbot Hugo, Samson, and Bozzy Jocelin—we find a world of lesser fictitious ones who appear and disappear when the occasion demands, representing the scales of virtues and vices, somewhat in the manner of Dante's *Inferno:* "Bobus Higgins, Sausage-maker on the great scale, . . . raising such a clamour for this Aristocracy of Talent" in the *Houndsditch Indicator* (a fictitious paper, incidentally) and whose arguments run "in a vicious circle, rounder than one of [his] own sausages" (*PP*, 31); Dryasdust, the pedantic historian; Sauerteig, one of Carlyle's imaginary philosophers; Blusterowski and Colacorde, "edito-

---

52. "*Sartor Resartus* and the Balance of Fiction"; cf. C. R. Sanders, "Carlyle, Poetry, and the Music of Humanity," *Western Humanities Review*, 16 (1962), 53–66.
53. "Carlyle's Creative Disregard," p. 19. In taking exception to Carlyle's "positively barbarous" language, John Sterling had objected amongst other things to the "heightened and plethoric fulness of the style" (letter to Carlyle, 29 May 1835, quoted by Calder, *Writing of 'Past and Present,'* pp. 123–24).

rial prophets of the Continental-Democratic Movement" (14); Teufelsdröckh, carried over from *Sartor*;
those arch-enemies, Sir Jabesh Windbag, Mr. Facing-
both-ways, Viscount Mealymouth, Earl of Windlestraw,
all antithetical to the real aristocracy of talent; "the
indomitable Plugson too, of the respected Firm of Plugson, Hunks and Company, in St. Dolly Undershot"
(189); or a Voltairean Prussian, "his Excellenz the
Titular-Herr Ritter Kauderwälsch von Pferdefuss-
Quacksalber" (216) ["Sir Gibberish Clovenfoot-Quack
Doctor"];[54] and so on. It may be Carlyle lacks the
verve and gusto of Byron, but they both have their
roots in eighteenth-century satire. We remember also
that among his contemporaries Carlyle's laugh was no-
torious.[55] In *Past and Present* he is willing to allow
even the near-scatological joke when he quotes Jocelin's description of my Lord of Clare: "The Earl,
crowded round (*constipatus*) with many barons and
men-at-arms" (102). "I love honest laughter," Carlyle
writes, "as I do sunlight, but not dishonest" (151). And
it is the tragic absurdity of the modern world his laughter makes us constantly aware of: in a society characterized by its overproduction and unfed, unclothed
masses, he sees only "millions of shirts, and empty
pairs of breeches, [which] hang there in judgment
against you" (170). His vision is sharper, his language
and tone more satirical, than Thomas Hood's in "The
Song of the Shirt," and his sympathy may be correspondingly more effective and convincing.

54. Richard D. Altick's translation, in his edition of *Past and
    Present*, Riverside ed. (Boston: Houghton Mifflin, 1965), p. 215
    n.11.
55. Wilson, *Life*, VI, 99, 253, 365, 386. Cf. *HHW*, 109, where Carlyle
    describes Shakespeare's laughter as "like sunshine on the deep
    sea" and as "very beautiful to me"; also *HHW*, 53; *SR*, 25–26;
    PP, 102; *CME*, II, 200–201. See also Thomas Wentworth
    Higginson, *Carlyle's Laugh and Other Surprises* (1909; rpt.
    Freeport, N.Y.: Books for Libraries Press, 1968), pp. 3–12.

The social commitment in all this is in part the
inevitable consequence of Carlyle's satirical intent and
in part the result of his uneasiness with his own profession of writing. Consequently, "Literature . . . is a
quarrel, and internecine duel, with the whole World
of Darkness that lies without one and within one"
(104). This much we have seen. Yet the social commitment did not entail the abandonment of literary techniques nor mean that Carlyle was unable to practise
them effectively. Certainly he became more desperate
in later life, more aware of society's unwillingness to
seek spiritual health, and certainly his later fictions
become increasingly transparent, his personae real people (Governor Eyre, Sir Robert Peel, Hudson, the railway tycoon).[56] We cannot conclude that his creative
vision is abandoned, that the greater practicality of the
Latter-Day Pamphlets or "Shooting Niagara" clashes
with the use of fictive techniques. To do so would be
to misread these works much as did his contemporaries. Fitzgerald himself wrote to a correspondent:
"Do you see Carlyle's Latter-Day Pamphlets? They
make the world laugh, and his friends rather sorry for
him. But that is because people will still look for practical measures from him. One must be content with him
as a great satirist who can make us feel when we are
wrong, though he cannot set us right. There is a bottom
of truth in Carlyle's wildest rhapsodies."[57] We in turn
overlook Carlyle's comic genius and, even in those
works denouncing literature as lying, his reliance upon
fictive and, more particularly, satirical techniques.

The structural image, for example, of "Shooting

56. Levine, "*Sartor Resartus* and the Balance of Fiction," p. 160,
    makes precisely this point, though argues excessively in favour
    of *Sartor* at the expense of later works.
57. *Tennyson and His Friends*, ed. Hallam, Lord Tennyson, p. 131.
    Cf. A. H. Clough's confidence to Emerson in 1848: "Carlyle
    led us out into the wilderness and left us there" (Wilson, *Life*,
    IV, 53).

Niagara" is that of Niagara Falls, that disastrous state to which England, by way of the 1867 Reform Act, is being drawn like a drowning man. The image is surprisingly undeveloped, but there remain other supporting images: of the whirlpool; the Pit of Hell; the swarmery of bees denoting the contemporary muddle; the "malodorous quagmires and ignominious pools" of the pestilential present (*CME*, V, 48); the inevitable imagery of light, fire, darkness, and sleep; and that animal imagery Carlyle was so fond of that his world seems full of rabid dogs and dumb cattle, or more fearful creatures (the chimera, boa constrictors, rattlesnakes, and apes). The concrete and dramatic sense is still here, though the tone is more abrasive and authoritarian, the irony more inclined to heavy sarcasm.[58]

Most important of all is Carlyle's distinction between the Speculative and the Industrial hero, a distinction which clarifies his final position and recurrent faith in the creative vision. While he may spend more time with the practical or Industrial hero, yet he is also insistent that both types belong to the "Aristocracy of Nature" as distinguished from the hereditary aristocracy. Though their functions are different—the Speculative hero fulfills himself in speech, the Industrial in silent action—

> these are of brother quality; but they go very different roads: "men of *genius*" they all emphatically are, the "inspired Gift of God" lodged in each of them. They do infinitely concern the world and us; especially that first or speaking class,—provided God *have* "touched their lips with his hallowed fire"! Supreme is the importance of these. They are our inspired speakers and seers, the light

58. Cf. Roberts, "Carlyle and the Rhetoric of Unreason," who argues that "the humour of *Sartor Resartus* and the irony at his [Carlyle's] own expense that we find in it turn respectively, in the later books, into scorn and into irony at the expense of others" (406).

of the world; who are to deliver the world from its swarm-
eries, its superstitions (*political* or other);—priceless and
indispensable to us that first Class! (*CME*, V, 23)

Carlyle does not fail to estimate either the worth of
the Speculative hero or the "visionary" (45) nature of
the task, for it is a role he took upon himself. What
needs noting, however, is the all-important qualifica-
tion: the Speculative hero's worth depends upon the
extent to which he is *truly* inspired—"provided God
have 'touched their lips with his hallowed fire'!" Likewise, while he might proceed to reject scornfully "Art,
Poetry and the like" as "that inane region," "a refined
Swarmery," and warn the Aristocrat against "Fiction"
with its "alarming cousinship . . . to *Lying*," he does
so to distinguish "real 'Art' . . . as Fact." Hence, the
Bible is "the *truest* of all Books," and "Homer's *Iliad*,
too, that great Bundle of old Greek Ballads, is nothing
of a *Fiction*" (24–25). In Shakespeare he admires "not
the Fiction" but "the Fact"; "the traces he
[Shakespeare] shows of a talent that could have turned
the *History of England* into a kind of *Iliad*, almost
perhaps into a kind of *Bible*" (26). This is indeed the
great work in hand for Victorian England, and we have
seen the extent to which Carlyle's own work, with its
elevation of heroes, its personae, imagery, dramatic
and concrete sense, above all its attempts at epic grandeur and revelation of the cosmic Divine Fact, approxi-
mates to the task.

While only halfway in his career Carlyle was described by Elizabeth Barrett in an enthusiastic letter to
Robert Browning (27 February 1845) as "the great
teacher of the age." She proceeded in more explicit
fashion to comment upon Carlyle's dual position
as artist-sage, seeing the two roles as by no means
antithetical:

He fills the office of a poet—does he not?—by analysing humanity back into its elements, to the destruction of the conventions of the hour. That is—strictly speaking—the office of the poet, is it not?—and he discharges it fully, and with a wider intelligibility perhaps as far as the contemporary period is concerned, than if he did forthwith "burst into a song."[59]

Whether we accept this view of the poet is irrelevant, though it is a view by no means foreign to either Yeats or Lawrence in their conceptions of the artist. In the case of Carlyle, his fictive world is certainly nothing like the sober fact he would have us believe, and his achievement lies in literature rather than in history or philosophy. For his creative vision leads him to enunciate in Victorian terms the familiar Romantic aesthetic principles—of energy, creativity, imagination, transcendence, symbol—and to express that creative vision through essentially literary means. His two roles—of historian and literary hero—are always together influencing his vision to make the Carlylean Fact indeed a *fictive* one.

59. *The Letters of Robert Browning and Elizabeth Barrett, 1845–1846*, 2 vols. (New York: Harper, 1899), I, 30.

CHAPTER THREE

W. B. Yeats and the Wisdom of Daimonic Images

W. H. Auden in his elegy "In Memory of W. B. Yeats" (1940) did not allow his genuine admiration for the recently dead poet to overwhelm his profound disagreement on certain fundamental issues of belief. "You were silly like us: your gift survived it all," he wrote;[1] and indeed Yeats continues to amaze us, transforming eccentric attitudes and philosophy into poetry which remains central to our time. The myth's cranky esotericism and Yeats's corresponding élitism and flirtation with fascism, nevertheless, have drawn disagreement and disapproval, at times provoking almost as violent a reaction as that from which Carlyle, Lawrence, and Ezra Pound have suffered also.[2] How-

1. For Auden's varying views on Yeats, see Richard Ellmann, *Eminent Domain: Yeats among Wilde, Joyce, Pound, Eliot and Auden* (New York: O.U.P., 1967), p. 105 ff.
2. See Louis MacNeice, *The Poetry of W. B. Yeats* (London: O.U.P., 1941); Robert Graves, *Crowning Privilege*, pp. 135–41; Yvor Winters, *The Poetry of W. B. Yeats*, Swallow Pamphlets 10 (Denver: Alan Swallow, 1960). Cf. Laurence Lerner, "W. B. Yeats: Poet and Crank," Chatterton Lecture, *Proc. Brit. Acad.*,

ever, when Yeats's myth, with its political as well as
metaphysical relevance, is placed within the context
of the Romantic vitalist tradition, its eccentricity, like
that of Blake's myth, is considerably diminished.
Moreover, the disagreement hinges upon a particularly
debatable critical position which seeks to correlate the
poetry's worth to the validity of the poet's ideas. Sean
O'Casey, in many ways antithetical to Yeats, took a
more defensible position. In 1964 when he himself was
dying, he recited the advice to Irish poets in "Under
Ben Bulben" and commented: "Good poetry, but bad
advice for Irish poets. Is it the Ireland of aristocratic
parasites and enslaved peasants he's asking us to go
back to? The Ireland of plaster saints and hedge
scholars? The Ireland of the Big House and the little
people? The Ireland of purple dust? Not bloody likely
we'll go back to those corpses. But it's still a damn fine

---

49 (London: O.U.P., 1963). Lerner found Yeats "the most splendid of modern poets" but saddled with "utterly crackpot ideas."
F. R. Leavis more recently took exception to "the cult and
industry" now surrounding Yeats, prescribing study of "Yeats's
life-long addiction to the occult and the esoteric, together with
the schematisms and the diagrammatics and the symbolical
elaborations that were its product," in English Literature in Our
Time and the University, The Clark Lectures, 1967 (London:
Chatto and Windus, 1969), pp. 137–38. The same objection is
made in F. R. Leavis and Q. D. Leavis, Lectures in America (New
York: Pantheon, 1969), p. 65, a lecture which also briefly distinguishes between Yeats and Blake. For discussion of Yeats's fascism, see Conor Cruise O'Brien, "Passion and Cunning: An
Essay on the Politics of W. B. Yeats," in In Excited Reverie,
ed. A. N. Jeffares and K. G. W. Cross (London: Macmillan,
1965), pp. 207–78; and cf. George Orwell, "W. B. Yeats" (1943),
in Critical Essays (London: Secker and Warburg, 1960), pp.
129–36; John R. Harrison, The Reactionaries (London: Gollancz, 1967), pp. 39–73; Francis Stuart, in The Yeats We Knew,
ed. Francis MacManus (Cork: Mercier Press, 1965), p. 34; and
Donald T. Torchiana, W. B. Yeats and Georgian Ireland (Evanston, Ill.: Northwestern Univ. Press, 1966), p. 159. Cf. Yeats's
own statement in Letters, pp. 881–82.

poem. And so like Yeats, to make good poetry out of bad opinions."[3]

Bad opinions or not—and Yeats's perceptions of the world and man, his traditional sense involving literature, history, and culture, his wrestling with the antinomies of time and eternity, cannot be lightly dismissed—it requires more than an Irish gift of the gab to elevate Yeats to the deserved stature his work now holds in the literature of this century. The silly Yeats "scarcely is to be encountered in the important poems and plays."[4] And while we might share at times O'Casey's view that Yeats often made "good poetry out of bad opinions," we recognize also the same terrifying honesty T. S. Eliot ascribed to Blake, who was for Yeats a favourite poet, a masterful precursor in song and prophecy, a spiritual mentor. When in 1940 Eliot, somewhat uncomfortably, offered his own pronouncement on Yeats, he used much the same terms he had previously applied to Blake. Eliot saw "an exceptional honesty and courage," shocking us with the "revelation of what a man really is and remains." We might conclude that Yeats's poetry, like that of Blake, has "the unpleasantness of great poetry."[5] If we are to believe

3. Quoted in David Krause, "Sean O'Casey: 1880–1964," in *Irish Renaissance: A Gathering of Essays, Memoirs, and Letters from The Massachusetts Review*, ed. Robin Skelton and David R. Clark (Dublin: Dolmen Press, 1965), p. 156. Cf. Oliver St. John Gogarty who viewed "Under Ben Bulben" as "a rap at the modern Woolworth Irishmen who ignorant of the country's history are contented to obtrude their vulgarity in the place of verse." Quoted in John Unterecker, "Yeats and Patrick McCartan, A Fenian Friendship," *Yeats Centenary Papers*, ed. Liam Miller (Dublin: Dolmen Press, 1965), X, 421.
4. Harold Bloom, "Yeats and the Romantics," in *Modern Poetry: Essays in Criticism*, ed. John Hollander (New York: O.U.P., 1968), p. 503.
5. "Blake" and "Yeats," in *Selected Prose* (Harmondsworth: Penguin, 1953), pp. 169, 203–4. Cf. Eliot's earlier pronouncements on Yeats's "greatness" arrived at "against the greatest odds" of

Allen Tate, it is "a poetry . . . nearer the centre of our main traditions of sensibility and thought than the poetry of Eliot or of Pound."[6]

My own purpose is to examine certain of Yeats's "opinions," bad or otherwise, as they are inherited from the Romantic vitalist tradition embracing Blake, Carlyle, and Lawrence, and rearticulated in the new and distinctive inflections characteristic of the Irish poet. I have chosen to concentrate for the most part upon *The Tower* (1928) and *The Winding Stair* (1933) because both volumes show Yeats at the height of his powers and most acutely aware of the dialectical vacillation experienced throughout his career. In Harold Bloom's words, these two volumes are "more in touch with justice and reality, Yeatsian tests for greatness, than are all but a few of the *Last Poems*."[7] An appreciation of the nature of Yeats's vision and the quality of expression gained in the composition of these poems is thus essential to an understanding and evaluation of his achievement and his place within the Romantic vitalist tradition.

1

In 1936, "at life's end," Yeats wrote with that intense self-examination he practised from the outset:

---

a philosophy weakened by "the trifling and eccentric, the provincial in time and place," in *After Strange Gods* (New York: Harcourt, Brace, 1934), pp. 47–51. For Eliot's "rapprochement" with Yeats, see Ellmann, *Eminent Domain*, pp. 94–95.

6. "Yeats's Romanticism: Notes and Suggestions," rpt. in *The Permanence of Yeats*, ed. James Hall and Martin Steinmann (New York: Collier, 1961), p. 105. I cannot accept, however, Tate's view of Yeats as "unromantic" (p. 98) any more than can Bloom, in *Modern Poetry*, ed. Hollander, p. 502. See also Stephen Spender, "The Influence of Yeats on Later English Poets," *Tri-Quarterly*, 4 (1965), 82–89.

7. *Yeats* (New York: O.U.P., 1970), p. 162.

> Grant me an old man's frenzy,
> Myself must I remake
> Till I am Timon and Lear
> Or that William Blake
> Who beat upon the wall
> Till Truth obeyed his call;

("An Acre of Grass," ll. 13–18)

Yeats manages to transform what in an inferior poet would be pretentious name-dropping or excessive gesture into a resonant sense of affinity with a tradition and a body of experience larger than mere self. Serving as touchstones, the figures remain subsidiary to the major Romantic concern with the making of self, and the inappropriateness of the portrait of Blake (resembling a Yeatsian mask more than the actual Blake) no more matters than the historical inaccuracies of Carlyle or Blake himself. "I am no stickler for the fact," as Yeats once admitted (*Myth*, p. 351), and as recent critics have shown, he constantly misinterpreted his sources to suit his own purpose.[8] His portraits are deliberately fictive constructions relevant more to himself than to his sitters.

Earlier, in 1908, Yeats had answered objections to his practice of revision in terms the later pronouncement echoes:

> *The friends that have it I do wrong*
> *When ever I remake a song,*
> *Should know what issue is at stake:*
> *It is myself that I remake.*

(*Var*, p. 778)

Indeed, precisely this pattern of reverberating echoes, whether of image, figure, theme, or concept, is the

8. Bloom, *Yeats*; George Bornstein, *Yeats and Shelley* (Chicago: Univ. of Chicago Press, 1970).

distinctive cumulative method which gives shape and
continuity to Yeats's poetry. The same preoccupation
with the process of making the self dominates his work
from *The Wanderings of Oisin* (1889) to *Last Poems*
(1939). Whether writing of Oisin or John O'Leary,
Cuchulain or Padraic Pearse, or adopting the mask of
lover, hero, poet, or saint, within settings ranging from
Arcady and ancient India to modern Ireland, the Romantic concern with the nature and fulfilment of the
self is the supreme theme out of which Yeats's entire
work comes.

What both verse statements reveal, moreover, is the
persistent recognition on Yeats's part of the central
Romantic and vitalist concentration upon the fictive
nature of the self. The reality which the self experiences is the direct consequence of the self's own nature; and more than mere perception, vision demands
a creativity on the part of the self kept continually busy
constructing both self and world. The more completely
real and total vision into the life of things is made
possible only when the self is itself most fictive and
harmonious. Just as the figures in Blake's myth see
wholly when they themselves are made whole, or as
Carlyle's heroes pierce through semblance to Fact by
a dynamic perception of the creative self, so too
throughout his poetry Yeats realizes the necessary re-
furnishing of self in its progression towards the peace,
harmony, and vision of fulfilment. The result is a constant vacillation between the antinomies of his dialectic—between self and soul, heart and intellect, aesthetic and heroic, swordsman and saint. "I have spent
my life saying the same thing in many different ways.
I denounced old age before I was twenty, and the
Swordsman throughout repudiates the Saint—though
with vacillation."[9]

9. MS note quoted in T. R. Henn, "Horseman, Pass By!" in *Yeats:
Last Poems*, ed. Jon Stallworthy (London: Macmillan, 1968),

That vacillation is more than an exploration of different and antagonistic mental states, more than psychological in relevance. It is in turn a discipline—moral, metaphysical, and aesthetic in scope—within which the self accumulates experience; is built, broken, rebuilt, and expanded in the process, that it might be brought to knowledge of "the heart's discovery of itself" (*Myth*, p. 325) or to dance "heart's truth" ("Crazy Jane Grown Old Looks at the Dancers"). And it is an action or process involving repetition, in the manner of the whirling dancer, winding stair, or spiralling gyre, Yeats's controlling or structural images. It also involves a kind of poetic ventriloquism and dramatic sense in which the more creative a self is the more roles he is able to adopt and explore. Hence the now familiar Yeats assertions, "The poet should know all classes of men as one of themselves"; "He will play with all masks" (*Auto*, p. 470).[10] Yeats's work, consequently, reveals a succession of masks, figures, and faces that parade, in his own image, like circus animals throughout his poetry, plays, and prose. Indeed, he proceeded to create and populate a whole world, sometimes inheriting masks from Celtic myth (like Cuchulain), sometimes inventing others of his own (Crazy Jane, Ribh, Tom the Lunatic), but also, and with increasing strength, transforming his own world and investing contemporaries like Maud Gonne, Lady Gregory, Synge, and himself with a symbolic, even

---

p. 121 n.1. Cf. Yeats to Olivia Shakespear, 30 June 1932, writing of his work as a whole: "The swordsman throughout repudiates the saint, but not without vacillation. Is that perhaps the sole theme—Usheen and Patrick—'so get you gone Von Hügel though with blessings on your head'?" (*Letters*, p. 798).

10. As early as 1869 J. B. Yeats wrote to Edward Dowden that he "would have a man know all emotions." *Letters to His Son and Others, 1869–1922*, ed. J. M. Hone (London: Faber, 1944), p. 48; cf. pp. 160–61. See also his *Early Memories* (Dundrum: Cuala, 1923), p. 10.

metaphysical, status. Denis Donoghue is anything but fanciful when he claims, "He invented a country, calling it Ireland"; "Yeats's Ireland is a fiction; so is his Poet."[11] For all Yeats's commitment to esoteric pursuits in magic and the occult and his indebtedness to transcendentalist philosophies, his is a poetry rooted in a humanism.

At the centre of that humanism is the concern with the dynamic and creative self. As insistently as Blake or Carlyle, Yeats could assert that man is the sole creator of his world. Lawrence too, recognizing support for his view in Bishop Berkeley, insisted, "Nothing exists beyond what I know" (*Ph. II*, p. 617). Adopting a subjectivism also akin to Berkeley's but given a deliberately arrogant and aristocratic turn, Yeats offered as "The First Principle" in "A General Introduction for My Work" (written 1937): "The world knows nothing because it has made nothing, we know everything because we have made everything" (*E & I*, p. 510). The claim has its source in the Romantic assertion of the self's primacy, while its somewhat haughty, imperious air is the consequence partly of Yeats's own arrogance but also of his Romantic faith in the autonomy of the self's fictive nature. A similar position we have seen in Blake, while Yeats himself knew also of its adoption by Shelley. In "The Philosophy of Shelley's Poetry" (1900; *E & I*, p. 70), for example, he quoted approvingly Shelley-Julian's affirmation in "Julian and Maddalo":

> "Where is the love, beauty, and truth we seek
> But in our mind? And if we were not weak,
> Should we be less in deed than in desire?"

(ll. 174–76)

11. *Yeats*, Fontana Modern Masters (London: Collins, 1971), pp. 14, 24.

The view is given in *A Vision* in more abstract and antinomial fashion: "The whole system is founded upon the belief that the ultimate reality, symbolised as the Sphere, falls in human consciousness, as Nicholas of Cusa was the first to demonstrate, into a series of antinomies" (p. 187).[12] But it accounts for Yeats's "Druid who answered, when someone asked him who made the world, 'The Druids made it'" (*Exp*, p. 24), and for Cuchulain, weak neither in deed nor desire, who in *The Death of Cuchulain* (1939) asserts, "I make the truth!" (*Var. Plays*, p. 1056). Indebted to platonic and idealist philosophers from Plotinus to Berkeley, Yeats in 1926 insisted to Sturge Moore that "nothing can exist that is not in the mind as 'an element of experience,'" a view which would "liberate us from all manner of abstractions and create at once a joyous artistic life" (*Y & TSM*, pp. 68–69). He found support in Giambattista Vico who argued, "We can know nothing that we have not made," and in his other authorities, Swift, Hegel, and Balzac (*Exp*, pp. 429–30). Similar assertions Yeats made at different times in his prose: "Somebody has said that all sound philosophy is but biography"; "History seems to me a human drama"; "All knowledge is biography" (*Exp*, pp. 235, 290, 397).

The stance has a political relevance also: Yeats shared with Carlyle that impulse to reduce all to the Great Man, an impulse which as an article of faith led both to a protofascism. Just as Carlyle justified the authority of an aristocratic hero or captain of industry by pointing to his esemplastic or creative character, moulding chaos into cosmos, so too Ezra Pound defended Mussolini much in the way Yeats's political views were formulated: "Treat him as *artifex* and all

12. I use the term "antinomial" in the same sense as Bornstein, *Yeats and Shelley*, p. 116: "an inclusive vision based on the tension between opposites like the ideal and the actual."

the details fall into place. Take him as anything save
the artist and you will get muddled with contradictions."[13] Thus far did the process of remaking the
self take Yeats, encouraging him to a naïve and cavalier
political faith, while at the same time providing him
with a distinctive view of history and philosophy and
an awareness of the dynamic creative self (the self as
lamp rather than mere reflecting mirror).

With such a supremely subjectivist faith in the individual self, Yeats went beyond the self's primacy to
stress the self's fictive character. As much as Blake and
any modern man after him, Yeats was aware of the
schizophrenic condition of man and from such an
awareness is derived his involvement with the making
of self. Upholding from the beginning of his poetic
career the dialectical nature of all things, he came to
conceive man as possessing both a contingent and an
essential self. The true and essential self was given to
man, while the contingent self could be refined and
purified by the energy and extent to which man might
desire and construct his anti-self, or mask. Union of
contingent self (or "Will," as Yeats called it in *A Vision*) with the mask would bring about a temporary
awareness of the daimonic essential self, a "Unity of
Being," which could be possessed completely only after
a series of purgatorial reincarnations or lives.

Yeats's doctrine of the Mask has, then, this psychological and metaphysical purpose—to complete the
partial self by union with one's daimonic eternal self.
Such a union brings release from further incarnations
and the peace of eternity, the Condition of Fire, upon
which he elaborated in *Per Amica Silentia Lunae*
(1917) in obviously Blakean terms:[14]

13. *Jefferson and/or Mussolini* (1935), quoted in Noel Stock, *The
Life of Ezra Pound* (New York: Pantheon, 1970), p. 331.
14. Although the terms are Blakean, Bloom is right to see Yeats's
clinamen from Blake's position (*Yeats*, p. 72).

When all sequence comes to an end, time comes to an end, and the soul puts on the rhythmic or spiritual body or luminous body and contemplates all the events of its memory and every possible impulse in an eternal possession of itself in one single moment. That condition is alone animate, all the rest is fantasy, and from thence [sic] come all the passions and, some have held, the very heat of the body. (Myth, p. 357)

The adoption of a mask may also be in part a disguise or pose, in the manner of Byron or Baudelaire rather than Blake, a fin-de-siècle defiance of the bourgeois. Hence, in his 1909 diary "Estrangement," he wrote, "Style, personality—deliberately adopted and therefore a mask—is the only escape from the hot-faced bargainers and the money-changers" (Auto, p. 461). More than simply an anti-bourgeois stance, however, Yeats's conception of the Mask took on a higher significance, for escape from "the hot-faced bargainers" was necessary if one were not to submit to that moral passivity and aesthetic impurity he associated with the bourgeois mind. The style gained from adoption of a mask involved that discipline Yeats saw as necessary to a virtuous life or to aesthetic creation.

There is a relation between discipline and the theatrical sense. If we cannot imagine ourselves as different from what we are and assume that second self, we cannot impose a discipline upon ourselves, though we may accept one from others. Active virtue as distinguished from the passive acceptance of a current code is therefore theatrical, consciously dramatic, the wearing of a mask. It is the condition of arduous full life. (Auto, p. 469)

Life is indeed a comédie humaine—Balzac constantly brought Yeats back from eastern meditative philosophies (E & I, p. 448)—and those creative selves, most capable of constructing an anti-self, or mask, out of their bitter, dissatisfied, and incomplete natures, are thus made aware of the nature of both themselves and existence. They learn the "wisdom of daemonic images" ("Meditations in Time of Civil War," VII, 39). When reality itself has as subjective a foundation as the creative self, it is no wonder that knowledge of one's self and the attainment of a spiritual psychic unity within leads inevitably to knowledge of the ultimate reality, the larger cosmic unity without. Hence, in another 1909 diary, "The Death of Synge," Yeats wrote what has by now come to be one of several central statements he made about his poetry and its fictive world:

> I think that all happiness depends on the energy to assume the mask of some other self; that all joyous or creative life is a rebirth as something not oneself, something which has no memory and is created in a moment and perpetually renewed. We put on a grotesque or solemn painted face to hide us from the terrors of judgment, invent an imaginative Saturnalia where one forgets reality, a game like that of a child, where one loses the infinite pain of self-realization. Perhaps all the sins and energies of the world are but its flight from an infinite blinding beam. (*Auto*, pp. 503–4)

Yet the mask must not be an evasion; "the infinite pain of self-realization" one must learn to endure; one must not perpetually forget "reality." Indeed, in a late essay, "Prometheus Unbound" (1932), he asked pointedly, "Why is Shelley terrified of the Last Day like a Victorian child? It was not terrible to Blake" (*E & I*, p. 420). But at the same time masks are a necessary piece of mental equipment in the self's progression towards fulfilment, towards reconciling the dichotomy of contingent and eternal selves, of what in *A Vision* he called "reality and justice" (p. 25).

Man's Mental Fight, to use Blake's terms, to reunite with his eternal self consists of more than a straightforward conflict between self and mask—that which a man is and that which he would most like to be. Somewhat in the manner of Blake's Four Zoas,[15] Yeats conceived of Four Faculties existing within man, imaged as conflicting within a pair of interpenetrating gyres or cones. Man's spiritual conflict consists not only of a war between what he is and what he desires to become, but also between his intellectual faculty (Creative Mind) and what that faculty knows, whether from environment, mental and physical, or from history (Body of Fate). The drama is thus both intellectual and emotional and pertains to both individual men and history. Moreover, the Four Faculties proceed to expand or contract through their pairs of cones, one subjective (or antithetical, as Yeats preferred to call it), the other objective (or primary).

> By the *antithetical* cone . . . we express more and more, as it broadens, our inner world of desire and imagination, whereas by the *primary* . . . we express more and more, as it broadens, that objectivity of mind which, in the words of Murray's Dictionary, lays "stress upon that which is external to the mind" or treats "of outward things and events rather than of inward thought" or seeks "to exhibit the actual facts, not coloured by the opinions or feelings." The *antithetical tincture* is emotional and aesthetic whereas the *primary tincture* is reasonable and moral. (*V*, p. 73)

However, we should always remember that "the sphere is reality" (p. 73), using that term as designating "the ultimate reality" in which "all things are present as an eternal instant to our *Daimon* (or *Ghostly Self* as it is called, when it inhabits the sphere), but that instant is of necessity unintelligible to all bound to the antinomies" (p. 193).

Although Yeats's abstract classification is complicated further by the possibility of a false as well as a

15. Richard Ellmann, *The Identity of Yeats* (London: Faber, 1964), pp. 28–29.

true mask, a false as well as a true creative mind, this much is clear: by using the Four Faculties he was capable of tracing the various complex tensions within and without man, in the mental and physical worlds he knows, inhabits, and constructs. The system Yeats formulated in *A Vision* was merely a framework— "metaphors for poetry," as his instructors described it (p. 8)—and surprisingly few poems fall foul of the system's abstractions. But the scope of the system enabled him to focus on the dynamic and dialectical nature of the self and its relationship to the larger design of history. For the gyres' movement from primary to antithetical has a threefold relevance: the movement describes the course taken by the individual self in a single lifetime; but it also constitutes the series of "cradles" or reincarnations the self undergoes before resting in the eternal peace of the sphere; while it includes further the historical cycle taken by an entire civilization and reflects the whole sweep of history. Man thus becomes truly the microcosmic image of the world, as Yeats's early interest in cabbalism and Hermes Trismegistus had revealed. In similar fashion, although he denounced Hermes Trismegistus (*J*, 91: 32–35), Blake traced the Fall and Redemption of man in the disharmony and reunion of the Four Zoas, moving freely from individual men to the Eternal Man, and used his own biography as emblematic of the larger cosmic process.

Yeats's own preference for the antithetical, "our inner world of desire and imagination," corresponds to Blake's insistence upon energy and the visionary faculty. For Vision incorporates intellect in a dynamic harmony of self, as opposed to the abstracting Urizenic intellect which divides, ultimately fragments, the self, thus fixing it in a deathly stasis. Yeats, on the other hand, with his antinomies of primary and antithetical, intellect and passion, talks of a harmony of self, Unity of Being, which is arrived at not by truly reconciling the antinomies but by a preponderance of one of them—passion.[16] The source for the elevation of passion is perhaps his father, J. B. Yeats, rather than a misreading of Blake. In *Autobiographies* we are told that his father's reading from the poets was always from their "most passionate moment," that "his chief word of praise" was "intensity," a quality his mother possessed and sought herself in the stories of the fishing people of Howth and Sligo (pp. 61–62, 65). Consequently, for W. B. Yeats the self is granted the numinous experience of the vortex vision—Unity of Being, which reconciles momentarily the war within—in the most preponderantly antithetical state of all, Phase 15, in his system of the phases of the moon.

Writing in 1922 of "Four Years: 1887–1891," Yeats noted, "A conviction that the world was now but a bundle of fragments possessed me without ceasing" (*Auto*, p. 189). Dominated by his awareness of the fragmentary nature of both self and world, Yeats "thought that in man and race alike there is something called 'Unity of Being', using that term as Dante used it when he compared beauty in the *Convito* to a perfectly proportioned human body. My father, from whom I had learned the term, preferred a comparison to a musical instrument so strung that if we touch a string all the strings murmer faintly" (p. 190). Preferring the older platonic image of the body to the Coleridgean Romantic aeolian harp, Yeats developed an organicism, much as did Blake, Carlyle, and Lawrence, to combat the now dominant mechanism and mammonism contributing to the Urizenic fragmentation of the present. In the manner of the vitalists, Yeats envisaged the battlefield as man's creative self. Consequently, he argued, Unity of Being is possible only

16. Bloom, *Yeats*, chap. 5, "Blake and Yeats," esp. pp. 70–74.

through the antithetical—through passionate intensity, that subjectivity of self which alone constituted the aesthetic or imaginative.

In a famous statement in *Autobiographies,* he offered his version of the myth of the dissociation of the sensibility, placing the contemporary chaos within the context of cultural history and stressing that wholeness of self through passion, in which the Four Faculties are momentarily harmonized.

Somewhere about 1450, though later in some parts of Europe by a hundred years or so, and in some earlier, men attained to personality in great numbers, "Unity of Being", and became like "a perfectly proportioned human body", and as men so fashioned held places of power, their nations had it too, prince and ploughman sharing that thought and feeling. What afterwards showed for rifts and cracks were there already, but imperious impulse held all together. . . . The men that Titian painted, the men that Jongsen painted,[17] even the men of Van Dyck seemed at moments like great hawks at rest. In the Dublin National Gallery there hung, perhaps there still hang, upon the same wall, a portrait of some Venetian gentleman by Strozzi, and Mr. Sargent's painting of President Wilson. Whatever thought broods in the dark eyes of that Venetian gentleman has drawn its life from his whole body; it feeds upon it as the flame feeds upon the candle—and should that thought be changed, his pose would change, his very cloak would rustle, for his whole body thinks. President Wilson lives only in the eyes, which are steady and intent; the flesh about the mouth is dead, and the hands are dead, and the clothes suggest no movement of his body, nor any movement but that of the valet, who has brushed and folded in mechanical routine. There all was an energy flowing outward from the nature itself; here all is the

17. See Denis Donoghue and Frank Kermode, letter to the editor, *TLS,* 11 Feb. 1972, p. 157. They note Yeats's confusion of Jongsen with the correct Cornelius Van Ceulen Jonson (or Janssen), a seventeenth-century Dutch painter.

anxious study and slight deflection of external force; there man's mind and body were predominantly subjective; here all is objective. (pp. 291–92)

The contrast elaborated upon here between the paintings by Strozzi and Sargent parallels the distinction drawn by T. S. Eliot between Donne and Tennyson or Browning. Both distinctions derive from the attainment of a unified self in a previous cultural period and the later disintegration. Both stress the wholeness of the perception—Yeats's the "whole body thinks" and Eliot's "A thought to Donne was an experience; it modified his sensibility."[18] What characterizes Yeats's version, however, is the marked vitalist emphasis upon the organic interaction of the whole self in a dynamic perception, and his Carlylean image of the valet as epitomizing the mechanical mind. Yeats further developed the myth by his elaborate phases of the moon, with the fullness of moon (complete subjectivity) corresponding approximately to the mid-Renaissance or to similar moments of unity, like fifth-century Byzantium or the Greece of Phidias. Approximation only is possible partly because Yeats refused to chart cultural movements with a mathematical precision, but also because man, being "composite" (composed of dialectical tensions), ceases to exist in either Phase 1 or Phase 15, when one of the dialectical antinomies—either complete subjectivity (antithetical) or complete plasticity (primary)—exclusively prevails. In Carlyle's terms, chaos is shaped into cosmos or cosmos falls away into chaos in these two states. Writing to Edmund Dulac in 1937, when his second and revised edition of *A Vision* appeared, Yeats described the purpose of his system in similar terms: "I do not know what my book will be to others—nothing perhaps. To me it

18. "The Metaphysical Poets," in *Selected Prose*, p. 117.

means a last act of defence against the chaos of the world, & I hope for ten years to write out of my renewed security."[19]

Yeats had in fact always striven for such a defence; in "If I Were Four-and-Twenty" (1919), he acknowledged the persistent need to "hammer [his] thoughts into unity," much as Blake had recognized the obligation to create a system. Indeed, what often proves remarkable in Yeats's work is the clarity with which he saw, even early on, the precise and complex nature of his dilemma. In the earliest poems commitment to one position is always counterbalanced by the attraction of its opposite: Oisin is answered by Patrick; the heroic by the contemplative and aesthetic; Fergus by the Druid; or faery by stolen child.

In 1888 to Katherine Tynan he wrote thus of his particular dilemma: that *The Wanderings of Oisin* volume was "not the poetry of insight and knowledge, but of longing and complaint—the cry of the heart against necessity"; and committed himself in the future to writing poetry of the former kind (*Letters*, p. 63). Characteristically that dilemma is cosmic rather than exclusively individual, as his Introduction to Lady Gregory's *Gods and Fighting Men* (1904) shows: "It sometimes seems as if there is a kind of day and night of religion, and that a period when the influences are those that shape the world is followed by a period when the greater power is in influences that would lure the soul out of the world, out of the body" (*Exp*, p. 24). Two years later he wrote to Florence Farr in more obviously vitalist and Nietzschean terms of his attempt "to lay hands upon some dynamic and substantialising force as distinguished from the eastern quiescent and supersensualizing state of the soul—a movement

---

19. Quoted in Richard Ellmann, *Yeats: The Man and the Masks* (London: Macmillan, 1948), p. 291. Cf. Yeats to Ethel Mannin, 20 Oct. 1938, in *Letters*, pp. 917–18.

downwards upon life, not upwards out of life" (*Letters*, p. 469). The two types of poetry defined to Katherine Tynan thus correspond to this further dialectic—of experience or transcendence, of acceptance or flight, responsibility or evasion, even West or East. In the same year, in *Discoveries*, this dialectical pattern posed "the choice of choices":

> In literature . . . we have lost in personality, in our delight in the whole man—blood, imagination, intellect, running together—but have found a new delight, in essences, in states of mind, in pure imagination, in all that comes to us most easily in elaborate music. There are two ways before literature—upward into ever-growing subtlety, with Verhaeren, with Mallarmé, with Maeterlinck, until at last, it may be, a new agreement among refined and studious men gives birth to a new passion, and what seems literature becomes religion; or downward, taking the soul with us until all is simplified and solidified again. That is the choice of choices—the way of the bird until common eyes have lost us, or to the market carts. (*E & I*, pp. 266–67)

By 1925 the downward path, redefined as "simplification through intensity," characterized the true mask of a man of Phase 17, that favourable phase to which Yeats assigned himself together with Dante, Shelley, and Landor (*V*, p. 140). In another section of *Discoveries*, "The Thinking of the Body," Yeats made clear his choice which was already evident in poems in *In the Seven Woods* (1904): "all good art" is characterized by "our thought" rushing "out to the edges of our flesh"; and acknowledging Blake whom he again distorts, "Art bids us touch and taste and hear and see the world, and shrinks from what Blake calls mathematic form, from every abstract thing, from all that is of the brain only, from all that is not a fountain jetting from the entire hopes, memories, and sensations of the body" (*E & I*, pp. 292–93). The distortion is clear in Yeats's polarization (abstraction or body), since neither pole satisfied Blake for whom each represented a false mode of thought. Yeats is closer to Lawrence when in *On the Boiler* he argued, "Our bodies are nearer to our coherence because nearer to the 'unconscious' than our thought" (*Exp*, pp. 446–47). The poems in *The Tower*, however, indicate the extent to which the counterimpulse of the way of the bird, gathering him into the artifice of eternity, pulled at him.

While Yeats used his Four Faculties, like Blake, to dramatize the war of opposites which images all existence, he again departs from Blake in his fascination with that war. For while the warring antinomies bring the fullness of moon and Vision, they also result inevitably in collapse and chaos. Yeats's position, unlike that of Blake, remained intrinsically cyclical and tragic. Indeed, he saw the tragedy of the cosmic and psychic wars as constituting the source of man's greatness as well as of his defeat and decline. Consequently, his work constantly justifies failure rather than triumph, offers resignation and reconciliation rather than transcendent and apocalyptic victory.[20] For it is with failure that the imagination is most fascinated and through failure that the self is refined.

> Does the imagination dwell the most
> Upon a woman won or woman lost?

> ("The Tower," ll. 113–14)

The question had been answered in part in the superior stance of the old crane of Gort in "The Three Beggars" in the volume *Responsibilities*. There King Guaire's question "Do men who least desire get most, / Or get the most who most desire?" provoked the beggars to a fruitless whirling frenzy lasting three days and nights.

---

20. Balachandra Rajan has argued for greater attention to Yeats's myth of failure, in "Yeats and the Absurd," *Tri-Quarterly*, 4 (1965), 133.

The crane, however, knows that the trout he seeks can be caught only "If but I do not seem to care." The appropriate mask to adopt in pursuit of desire and fulfilment is the seeming indifference of the hero, as Yeats in the same volume advised Lady Gregory in "To a Friend Whose Work Has Come to Nothing." But the beggars' frenzy has its value too and in *Per Amica Silentia Lunae* Yeats affirmed: "The poet finds and makes his mask in disappointment, the hero in defeat. The desire that is satisfied is not a great desire, nor has the shoulder used all its might that an unbreakable gate has never strained" (*Myth*, p. 337). The result is the daimonic crisis to which all men are eventually brought to be purified, but it is a purification through failure which the passionate self must learn to endure.

Both Blake and Yeats use certain physical and mental states to symbolize the spiritual health or disease of the self, tracing the different stages in the self's progression towards fulfilment. And Yeats's terms (joy and ecstasy), his elevation of passion, and his scourging of abstraction are clearly inherited from Blake and the Romantic vitalist tradition. More peculiarly Yeats prefers heroic indifference and tragic gaiety to concern with personal salvation and triumph, the pettiness of which he saw as particularly bourgeois. An examination of these attitudes and their relationship to the wisdom gained from daimonic images is thus a necessary preliminary to fuller appreciation of Yeats's distinctive vision.

Yeats's divergence from Blake is once more evident in his discussion of joy and tragedy. In 1909, when his ideas on tragedy were acquiring sharper focus, he distinguished tragedy from comedy, the one offering ecstasy, the other joy.

Comedy is joyous because all assumption of a part, of a personal mask, whether of the individualized face of comedy or of the grotesque face of farce, is a display of energy, and all energy is joyous. A poet creates tragedy from his own soul, that soul which is alike in all men. It has not joy, as we understand that word, but ecstasy, which is from the contemplation of things vaster than the individual and imperfectly seen, perhaps, by all those that still live. The masks of tragedy contain neither character nor personal energy. They are allied to decoration and to the abstract figures of Egyptian temples. Before the mind can look out of their eyes the active will perishes, hence their sorrowful calm. Joy is of the will which labours, which overcomes obstacles, which knows triumph. . . . is not ecstasy some fulfilment of the soul in itself, some slow or sudden expansion of it like an overflowing well? Is not this what is meant by beauty? (*Auto*, p. 471)[21]

The superiority of tragedy lies then in its revelation of eternal truth: we pass beyond "the individualized face of comedy" to "contemplation of things vaster than the individual." A similar movement can be traced in Yeats's own development—from a *fin-de-siècle* narcissism and debilitating Romantic introspection to that position in which his personal experiences acquire archetypal stature and his biography becomes a history of our time. In his pursuit of the soul's progression to the state of beauty, which is both the condition of Unity of Being and eternity itself, Yeats proceeded to use not only the above distinction of comedy and tragedy but its various terms and images. Joy and ecstasy, will and triumph, labour and overflowing well, all take their place in his system of thought and symbol. Likewise, in 1910 he wrote of tragedy in these terms: "Tragic art, passionate art, the

21. As Thomas R. Whitaker has noted, Yeats's views of joy changed in the course of time. The term "ecstasy" supplanted that of "joy" in the middle years, but in later works he preferred terms like "shaping joy" or "tragic joy." *Swan and Shadow: Yeats's Dialogue with History* (Chapel Hill: Univ. of North Carolina Press, 1964), p. 275. Cf. *E & I*, pp. 239, 321; *Exp*, pp. 448–49.

drowner of dykes, the confounder of understanding, moves us by setting us to reverie, by alluring us almost to the intensity of trance. The persons upon the stage, let us say, greaten till they are humanity itself. We feel our minds expand convulsively or spread out slowly like some moon-brightened image-crowded sea" (*E & I*, p. 245). The "reverie," "trance," and, above all, that "moon-brightened image-crowded sea" are also to recur at crucial moments in Yeats's poetry and vision.

What is characteristic of Yeats is that the state of reverie or trance in which our minds expand occurs only through an awareness of life's tragedy. "We begin to live when we have conceived life as tragedy" (*Auto*, p. 189). Hence, although he could uphold the conjunction of energy and joy—"I think that all happiness depends on the energy to assume the mask of some other self; that all joyous or creative life is a rebirth as something not oneself" (p. 503)—the fearful labour within a tragic process became his more characteristic emphasis.

> The fascination of what's difficult
> Has dried the sap out of my veins, and rent
> Spontaneous joy and natural content
> Out of my heart.
>
> ("The Fascination of What's Difficult")

As he proceeded to point out in that poem, the creative life was not restricted to aesthetics or the psychology of the Mask, but, like Blake's catholic definition of Art, included everyday life ("the day's war with every knave and dolt") and his work at the Abbey ("Theatre business, management of men"). In other poems he saw such creativity present also in the labouring creation of a woman's beauty ("Adam's Curse") and even in the shaping of political events ("Easter 1916"). Indeed, contemporary politics in Ireland proved tragic,

in much the same way Irish history has been persistently tragic, demanding sacrifice of Oisin, Cuchulain,
or Usna's sons. For Yeats as poet the tragedy took the
particular form of a choice, his distinctive dialectical
stance, between life and art:

> The intellect of man is forced to choose
> Perfection of the life, or of the work,
> And if it take the second must refuse
> A heavenly mansion, raging in the dark.

> ("The Choice")

Whatever fatalism may or may not be found in Yeats's
myth, he reiterated frequently the necessity of choice
within the cyclical tragic process, and the considerable
temptation for himself as poet: "All things can tempt
me from this craft of verse," he admitted ("All Things
can Tempt Me"), even to the extent of throwing away
"poor words" and being "content to live" ("Words").

With tragedy, however, and its concomitant temptations and arduous choices, come not the Blakean innocent joy in the face of Experience, not the annihilation
of self Milton took upon himself to redeem the world,
not the forgiveness of sins promulgated by Jesus, but
hatred, frenzy, and madness, themselves mental states
or passions which Blake classified under Experience
itself. And Yeats became correspondingly preoccupied
with what he called a "Vision of Evil," that awareness
indispensable in his eyes to the great poet, redeeming
one's work from bourgeois sentimentality and trivi-
ality. Precisely these bourgeois values were set off
against the Mask. Indeed, the two concepts (the Vision
of Evil and the Mask) came to fruition at the same
time in Yeats's mind and support one another.

Again in a significant and characteristic way he departs from Blake. For while Blake was hardly lacking
an awareness of evil, he was not committed, any more

than Shelley, to that antinomial metaphysics intrinsic to Yeats. George Bornstein very properly argues that "Yeats insisted upon capitalizing the phrase Vision of Evil in order to distinguish it from a mere vision of evil,"[22] and that the clearest he comes to defining the phrase is in his description of Shelley in *A Vision*. "He [Shelley] lacked the Vision of Evil, could not conceive of the world as a continual conflict, so, though great poet he certainly was, he was not of the greatest kind. Dante suffering injustice and the loss of Beatrice, found divine justice and the heavenly Beatrice, but the justice of *Prometheus Unbound* is a vague propagandist emotion and the women that await its coming are but clouds" (p. 144). The description of Blake, assigned to Phase 16 (pp. 137–40), makes no mention of a Vision of Evil; notes the "ceaseless struggle" within the mind, as in Blake's hatred, "always close to madness," or "frenzy" accompanied by "a delight"; but offers the blanket evaluation, "Capable of nothing but an incapable idealism (for it has no thought but in myth, or in defence of myth)"—a strange dismissal of Blake as Yeats dismissed Shelley also. Yet while Blake too upheld a dialectic, he was no dualist Gnostic. Like Carlyle later, he was always certain of the ultimate victory of good over evil, justice over reality, and the eventual transcendence of the dialectical negatives to a dynamic marriage of contraries in Jerusalem.

Yeats's cycles, however, proceed less surely through a Heraclitean process of expansion, contraction, reversal, and repetition: "Each age unwinds the thread another age had wound, and it amuses one to remember that before Phidias, and his westward-moving art, Persia fell, and that when full moon came round again, amid eastward-moving thought, and brought Byzantine glory, Rome fell; and that at the outset of our westward-moving Renaissance Byzantium fell; all things

22. *Yeats and Shelley*, p. 201.

dying each other's life, living each other's death" (*V*, pp. 270–71). Only through the completest "expiation" (p. 236) is the soul taken out of the cyclism into the peace of the Thirteenth Cycle or Cone or Sphere (p. 210). As Bornstein shows, "both Shelley and Yeats remake Dante in their own images," while Hazard Adams and Harold Bloom have indicated Yeats's deliberate misreading of Blake to accommodate him in his own visionary company.[23] Moreover, the artifice, theatricality, posing, and mask-making contingent upon Yeats's Vision of Evil were to Blake evidence of a fallen state. And we remember Samuel Palmer's praise, that Blake was a man without a mask. That which for Blake constituted a weakness Yeats turned into a particular strength.

The consequent revelation to the self capable of attaining and enduring a Vision of Evil, or of undertaking the playing with all masks, is "ecstasy."

> Nor has any poet I have read of or heard of or met with been a sentimentalist. The other self, the anti-self or the antithetical self, as one may choose to name it, comes but to those who are no longer deceived, whose passion is reality. The sentimentalists are practical men who believe in money, in position, in a marriage bell, and whose understanding of happiness is to be so busy whether at work or at play that all is forgotten but the momentary aim. They find their pleasure in a cup that is filled from Lethe's wharf, and for the awakening, for the vision, for the revelation of reality, tradition offers us a different word—ecstasy. (*Myth*, p. 331)

In "Ego Dominus Tuus," which serves as exposition of the Mask doctrine as "The Phases of the Moon" does to that part of *A Vision*, Yeats elevated Dante, "The

23. *Yeats and Shelley*, p. 218; cf. Bloom, *Yeats*; and Hazard Adams, *Blake and Yeats: The Contrary Vision* (1955; reissued New York: Russell and Russell, 1968).

chief imagination of Christendom," as capable of climbing the winding stair to anti-self and eating "bitter bread." The result was the aesthetic and metaphysical ecstasy of his union with Beatrice. On the other hand, he who would "keep his mask and his vision without new bitterness, new disappointment" should remember Wordsworth, whom Yeats criticized for lacking the theatrical sense necessary for mask-making, and subsequent upon that remembrance eat "some bitter crust" (*Myth*, p. 342). Yeats likewise criticized Emerson and Whitman as "writers who have begun to seem superficial precisely because they lack the Vision of Evil" (*Auto*, p. 246). Consequently, in "Ego Dominus Tuus" Yeats mistakenly objected to Keats, whose nose he saw "pressed to a sweet-shop window," a curious echo of Carlyle's own objections to the Romantic poet and as much the "nineteenth-century caricature" to which Bloom has accused Yeats of reducing Blake.[24] In Yeats's eyes, Keats's "Luxuriant song" evades the tragic; candy is no substitute for bitter bread. As he wrote in 1935 to Lady Dorothy Wellesley, "To me the supreme aim is an act of faith and reason to make one rejoice in the midst of tragedy" (*LP*, p. 12).

In an important statement in *Autobiographies* Yeats brings these concepts together in a distinctive unity:

> I know now [1922] that revelation is from the self, but from that age-long memoried self, that shapes the elaborate shell of the mollusc and the child in the womb, that

24. *Yeats*, p. 247. See Brian John, "Yeats and Carlyle," *N & Q*, NS 17 (Dec. 1970), 455. Cf. D. H. Lawrence, Preface to A. F. Grazzini, *The Story of Dr. Manente*, in *Ph*, p. 277: "We badly need some of it [the courage of life] today, in this self-pitying age when we are so sorry for ourselves that we have to be soothed by art as by candy." Cf. Lawrence to A. W. Macleod, 26 Apr. 1913, *CL*, p. 203, in which Lawrence describes H. G. Wells as "looking at life as a cold and hungry little boy in the street stares at a shop where there is hot pork."

teaches the birds to make their nest; and that genius is a crisis that joins that buried self for certain moments to our trivial daily mind. There are, indeed, personifying spirits that we had best call but Gates and Gate-keepers, because through their dramatic power they bring our souls to crisis, to Mask and Image, caring not a straw whether we be Juliet going to her wedding, or Cleopatra to her death; for in their eyes nothing has weight but passion. We have dreamed a foolish dream these many centuries in thinking that they value a life of contemplation, for they scorn that more than any possible life, unless it be but a name for the worst crisis of all. They have but one purpose, to bring their chosen man to the greatest obstacle he may confront without despair. They contrived Dante's banishment, and snatched away his Beatrice, and thrust Villon into the arms of harlots, and sent him to gather cronies at the foot of the gallows, that Dante and Villon might through passion become conjoint to their buried selves, turn all to Mask and Image, and so be phantoms in their own eyes. (pp. 272–73)

The desired state is not joy but passion, which Yeats identified with Blake's Energy, and the passionate man can best face the daimonic crisis by evidencing gaiety, the response of the hero, indifferent to his own salvation, or of the poet labouring to create beauty. The first figure finds his mask in defeat, the second in disappointment. The pain and suffering are both obstacles and instruments, both hindering and furthering the self in its search for fulfilment.

Consequently, in "Upon a Dying Lady" Yeats praised Mabel Beardsley, "great enemy," as possessing "a laughing eye" and a courage which will after death grant her visions of, and presumably communion with, similar heroic laughing selves.

When her soul flies to the predestined dancing-place
(I have no speech but symbol, the pagan speech I made
Amid the dreams of youth) let her come face to face,
Amid that first astonishment, with Grania's shade,

All but the terrors of the woodland flight forgot
That made her Diarmuid dear, and some old cardinal
Pacing with half-closed eyelids in a sunny spot
Who had murmured of Giorgione at his latest breath—
Aye, and Achilles, Timor, Babar, Barhaim, all
Who have lived in joy and laughed into the face
    of Death.

(VI, "Her Courage")

Hers is a defiance which knows and rejects the ignominy of defeat and despair—the final accolade which places her with the great and archetypal heroes—and she responds with a gaiety which, in "Poetry and Tradition" (1907), he had previously defined as a Castiglione-like "recklessness" allied to the artist's style (*E & I*, p. 256). The mastery that comes in life to the aristocrat and in the arts to the possessors of "style, which is but high breeding in words and in argument" (p. 253), is also necessary to the lover: "For only when we are gay over a thing, and can play with it, do we show ourselves its master, and have minds clear enough for strength" (p. 252). Yeats wrote similarly in poems like "The Mask" (1910) and "Before the World Was Made" (1929). "That we may be free from all the rest, sullen anger, solemn virtue, calculating anxiety, gloomy suspicion, prevaricating hope, we should be reborn in gaiety" (p. 252). This it is which in a later poem, "Lapis Lazuli," he grandly claims capable of "transfiguring all that dread."

However, the gaiety in "Lapis Lazuli" is the attribute gained by all those players in the *comédie humaine* rendered capable of performing their parts in the tragic process. Sometimes the players crack and, instead of provoking heroic gaiety, the tragedy is such as to bring madness, hatred, frenzy, and rage—the tormented agony of the self broken on the wheel, heart and head exploding under the strain. These states, nevertheless, remain superior to the evasiveness of sentimentality, to those who would drink the cup of oblivion and thus prolong their ultimate redemption. For madness and its related states are preferable to hypocrisy and evasion: the wild crazed figures experience passionate intensity, crisis, and, above all, the tragedy which constitutes the foundation of their illuminating vision. Other states too are explored in Yeats's work: he recognized the recurrence in himself of remorse, destructive of both joy and a Blakean blessedness. "When such as I cast out remorse," he sang in "A Dialogue of Self and Soul," the subsequent vision is one of blessedness: "Everything we look upon is blest." That vision, however, came rarely to Yeats; rather, "the common condition of our life is hatred" (*Myth*, p. 365), and when not provoked into a *saeva indignatio*, Yeats was often burdened by remorse, guilt, and an overwhelming sense of responsibilities. At other times, he describes the mere confrontation of forces, as in the late poem "The Man and the Echo." The scene is stark, bare, essential: "What do we know but that we face / One another in this place?" (ll. 39–40). The stricken rabbit's distracting cry indicates the continuing tragic process. But the man is neither joyful nor remorseful, neither exultant nor evasive, and his persistent attention to "The spiritual intellect's great work" (l. 20) is a fit mask for Yeats himself.

The discipline of self-fulfilment depends upon such a confrontation—of man and his ghostly eternal self, or daimon—taking the inevitable form of war or dialectical conflict: "The Daimon comes not as like to like but seeking its own opposite, for man and Daimon feed the hunger in one another's hearts. Because the ghost is simple, the man heterogeneous and confused, they are but knit together when the man has found a mask whose lineaments permit the expression of all the man most lacks, and it may be dreads, and of that only" (*Myth*, p. 335). Quoting Heraclitus, "the Daimon is our destiny," Yeats saw "life as a struggle with the

Daimon who would ever set us to the hardest work among those not impossible" (p. 336). Similarly, the Blake apothegm, much favoured though also much misunderstood by Yeats, that "sexual love is founded upon spiritual hate," is thus "an image of the warfare of man and Daimon" (p. 336). Using the daimon as ghostly mediator somewhat in the manner of Blake's Divine Image or Jesus, though lacking Jesus' central principle of the forgiveness of sins, Yeats saw a similar revelation to be gained in Blake's temporal Minute Particular, the pulsation of the artery: "The Daimon, by using his mediatorial shades, brings man again and again to the place of choice, heightening temptation that the choice may be as final as possible, imposing his own lucidity upon events, leading his victim to whatever among works not impossible is the most difficult. . . . We perceive in a pulsation of the artery, and after slowly decline" (p. 361).[25]

Yeats's indebtedness to and participation in the Romantic vitalist tradition takes many forms. Recognizing early the artist's mythopoeic obligations—to create a system or be enslaved by another man's—Yeats sought to hammer his thoughts into a unity and upheld, like Blake and Carlyle, the importance of symbols. Although his is a more Gnostic and antinomian stance than that of either Blake or Carlyle, he shares with them the vitalist insistence upon the dialectical structure of all things. In Yeats's case the dialectic takes the form not only of the mental fight experienced by all men but also the warfare of man and daimon, time and eternity, so that he moves between individual biography and the two-thousand-year cycles of history to the Platonic *Magnus Annus* itself. Moreover, he transforms the vitalist principle of Force, or energy, into man's passionate pursuit of an eternal beauty or completeness with the subsequent purgatorial refine-

25. See Blake, *M*, 28: 47; 29: 1–3; cf. *E & I*, pp. 159, 195, 197.

ment of self and soul. Likewise, he argued, "I cannot discover truth by logic unless that logic serve passion, and only then if the logic be ready to cut its own throat, tear out its own eyes—the cry of Hafiz, 'I made a bargain with that hair before the beginning of time', the cry of every lover" (*Exp*, p. 301). In the face of increasing mechanism and materialism, he adopted an organicism, seeing the encroachment of the scientific method as deadening the spirit and man's means to wholeness and salvation. His occultism and magic are in some part his calculated defiance of logical and intellectual methodologies. As much as Carlyle and Lawrence, he could be tempted into a quasi-primitivism, preferring the less technologically advanced Irish peasant as the more spiritually perceptive. Even his political views, like those of Carlyle and Lawrence also, were founded upon an élitism and a corresponding distrust of democracy, both of which seem to accompany most vitalist philosophies.

In all these ways and more, Yeats was profoundly indebted to the vitalists and, despite his deliberate misinterpretation of Blake and others, might be said to share a common ground. All these directions require fuller treatment than can be provided here. Nevertheless, my own concentration upon Yeats's elevation of the creative self, constructing both self and world in an essentially vital and fictive way, touches upon these matters and, above all, illuminates that aspect of his work central to his vision and achievement. Indeed, Denis Donoghue has recently claimed that Yeats's "sense of consciousness as conflict is the most important article in Yeats's faith as a poet,"[26] and proceeds to quote from *A Vision:* "My instructors identify con-

26. *Yeats*, p. 40; cf. Frank Lentricchia, *The Gaiety of Language: An Essay on the Radical Poetics of W. B. Yeats and Wallace Stevens*, Perspectives in Criticism, 19 (Berkeley and Los Angeles: Univ. of California Press, 1968), pp. 78–79.

sciousness with conflict, not with knowledge, substitute for subject and object and their attendant logic a struggle towards harmony, towards Unity of Being. Logical and emotional conflict alike lead towards a reality which is concrete, sensuous, bodily" (p. 214). As much as any other vitalist Yeats could assert the dignity and greatness of man when refined by the very nature of his being. Seeing the blessedness of life and being made capable, like his own heroes, of transforming defeat into victory, tragedy into ecstasy, Yeats thus created his own supreme fictions out of that matrix which, in "The Circus Animals' Desertion," he described as "the foul rag-and-bone shop of the heart."

In *A Vision* Yeats described the effect of the tragic process upon a civilization in these terms: "A civilisation is a struggle to keep self-control, and in this it is like some great tragic person, some Niobe who must display an almost superhuman will or the cry will not touch our sympathy" (p. 268). However, we must always remember the reverse is also true: that man too is asked to learn to display such superhuman will, such self-control, while also learning to endure the ravages of self and heart and even of time itself.

Precisely this historical perspective is provided in a poem central to *The Tower* volume, "Two Songs from a Play."[27] Here is to be found that discipline involving the daimon who brings his chosen man to crisis through passionate intensity and tragic awareness. But the discipline is not fully appreciated without the historical framework which the poem provides. For the historical pattern explored in the poem establishes the relevant perspective with which to place both individual and all time.

Yeats traces the rise and fall of the classical era in

27. I cannot accept Bornstein's reading of this poem, that Yeats's "bitterness encompasses the entire pattern of history" and that "antinomially, history is bunk" (*Yeats and Shelley*, p. 195).

the first song, from its initiation in Zeus' swallowing of Dionysus' heart, to its replacement, in the second, by the Christian civilization, imaged in the beating of Christ's phantom heart. Clearly a distinct pattern is being established, centring on the sacrificial slain god figure and his consumption of heart which is a necessary prelude to the consummation within the civilization his birth and death set in motion. Similarly, as critics have pointed out,[28] the virgin figures and their respective stars merge together to form another distinctive pattern—Pallas Athene; Astraea, the star-maiden, who became Virgo the constellation, who holds the star Spica in her hand; and the Virgin Mary and the Star of Bethlehem. All such figures and events are part of the largest cycle of all, the twenty-six-thousand-year cycle of the Platonic Year ("Magnus Annus"). And just as the classical era blotted out "the Babylonian mathematical starlight" (*V*, p. 268), giving birth both to the Greek visionary perfection of Homer and Phidias and to the inferior, because practical, administrative mind of Rome, so too the Christian era offers pity in place of love and reverses the classical virtues of "Platonic tolerance" and "Doric discipline," providing modern man with the need for a future annunciation.

But it is to the final stanza of the second song that we must attend.[29] The final stanza directs us to the equally significant heart of man and sees the consum-

28. John Unterecker, *A Reader's Guide to William Butler Yeats* (New York: Noonday, 1959), p. 186; A. Norman Jeffares, *A Commentary on the Collected Poems of W. B. Yeats* (London: Macmillan, 1968), pp. 289–90.

29. I reject Ellmann's view that the last stanza's insistence upon man-made qualities as opposed to the previous stanzas' insistence upon divine miracle is "slightly out of key" (*Identity of Yeats*, p. 262). Cf. Whitaker, who also rejects Ellmann and properly places the poem with "Leda and the Swan" in which a similarly tragic historical pattern is drawn (*Swan and Shadow*, pp. 107–9).

ing agony of individual men against the creative nature of the cyclical tragic process of time itself. For just as history moves within a pattern which resigns us to the disastrously anarchic present, in the expectation of a better era about to be born, so too the nature of existence is contained in the microcosmic image of man, reconciling us to the agony of our passions. Our desires, images, self-projections, loves and hates, triumphs and despairs, are part of the purificatory process imposed on the self by the daimons, who in turn are sustained by precisely those tensions within the self.

> Everything that man esteems
> Endures a moment or a day.
> Love's pleasure drives his love away,
> The painter's brush consumes his dreams;
> The herald's cry, the soldier's tread
> Exhaust his glory and his might:
> Whatever flames upon the night
> Man's own resinous heart has fed.

This relationship between man and daimon, paralleled in history's dialectic, clarifies the transient and tragic character of man's passions, dreams, and actions, while at the same time justifying that very character. The experiences of the contingent self are the necessary means by which the daimon leads man to crisis and defeat. But, with the dialectical logic of paradox, the daimonic discipline leads man from creation of image to destruction of self and, ultimately, to that self's re-creation and redemption. The daimons flaming upon the night, in their participation in the Condition of Fire, play a significant role in both the Byzantium poems. What must be made clear is the interdependence of man and daimon, whose meeting place is man's heart. Precisely this meeting of man and daimon in the individual heart is behind Yeats's question, "Why should we honour those that die upon the field of battle, a man may show as reckless a courage in entering into the abyss of himself."[30] To enter that abyss would be to emulate Jonathan Swift and Parnell and pluck "bitter wisdom that enriched his blood" ("Parnell's Funeral," II, 12).

2

Not always is the tension within the self overcome by such a reconciliation to "Man's own resinous heart." There are occasions when the influence of intellect predominates. In the opening poem of *The Tower*, "Sailing to Byzantium," in place of heart, both meeting place and battlefield of man and daimon, the protagonist elevates "Monuments of unageing intellect." Instead of tragedy, the eternal world of Byzantium is preferred because it transcends the tragic dialectic. And, it must be remembered, such a transcendence has always been Yeats's ultimate goal, as the Thirteenth Cone remains man's ultimate resting place. Yet the visionary state epitomized in Byzantium remains curiously unconvincing, even unattractive, and the poet is unconsciously pulled back towards that country of the heart from which he has determinedly set sail. The poem thus reflects in typical, but here unconscious, fashion that dialectical vacillation inherent in Yeats's vision which makes his best work particularly dramatic. For while in intention the poet sets his face against time and heart and yearns for the completeness and peace of "the artifice of eternity," the quality of the descriptions together with particular images reflects Yeats's characteristic crisis. But that is as it should be: the tension between self and soul, which runs constantly through both *The Tower* and *The Winding Stair*, is never totally relinquished nor finally resolved.

30. Quoted in Ellmann, *Yeats: The Man and the Masks*, p. 6.

It is curious, however, that for once the tension seems unconsciously present rather than deliberately sought.[31]

The poem begins with the protagonist recognizing that temporal existence can offer only the ironic paradox of death implicit in birth ("Those dying generations"); that the "sensual music" constitutes one more net by which, Daedalus-like, he must fly;[32] that the "country" he abandons (the entire world of Becoming and not merely Ireland)[33] is unproductive for old men, towards whom it proves unreceptive and disdainful. Yet what is striking about the images in stanza I is Yeats's obvious attraction to that state from which he is fleeing. Nevertheless, using imagery derived in part from neoplatonic myth which conceived man as a beggar wearing the rags of mortality, and in part from Blake's description of his brother's soul rising to the ceiling clapping its hands for joy, Yeats sets himself against the temporal nature of man's existence. Aged man is encouraged in his decline towards death: "Soul clap its hands and sing, and louder sing / For every tatter in its mortal dress." The polarity of time and eternity is charted by way of images of music and monument, natural tree and golden bough, worldly fowl and artificial bird, self (here called heart) and soul, the fire of lust and the purificatory holy fire of God. In a 1937 BBC broadcast Yeats defined the Byzantine tree of stanza IV "as a symbol of the intellectual

31. Lentricchia argues that the tension is conscious and that "Yeats wants it both ways" (*Gaiety of Language*, p. 107).
32. Yeats originally thought in terms of flight imagery. See Curtis Bradford, "Yeats's Byzantium Poems: A Study of Their Development," in *Yeats, A Collection of Critical Essays*, ed. John Unterecker (Englewood Cliffs, N.J.: Prentice-Hall, 1963), p. 99.
33. A. Norman Jeffares thinks merely in terms of Ireland. *The Poetry of W. B. Yeats*, Studies in English Literature, 4 (London: Arnold, 1967), p. 43.

joy of eternity, as contrasted with the instinctive joy
of human life."[34]

The irony, always present in Yeats's moments of
fullest vision, centres on the term "consume." For indeed the temporal world is a consumption, a gnawing,
contentious, self-absorbing state in which the heart,
like that of Swift in "Blood and the Moon" (II), drags
one down into mankind, and one suffers with age the
wrack of body expressed in the next poem, "The
Tower." But the eternal world also consumes, eats away
at heart, swallows heart indeed, as in those apocalyptic
moments when a new civilization is born ("Two Songs
from a Play"). In fact, as we have already seen in
Yeats's more abstract statements or in the final stanza
of "Two Songs from a Play," even the temporal experience of heart's consumption—in desires frustrated or
actions defeated—can bring the chosen man to crisis
and daimonic awareness. In an early essay, "The
Moods," he had defined this as the artist's discovery
of "immortal moods in mortal desires, an undecaying
hope in our trivial ambitions, a divine love in sexual
passion" (E & I, p. 195). Yet in "Sailing to Byzantium"
the temporal brings only consumption; the eternal,
consummation; and the latter's immediate consequence is agony, its lasting state, peace. As he asserted
in Per Amica Silentia Lunae, "In the condition of fire
is all music and all rest" (Myth, p. 357). The "sages
standing in God's holy fire" then are our daimons with
whom through mask we unite. To descend to their
chosen man, whom they have led to crisis—the torment of the temporal expressed in stanza I—the
daimons must "perne in a gyre," a movement reminiscent of Blake's Milton (M, 15: 17–35) and "gather
[him] / Into the artifice of eternity." The imagery of
retreat and protection ("gather"), predominant in the

34. Quoted in Bradford, in Yeats, ed. Unterecker, p. 95.

early poetry, is used once more to project the nature of the created paradise of Byzantium.[35]

Whatever terms Yeats may use to articulate his vision of eternity, the result is preponderantly static (as evidenced also in the passive verb "set") and two-dimensional (here/there, time/eternity). The real strength of the poem lies not in any attainment of vision but in the crisis experienced by the "I" labouring to transcend the dialectic. For indeed the condition of existential crisis, rather than the eternal peace, is the source of illumination, as Yeats's thought and poetic practice indicate. To return to the image of the consumed heart, Yeats has already seen that only by experiencing heart's consumption by frustration, defeat, decay, and despair can any consummation be attained. In this respect the next poem, "The Tower," is more in line with the emphasis of the later work. Moreover, the music the artificial Byzantine bird sings is surprisingly temporal ("Of what is past, or passing, or to come"),[36] and precisely this interrelationship of all time in a numinous moment, known through passion and daimonic crisis, is explored in other poems in *The Tower*. In "Sailing to Byzantium," however, the moment of vision is set off against the imperfect experience of the contingent self. In successive poems in both the 1928 and 1933 volumes, on the other hand, the poet is to express precisely that numinous moment *within*

35. See "The Indian to His Love," "The Lake Isle of Innisfree," "The Secret Rose," "The Poet Pleads with the Elemental Powers"; cf. *Myth*, pp. 300–301, noted by Jeffares, *Commentary*, p. 256.
36. The line is reminiscent of Ahasuerus in Shelley's *Hellas*, l. 148, "The Present, and the Past, and the To-come," as Bornstein has convincingly shown (*Yeats and Shelley*, pp. 187–88). Moreover, Bornstein notes, Ahasuerus is Asiatic and lives in a cave near Byzantium. The parallel illustrates Yeats's manipulation of sources, for Ahasuerus is used to express not Shelley's affirmation of life but Yeats's affirmation of art.

time and through the very nature of temporal existence itself.

The structure of "The Tower" is more complex than the two-dimensional "Sailing to Byzantium." In each section of this poem Yeats employs a variety of tone, metre, and attitude which shift as the poem proceeds. Moreover, in each section we find the poet shuttling back and fore in time: from bodily decrepitude of old age to boyhood energy and forward to future abstract speculation (section I); from the present scene on the tower's battlements to the "Images and memories" called forth "From ruin or from ancient trees" to his future peace (II); from the present deepening of night and life to the past achievements of the Greek and the eighteenth-century Irish traditions to Yeats's heirs and his own future self-making (III). Indeed, the poem proceeds through a series of triads, thus making the structure three-dimensional and suggesting also the increasing penetration to the heart of the poem's problem. Reconciling rather than separating opposites, the poem offers not only past, present, and future, but Muse, abstraction, and action; imagination, intellect, and senses; moon, sun, and their "One inextricable beam"; death, life, and "Translunar Paradise." For these are the elements in the individual and the civilization which make the whole self—Unity of Being or Unity of Culture. Likewise, the predominant design of the poet's experiences is that of resolution of antinomies, a whirling of gyres, and the dancelike movement to the position Yeats attains. Having climbed the tower's staircase, his position on the battlements reminds us of the wars of self and soul. For this is the reconciliation to loss of the youthful antithesis of climbing "Ben Bulben's back": the wisdom that comes with age.

Yeats's position bears comparison with that of Blake in his final year. To his friend George Cumberland, Blake wrote (12 April 1827) in one of his last letters: "I have been very near the Gates of Death & have returned very weak & an Old Man feeble & tottering, but not in Spirit & Life not in The Real Man The Imagination which Liveth for Ever. In that I am stronger & stronger as this Foolish Body decays" (E, p. 707). Blake, however, remained more of the visionary than Yeats ever became and from the outset had denounced the empirical world as unreal. Yeat's wisdom, won through age and bodily decrepitude, consists of a different order. Wisdom consists of neither the less desirable alternative of Plato and Plotinus (abstract idealist philosophy) nor the passionate boyhood which still cannot match the old man's "Excited, passionate, fantastical / Imagination." Rather, wisdom evidences the newly acquired ability to see things in their proper perspective, as parts of a continuous process. That process is indeed cyclical and tragic, but is nevertheless the source of man's greatness as well as of his despair and decay.

This cyclical design is supported and expressed further by particular images of tree, house, and tower. The description of the tree, for example, contains the very dualistic nature of the world Yeats is now surveying. His simile, "like a sooty finger," suggests a more ironic version than the thrilling dynamic tree in "Among School Children," though the tree here too "*starts* from the earth" (my italics). The verb directs us to origins while also giving us a sense of vital force. The tree's very nature of roots, trunk, and branches participates in the opposites of earth and air and is related to more esoteric and cabbalistic trees in the early poems. "The foundations of a house" upon which he stares is indicative as well of man's refusal to give way to chaos; the Great House, with its obvious reverberations in Yeats's mind of the greatness of the Anglo-Irish eighteenth century and of aristocrats of the Ascendancy like the Gregorys, epitomizes man's rage for order. Yet the house is in ruin like the embattled protagonist. The tower likewise is a monument Yeats has chosen to inherit and pass on to his children, and from the vantage point of the battlements he can take in the entire countryside.

More important is the illuminating nature of the perception this vantage point brings. For the poet himself is as much an emblem of a dark night of the soul as "the day's declining beam" and the increasingly anarchic society, and seeks information via the "Images and memories / From ruin or from ancient trees." Even Hanrahan, whose "deep considering mind" now made even more knowledgeable from his experiences in the grave, can be placed in the same category. For tree, house, tower, and now Hanrahan himself are all images of that wisdom which comes from embracing rather than separating the antinomies. Hanrahan's mind has plumbed the depths of the abyss as the tree has put down roots or the house and tower their foundations. All four images suggest a matrix to which the self must be brought. Consequently, the labyrinth image which follows indicates both the pattern and the salvation. For the labyrinth suggests the gyring movement of the self and of all time and is repeated in the poet's climbing of the winding stairs to the battlements. It refers also to the riddle of both self and universe that the poet, and all such travellers in quest of self-discovery, seeks to solve. But when the labyrinth is applied specifically to the sexual experience, Yeats is brought to ask the central question and to gain the necessary insight into heart's consumption and heart's truth:

> Does the imagination dwell the most
> Upon a woman won or woman lost?

> (ll. 113–14)

The question has in fact been answered in previous poems like "The Three Beggars" or "The Cold Heaven" and in *Per Amica Silentia Lunae.* It will reappear in "A Dialogue of Self and Soul" imaged not as a labyrinth, with its aesthetic associations, but as a cruder, more bestially sexual ditch:

> . . . that most fecund ditch of all,
> The folly that man does
> Or must suffer, if he woos
> A proud woman not kindred of his soul.
>
> (ll. 61–64)

Just as the artificial bird in "Sailing to Byzantium" is meant to supply the fitting climactic image to Yeats's vision in that poem, so too birds, though of a very natural kind, dominate the final section of "The Tower." The swan's proud last song allies it to the poet, whose song is likewise proud and who has relied upon swans in earlier poems to project his particular preferences; to the fishermen, "upstanding men" whom the poet chooses as his inheritors; and to "The people of Burke and of Grattan" who now figure prominently in the myth. The extended simile of the daws in lines 116–72 is of even greater significance:

> As at the loophole there
> The daws chatter and scream,
> And drop twigs layer upon layer.
> When they have mounted up,
> The mother bird will rest
> On their hollow top,
> And so warm her wild nest.

Though no longer the romantic, even archetypal, swan but mere jackdaws, whose cries can hardly be called either proud or musical, the birds' nest-building is analogous to man's impulse to build towers and Great Houses; to climb battlements or mountains like Ben Bulben; to progress through the labyrinthine abyss of the self "to hold in a single thought reality and justice" (*V*, p. 25). The analogy is made even more explicit by the repetition of the verb "mount": it has been applied to the climbing of mountain and tower; to the bankrupt master ("old, necessitous, half-mounted man," l. 90); and is implicit in the sexual mounting to which Hanrahan had set his heart and devoted his life. But like the bankrupt master, he too is only "half-mounted," caught by necessity to experience the awful bitterness of frustration. In the tale "Red Hanrahan" (*Myth*, pp. 213–24) of which Yeats reminds us here, the "great labyrinth" Hanrahan spurned was the immortal Echtge, daughter of the Silver Hand, "a woman, the most beautiful the world ever saw," surrounded by the four talismans of the Tuatha de Danaan (cauldron, spear, stone, and sword). The consequences were fearful, but the emotional crisis would nevertheless help Hanrahan's progress towards expiation and rebirth into the Thirteenth Cone. Certainly in "The Death of Hanrahan," the last of the *Stories of Red Hanrahan* (*Myth*, pp. 253–61), he is united in death with "one of the lasting people."

However, the daws' mounting of twigs derives from that impulse which in *Autobiographies* is related to "revelation . . . from that age-long memoried self . . . that teaches the birds to make their nest" (p. 272). The definition there of "genius" as "a crisis that joins that buried self for certain moments to our trivial daily mind" thus brings the reader back to the declaration of faith in "The Tower" in lines preceding the bird-nesting image. The lines are central to Yeats, not merely because they express a theme dominant in his mature work, but because they constitute a blossoming into order of that concern with tragedy, crisis, and mask—the wisdom learnt from daimonic images—and indicate the relevance to his system of particular masks like the poet, lover, beautiful woman.

I mock Plotinus' thought
And cry in Plato's teeth,
Death and life were not
Till man made up the whole,
Made lock, stock and barrel
Out of his bitter soul,
Aye, sun and moon and star, all,
And further add to that
That, being dead, we rise,
Dream and so create
Translunar Paradise.
I have prepared my peace
With learned Italian things
And the proud stones of Greece,
Poet's imaginings
And memories of love,
Memories of the words of women,
All those things whereof
Man makes a superhuman
Mirror-resembling dream.

(ll. 146–65)

Yeats's faith in man's fictive self is thus given its most explicit and most defiant expression. All things—death and life, sun, moon, and star; even "Translunar Paradise"—now depend upon man's capacity both to endure the bitter consumption of heart and to construct out of that experience one's "peace," one's "super-human / Mirror-resembling dream."[37]

37. Torchiana indicates Plotinus, Boehme, Blake, Gentile, Croce, and Vico as sources of Yeats's faith. In his copy of Croce's *The Philosophy of Giambattista Vico*, trans. R. G. Collingwood (London, 1913), p. 29, Yeats in 1924 annotated these lines of Vico: "Man creates the human world, creates it by transforming himself into the facts of society: by thinking it he recreates his own creations, traverses over again the paths he has already traversed, reconstructs the whole ideally, and thus knows it with full and true knowledge. Here is a real world; and of this world man is truly the God" (*Yeats and Georgian Ireland*, p. 262).

Both faith and pride, however, are left to the "young upstanding men" capable of practising them. Yeats, on the other hand, is confronted with a different and altogether contrary labour: the compulsion to choose the "learned school" of intellect or soul and thus resign himself to the destruction of those things on which he had previously set such store. The diminished tone of the poem's conclusion should not deceive us into believing that the choice has been easy. Yeats's dignity and courage in the face of defeat are impressively tragic and moving.

The next ten poems in *The Tower* volume are devoted to less personal and more historical perspectives, but their conclusions do not differ radically from that arrived at in "The Tower." For despite expressions of disillusionment and even near-nihilism, Yeats's view of the disastrous present in "Meditations in Time of Civil War" and "Nineteen Hundred and Nineteen" is brought ultimately to that same reconciliation as evidenced in "Two Songs from a Play," "The Tower," and other shorter and less significant poems of this group ("The Wheel" and "Youth and Age").

"Meditations in Time of Civil War" consists of seven sections, I–IV juxtaposing the past with the present, V and VI more particularly rooted in the present, with the last, VII, synthesizing all time into an inclusive vision proceeding through past and present to future. The opening section, "Ancestral Houses," with its contrary images of fountain ("life's own self-delight") and shell (originally an image of order and disciplined containment, but now rendered empty),[38] establishes the

38. The images of fountain and shell recur throughout Yeats's work. He found fountains in Blake, Shelley, and Porphyry (*E & I*, pp. 78–87); associated the image with "noble extravagance" in men of Phase 12 (*V*, p. 128); while the shell he related to order (note to "Three Songs to the Same Tune," *Var*, p. 543; cf. *Auto*, pp. 539–40). The conjunction of violence and art is proclaimed also in "Under Ben Bulben," ll. 25–36.

tragic dialectic running through all things. That dialectic in previous times was reconciled by those creators of ancestral houses who could fuse their personal violence and bitterness with sweetness and gentleness in the foundation of a Great House. The artefact, when born of the harmonious creative self, withstands time in the manner of Keats's Grecian Urn. But when we ask how we shall be judged by history, Yeats concludes that the present has only violence and bitterness untempered by the creative life. The fountain, rather than being balanced by the shell, has been replaced by it.

The next three sections are more personal, dealing with "My House," "My Table," "My Descendants," yet centre still upon the creative life. That life may be imaged in the artefacts of tower, sword, and even of family, but bears ultimately on the making of self and is set off against the inevitable dialectic. In a setting where age and stoniness are emphasized, Yeats sees himself in the manner of Milton's platonist illuminated by "daemonic rage" and seeking "emblems of adversity." Or, confronted with the changeless aspect of Sato's sword (a gift from a Japanese admirer),[39] he can be reconciled to the irrevocable interrelationship of change and changelessness. For the sword as artefact is changeless but born of change: "only an aching heart / Conceives a changeless work of art." Similarly, the importance of art is such that it is both reflective of the soul's beauty (or harmony) and conducive to that beauty. Hence, the sword's creator would know "that none could pass Heaven's door / That loved inferior art," but in that wisdom would experience time in its totality—whether the moon in its fullness in Phase 15 ("Soul's beauty being most adored") or at the dark in Phase 1 ("Juno's peacock screamed," which Yeats identifies in A Vision, p. 268). In the fourth

39. Yeats to Edmund Dulac, 22 Mar. 1920, in Letters, p. 662.

section, Yeats recognizes that transience makes any achievement short and that his descendants can decline from a variety of causes (at best the inevitable cyclism, at worst the mistaken choice). "The Primum Mobile that fashioned us / Has made the very owls in circles move." Such a recognition has motivated Yeats to build his tower as a monument of self, out of love and friendship. As such, the monument stands in contrast to the monuments of unageing intellect in "Sailing to Byzantium."

Neither love nor friendship exists in the external world of Ireland, fraught with the dissensions of the Civil War. The distracting world of action to which Yeats remains tempted is put aside, and instead of war and violence he offers first the bird image of the moorhen, analogous to the daws in "The Tower," and the more extended bee image of section VI. Associated not only with sweetness and love, but with a Golden Age, as in the Virgilian-Mandevillian sense,[40] the bees are emblematic of a life contrary to the present: ordered and hierarchical, regulated by a sense of authority, class, and unity. In "The Gift of Harun Al-Rashid" the image is repeated in Yeats's urging "all the chroniclers / To show how violent great hearts can lose / Their bitterness and find the honeycomb" (ll. 46–48). While section VI of "Meditations" provides an awful indictment of the Irish present—with its killing, burning of houses, and erecting of road barricades, and the corresponding loosening of Yeats's own wall—the persistent urging, "Come build in the empty house of the stare," suggests the means to overcome the dissension.

> We had fed the heart on fantasies,
> The heart's grown brutal from the fare;
> More substance in our enmities

40. Torchiana shows Swift's *The Battle of the Books* also as a source (*Yeats and Georgian Ireland*, p. 315).

Than in our love; O honey-bees,
Come build in the empty house of the stare.

The final section, "I See Phantoms of Hatred and of
the Heart's Fullness and of the Coming Emptiness,"
provides through a succession of visions a telescoped
history of the tragic cyclism. Climbing to the vantage
point of his tower, Yeats is illuminated, like the countryside around, by a moon no longer emblematic of
change but resembling more the artefact, Sato's sword:
"under the light of a moon / That seems unlike itself,
that seems unchangeable, / A glittering sword out of
the east." The lines not only refer back to the Japanese
sword but echo Yeats's description of the anti-self in
"Ego Dominus Tuus," which proves "of all imaginable
things / The most unlike" (ll. 73–74). Both sword and
anti-self depend for their creation upon man's aching
heart; only by acquiring such a wholeness through
heart's consumption can a total vision be experienced.
The image of the eye, as central to Yeats as it proved
to Blake and Carlyle, varies from vision to vision: "the
mind's eye" of Yeats sees visions of "eyes that rage has
brightened" (those seeking vengeance for the murder
of Jacques Molay); of the "musing eyes" of the lovely
ladies (Yeats cannot resist punning on the word "musing" and follows with a reference to the mind's pool,
a variation on the archetypal well associated with the
Muses); and finally of "the eye's complacency." These
are indeed the variations, reflected in the eye's pupil,
Minnaloushe knew in "The Cat and the Moon" in the
volume The Wild Swans at Coole. The moon's cyclism
provides for the moment of illumination in Phase 15
(that of the lovely ladies) but also and inevitably for
the decline into fanatical rage of the Templars or the
indifference of the multitude, given over to mechanical
logic and abstraction ("brazen hawks"), the latter emotions indicative of the primary phases around Phase 1,
as Yeats's note proves (Var, p. 827).

Again the temptation returns—the daimonic choice perpetually confronting the self—whether or not a life different from that Yeats chose would have been more valuable. Again the solitude of the visionary state is set off against the gregarious common life. What ease and comfort might have come, however, would have been illusory: "It had but made us pine the more." The "ambitious heart" addressed is both the source and battleground of such conflicting temptations; it is also, nevertheless, the means by which the historical cyclism traced in the three visions is overcome. The conclusion is thus one of reconciliation and of recognition: further solitude and further suffering in the face of tragedy—the wisdom of daimonic images—must be sought rather than avoided.

"Nineteen Hundred and Nineteen" (written four years earlier and originally entitled "Thoughts upon the Present State of the World") expresses further Yeats's conception of the anarchic present and explores the dichotomy of triumph and solitude. The artefact also retains its significance in the historical design, as emblematic of that creative life which at best confronts and in one sense defeats the cycles. In a more obvious sense the artefact remains subject to time and suffers defeat at its hands:

> Many ingenious lovely things are gone
> That seemed sheer miracle to the multitude,
> Protected from the circle of the moon
> That pitches common things about. There stood
> Amid the ornamental bronze and stone
> An ancient image made of olive wood—
> And gone are Phidias' famous ivories
> And all the golden grasshoppers and bees.

(ll. 1–8)

But the artefact is also the product of the creative self working at its highest level, experiencing at best existence in its totality. And the creative self capable of producing such "ingenious lovely things" learns also the wisdom that brings reconciliation to the cyclism and recognizes the need for solitude and endurance in the face of defeat. Hence, the dichotomy of triumph and solitude, pursued throughout this poem, postulates the awful temptation or choice Yeats saw confronting all men in the process of self-making. While he might recognize the fearful substitution of a "dragon-ridden" present in the place of a Blakean vision of Isaiah, converting cannon into ploughshares, nevertheless the need for solitude is all the greater. Yeats is placing the individual's purpose in finding himself in the daimonic crisis against the larger purpose of time finding its true self in the cycles of history.

The Vision of Evil remains crucial, and the temptations of evasion or triumph must still be firmly renounced:

> He who can read the signs nor sink unmanned
> Into the half-deceit of some intoxicant
> From shallow wits; who knows no work can stand,
> Whether health, wealth or peace of mind were spent
> On master-work of intellect or hand,
> No honour leave its mighty monument,
> Has but one comfort left: all triumph would
> But break upon his ghostly solitude.

(ll. 33–40)

The adjective "ghostly" directs us to the interplay of self and daimon—the daimon is called the "*Ghostly Self*. . . when it inhabits the sphere" (*V*, p. 193)[41]—and prepares us for the next question and answer:

41. This seems to be the basis of Yeats's distinction between permanent and impermanent daimons (*Myth*, p. 335 n.1).

> But is there any comfort to be found?
> Man is in love and loves what vanishes,
> What more is there to say?

(ll. 41–43)

The question grows out of the constant temptation confronting man, tormented by the daimonic crisis, but the answer brings us back to that torment and the heart's relevance, while the blank, uncompromising tone and word choice impress upon the reader the honesty and insight of the poet's perception.

Because the dragon-ridden days of section I are still capable of producing other dragons—this time of air, in the form of Loie Fuller's Chinese dancers—the whirling image, with its obvious connotations also of celebrations of the Chinese New Year, reminds Yeats of the larger cosmic dance of the Platonic Year and man's participation in it: "All men are dancers and their tread / Goes to the barbarous clamour of a gong." However, the striking image of the swan, symbolic of the solitary soul, flying off "into the desolate heaven," can still overturn the poet's mind, "lost amid the labyrinth that he has made," with desires of transcendence, only to be counterbalanced by the recognition of another "crack-pated" dream, to "mend" mankind's afflictions. The effect of both dreams—for transcendence or for futile political action—is to be found in the fearful expression of despair and nihilism in sections IV and V, the latter preluding the equally fierce and fearful ballad songs of the thirties.

Despite its expression of violence and its vision of the apocalyptic terror associated with Phase 1, the poem's final section is the consequence of a regained solitude. Instead of sharing in the mob feeling of section V ("Come let us mock at the great"), Yeats's position as agonized but enduring observer returns. This section clearly parallels the final section of "Meditations in Time of Civil War," but lacks the compensating vision of the lovely ladies. Instead, we are shown only Salome and "That insolent fiend Robert Artisson"—the one associated in the myth with the end of the classical era, the other a famous fourteenth-century Kilkenny incubus invoked to satisfy the lusts of Lady Kyteler. Lady Kyteler's gifts of "Bronzed peacock feathers, red combs of her cocks," clearly relate her unnatural love also to the end of an era. The juxtaposition of Salome and Artisson makes sense in another way: both are traditionally seen as a perversion of natural love, whether in Herod's taking Herodias, his brother's wife, mother of Salome, or in Lady Kyteler's demonic love of an incubus. Yeats's own note provides this rhetorical question: "Are not those who travel in the whirling dust also in the Platonic Year?" (*Var*, p. 433). The question is only rhetorical, and the reader is left with knowledge of the inevitable cyclism and the necessity for tragic endurance and solitude.

3

"Among School Children," although sharing the several themes and images expressed and explored in the previous poems from *The Tower* volume, provides a more joyful and exultant conclusion. The elements for tragedy remain; the daimonic crisis, the existential dialectic of time, the tension between self and soul, the agony of heart's truth, continue. However, no other poem in the volume so firmly refutes "Sailing to Byzantium," and the affirming voice prepares us for *The Winding Stair*. Instead of the static, mechanical, non-vital Byzantine bird we are directed to the organic and vitalist tree, rooted in earth and reaching out into air, embracing the dialectic out of which the poet's vision now triumphantly comes.

The poem proceeds out of a series of triads,[42] a

42. Unterecker's term is "trinities" (*Reader's Guide*, p. 191).

design already noted in "The Tower." Whether of
Maud as a child, lover, and old woman; or Yeats himself as baby, lover, and aged scarecrow; or the nun,
mother, and lover set off against Plato, Aristotle, and
Pythagoras—all direct us to the conjunction here and
now of past, present, and future, made concrete by the
richness of the ordering and ordered experiencing self.
The climax centres on the image of the tripartite tree,
neither leaf, blossom, nor bole. The poem's remarkable
achievement consists not merely in the nature of the
vision—glorious as that may be—but in the manner
in which the poem itself becomes the most appropriate
vehicle possible for that vision. There is no finer poem
in Yeats's entire work and no other which so clearly
demonstrates the irreducibility of great art to prosaic
paraphrase.[43]

Visiting the Montessori school at the Convent of
Mercy, Waterford, as part of his senatorial obligations,
Yeats found an ideal educational system in practice.
There could be no more appropriate setting for the
educating experience he himself undergoes. The children's scrutiny of and only "momentary wonder" at
"A sixty-year-old smiling public man" enable him to
apply a similar scrutiny towards himself. For the public
image and private vision contradict each other, and the
occasion gives rise to that self-examination Yeats always found necessary and productive. By the time
poem and vision reach conclusion, private and public
images are resolved, not in the stoic resignation which
marked "Meditations in Time of Civil War" or "Nine-

---

43. Cf. F. R. Leavis and Q. D. Leavis, *Lectures in America*, p. 78.
For a contrary view, see Bloom, *Yeats*, p. 369; George Brandon
Saul, "In . . . Luminous Wind," *Yeats Centenary Papers*, VII,
229. For a useful discussion of the poem and Yeats's visit to
the school, see Donald T. Torchiana, "'Among School Children' and the Education of the Irish Spirit," in *In Excited
Reverie*, ed. Jeffares and Cross, pp. 123–50.

teen Hundred and Nineteen," but in a glorious, affirming harmony.

The daimonic crisis still informs the poet: the schoolchildren provoke him to "dream of a Ledaean body" (Maud) and of her tale "That changed some childish day to tragedy." The term "tragedy" is not used idly; Yeats valued it too highly for that. The tragic vision underlies the various experiences the poet is led to in the course of the poem: the previous sympathetic union of Maud and Yeats, imaged in "Plato's parable" in *The Symposium*, and the present state of being "driven wild" by his imagining a youthful Maud; the present state of Maud, his Rose, Ideal Beauty, and Helen, now possessed of "Hollow of cheek," an image appropriately echoing Dante's "hollow face" in "Ego Dominus Tuus"; his own state of physical decrepitude; the suffering of a mother in childbirth and in parental love and concern; the heartbreak known by nuns, mothers, and lovers, but of which abstract philosophy (Plato, Aristotle, and Pythagoras) remains ignorant; and, finally, the tragic nature of the relationship between man's self and the Presences, or daimons. Yeats could "think of life as a struggle with the Daimon who would ever set us to the hardest work among those not impossible," or see that "man and Daimon feed the hunger in one another's hearts" (*Myth*, pp. 335–36). Consequently, the daimons become in the poem the "Presences" who are "self-born mockers of man's enterprise":[44] mockery of man's enterprise has been their constant attitude, while the epithet "self-born" refers to both their unique origin (not created by any being

44. Thomas Parkinson argues mistakenly that "the 'Presences' can only be taken to mean the statues and children that are knowable by passion, piety or affection." *W. B. Yeats: The Later Poetry* (Berkeley and Los Angeles: Univ. of California Press, 1964), p. 105.

other than themselves) and the element in which they
operate (man's self). This definition has been prepared
by Yeats in his declaration of faith in section III of
"The Tower" and in the concluding stanza of "Two
Songs from a Play." The irony is, however, that only
by such mocking tension between man and daimon
can the jubilant celebration of "Man's own resinous
heart" be offered. The tragic relationship of man and
daimon is positive in its very tragedy. For just as Dante
climbed the stair to eat the bitter bread, thus "found
the unpersuadable justice, . . . / The most exalted lady
loved by a man" in "Ego Dominus Tuus" (ll. 36–37),
so too Yeats can declare:

> Labour is blossoming or dancing where
> The body is not bruised to pleasure soul,
> Nor beauty born out of its own despair,
> Nor blear-eyed wisdom out of midnight oil.
> O chestnut-tree, great-rooted blossomer,
> Are you the leaf, the blossom or the bole?
> O body swayed to music, O brightening glance,
> How can we know the dancer from the dance?

>   (ll. 57–64)

Harold Bloom is right to characterize the poem as
one "in which . . . Yeats knows his own limitations
and the limitations of poetry, and of thought,"[45]
though he fails to appreciate the dignity and worth
with which the poem endows man and temporal existence. The questions are rhetorical apostrophes and
contain none of "the genuine doubt" Bloom sees. The
lines extol time and change and place man's greatness
and capacity for an all-inclusive vision with, rather
than against, "the barbarous clangour of a gong"
("Nineteen Hundred and Nineteen," l. 58). Indeed, the
conclusion is paralleled in a poem written some twenty

45. *Yeats*, p. 369.

years later, Wallace Stevens' "A Primitive Like an Orb,"
which offers a similar elevation of the temporal flux
and the creative self's capacity to construct a paradise
of the present out of its very fluctuating nature. The
opening lines of Stevens' final stanza, moreover, offer
remarkable verbal echoes of the final stanza to "Two
Songs from a Play":

> That's it. The lover writes, the believer hears,
> The poet mumbles and the painter sees,
> Each one, his fated eccentricity,
> As a part, but part, but tenacious particle,
> Of the skeleton of the ether, the total
> Of letters, prophecies, perceptions, clods
> Of color, the giant of nothingness, each one
> And the giant ever changing, living in change.[46]

At the end of his life Yeats declared, "Man can
embody truth but he cannot know it" (*Letters*, p. 922).
His own work is a direct attempt to attain that embodi-
ment of truth. This is what is meant by Unity of Being
or the whole man—blood, intellect, and imagination

---

46. *Collected Poems of Wallace Stevens*, p. 443. Another close
parallel, however, is Paul Valéry in *Mélange* (Paris: Gallimard,
1941), p. 97; noted by Ian W. Alexander, "Valéry and Yeats:
The Rehabilitation of Time," *Scottish Periodical*, 1 (Summer
1947), 77–106:
> O plante, arbre, répétition rayonnante
> Tu rayonnes ton âge par saisons et par germes
> Tu répètes ton motif régulièrement à chaque angle
> De chaque étage de ta croissante stature, et tu répètes
> Ton essence en chaque graine, tu te produis, tu te jettes
> Autour de toi périodiquement sous forme de chances—en
>   tel nombre
> Tu élimines tes similitudes.
The lines are first to be found in the *Cahiers*, XII, 295, written
1926–28, at the time of Yeats's "Among School Children." See
Pierre Laurette, *Le Thème de l'Arbre chez Paul Valéry*, Bib-
liothèque Française et Romane, Série C, Études Littéraires, 14
(Paris: Librairie C. Klincksieck, 1967), p. 58.

running together—which Blake called Vision. It is the integration of the Four Zoas, the various parts of the self, in a divine harmony which transforms both self and world. What amongst other things distinguishes Yeats, however, is his recurrent insistence upon the tragic nature of the vision which allows men such moments of epiphany. The poem has illustrated the good Romantic doctrine that the nature of the world depends upon the nature and constitution of the self. A more complete self sees more fully and more truthfully. The unifying and unified quality of the vision imaged in the chestnut tree defies analysis, because analysis operates on a narrower, more rigid level of experience, reducing the unified to the fragmentary and separate. Or, as Wordsworth put it in "The Tables Turned," "We murder to dissect." In its very structure, moving through all time, and in its synthesizing of experiences, Yeats's poem demonstrates the limitation and inaccuracy of the nonvisionary perception. We are given the texture of a heightened experience. But, as the experience among schoolchildren shows, the illumination comes not merely as a reconciliation to the tragedy of existence but out of that very tragedy itself. The numinous experience, rather than set apart in the eternal city of Byzantium, is possible within existence; moreover, it is known through, rather than despite, the temporal nature.

The rehabilitation of time, which provides a major concern in *The Tower*, is more firmly upheld in *The Winding Stair*. The tensions evident in the former volume remain. The beautiful woman continues to choose her false mask and, becoming opinionated, is reduced to a scarecrow ("In Memory of Eva Gore-Booth and Con Markiewicz"). The proud heroic man is still elevated as emblematic of the creative self, or in Yeats's startling terms, "Man has created death" ("Death"). The dialogue persists between self and soul, dramatizing the fearful tension between imagination and intellect, time and eternity. Likewise, men go on constructing towers in the familiar pattern known to the Alexandrian, the Babylonian, and, more recently, to the Romantic Shelley, only to experience the contrary pull by the heart in the direction of mankind ("Blood and the Moon"). The Great House remains the epitome of culture, breeding, poise, and grace in a world ranged against it and the values it represents ("Coole Park, 1929" and "Coole Park and Ballylee, 1931"). Indeed, *The Winding Stair* begins with dreams of an incendiary apocalypse to purge a declining world and ends with a prayer to "Overcome the Empyrean; hurl / Heaven and Earth out of their places" ("From the 'Antigone'").

It would be tempting to conclude that Yeats has abandoned heart and its temporal nature, now imaged as "The fury and the mire of human veins" ("Byzantium"), preferring the eternal state of Byzantium. Yet what is evident about the volume is that while Yeats might continue to experience his distinctive vacillation ("A Dialogue of Self and Soul," "Vacillation," "Blood and the Moon"), nevertheless his conclusions more firmly than ever direct us to temporal existence and the tragic human condition, to what Crazy Jane calls "heart's truth." Indeed, "Byzantium" is more expressive of the dynamic whirling of the gyres than its predecessor, "Sailing to Byzantium." The static artificial bird is replaced not only by dancing daimons but by dolphins, whose mire and blood are the necessary and sole vehicles by which spirits are transported to the holy city.

> At midnight on the Emperor's pavement flit
> Flames that no faggot feeds, nor steel has lit,
> Nor storm disturbs, flames begotten of flame,
> Where blood-begotten spirits come
> And all complexities of fury leave,
> Dying into a dance,

An agony of trance,
An agony of flame that cannot singe a sleeve.

Astraddle on the dolphin's mire and blood,
Spirit after spirit! The smithies break the flood,
The golden smithies of the Emperor!
Marbles of the dancing floor
Break bitter furies of complexity,
Those images that yet
Fresh images beget,
That dolphin-torn, that gong-tormented sea.

The ascension to Heaven, so avidly sought by Soul in "A Dialogue of Self and Soul," is now conceived as possible only through the relationship of man and daimon. The spirits that come, like those perning in a gyre in "Sailing," are "blood-begotten," begotten out of blood and man's experience of crisis which sustains them and keeps them in being: "man and Daimon feed the hunger *in one another's* hearts" (*Myth*, p. 335; my italics); or, as Yeats puts it in *A Vision*, p. 238, "The expiation, because offered to the living for the dead, is called 'expiation for the dead' but is in reality expiation for the *Daimon*, for passionate love is from the *Daimon* which seeks by union with some other *Daimon* to reconstruct above the antinomies its own true nature." The tragedy of man's self is now made clear and seen as part of that total process which is both existence and redemption. For man is confronted with crisis through the perpetual watchfulness of his daimon—Yeats's version of the watchman duties of Blake's Los—and ecstasy or union with one's eternal daimonic self is possible only through agony. Likewise, the redemptive process, imaged in the dolphin's transporting spirits to Byzantium, is made possible through "the dolphin's mire and blood." The irony is implicit in the last lines of the poem. The image of the creative elements ("Marbles of the dancing floor") is superbly appropriate, capturing as it does that "marmorean

Muse" Yeats sought (*Myth*, p. 325); while suggesting also a finished and ordered completeness and its resistance to time; together with a sense of a mosaic pieced together into an eternal unity, as the composite or complex self too must be pieced together into new composition with its daimon. The smithies are similarly modelled on Blake's Los, the creative imagination continually at work as blacksmith with anvil, hammer, and furnaces. The irony contained in the verb "break" is, however, one indication of Yeats's major divergence from Blake. For while Los creates the City of Art, Golgonooza, which bears a superficial resemblance to Byzantium, he does so as one of several preparations for threefold man to proceed to the final city of the fourfold Jerusalem. Byzantium seems more of a final resting place than Golgonooza ever was, and is certainly a more frenzied, furious, and agonizing state than the "building of pity and compassion" Blake described (*J*, 12: 25–44). Yeats's verb "break" includes the breaking out of the cyclical pattern to the breakthrough into the Thirteenth Cone, but also the constant heartbreak that for him constituted the means by which such a blossoming of self takes place. But in another sense man's created self (his image or desire) is that which can lead him two ways: either to salvation through the daimonic possession in Byzantium, or to further reincarnation and future purgation of self tormented by desire.

Likewise, in "A Dialogue of Self and Soul" the dramatic conflict remains; the temptation of transcendence still allures. The voices of Self and Soul persistently talk at cross-purposes, continuing in a particular train of thought regardless of the other's assertions. Soul concentrates his gaze on the ascent of the winding stair and the ultimate reward of transcendence, offering in the place of the affirmative voice of "Among School Children" ("How can we know the dancer from the dance?") its own negation: "Who can distinguish

darkness from the soul?" Both questions address the
same situation: the creative potentiality of the individual who contains the whole world in himself, whose
progress and decline correspond to the larger cosmic
cyclism. But Soul chooses to stress the "ancestral
night" which brings deliverance. Again the parallel
with "Among School Children" holds true. Instead of
the exultant blossoming of "labour" we get deliverance: the imagery of birth persists, but now in the form
of transcendental rebirth. In its stead, Self offers only
continual labour; in place of winding stair, Self holds
out Sato's sword, "Emblematical of love and war." And
in the second section, once Soul has been rendered
silent as a stone, Self proceeds to move gradually from
stoic resignation ("What matter . . . ?") to content
and, finally, to a Blakean blessedness which can hold
in balance the antinomies of Soul's intellect (measure-
ment) and Self's imagination (forgiveness):[47]

> I am content to follow to its source
> Every event in action or in thought;
> Measure the lot; forgive myself the lot!
> When such as I cast out remorse
> So great a sweetness flows into the breast
> We must laugh and we must sing,
> We are blest by everything,
> Everything we look upon is blest.

(ll. 65–72)

Instead of the fragmentation of Self and Soul, we are
offered their transformation through the passionate

47. As Whitaker has noted, under the influence of Blake Yeats
    rather surprisingly identified the imagination with forgiveness
    of sins (*Swan and Shadow*, p. 154). See *E & I*, pp. 102, 112;
    Plays and Controversies (London: Macmillan, 1923), p. 113;
    and cf. his statement that "the common condition of life is
    hatred" and that only in moments when love and forgiveness
    overcome hate can happiness come (*Myth*, p. 365).

intensity of "Heart's purple" experienced by Self or heart.

With this awareness Yeats ventures in "Vacillation" to explore the crucial question "What is joy?" beginning with inevitable reference to the dialectic: "Between extremities / Man runs his course." The poem itself proceeds in dialectical vacillation, posing those alternatives man takes in his search and employing the familiar Yeats imagery (tree, fire, heart, and soul) and masks (lover, bourgeois, solitary, man of action, and saint). The first alternative is that of the Attis worshipper, granted an ecstatic revelation (II). The tree he experiences is miraculously "half all glittering flame and half all green / Abounding foliage," an image which clearly embraces the dialectical contraries and momentarily resolves them.[48] Yeats's cryptic comment— "And half is half and yet is all the scene; / And half and half consume what they renew"—relates the situation to the heart's consumption and the self's consummation already noted in *The Tower*, and parallels the fertility-resurrection myth associated with Attis. Indeed, the conjunction of eternity and time, god and man, is epitomized in the dual nature of the tree: "That staring fury" of the purificatory fire is set off against "the blind lush leaf" of the natural. We have seen other similar staring eyes in Yeats's myth, from the eagle eye of the hero to that of Pallas Athene. Sections III, V, and VI pursue other variations on the heart's consumption, whether misled by material wealth and ambition or guided by love (III); or burdened by responsibility and conscience (V); or capable of indifference as experienced by conquerors (VI). The fourth section brings a moment of bliss with the body's

48. Raine sees this as a Heraclitean "comparison of nature to an everlasting fire, parts kindling, parts going out" (*Blake and Tradition*, II, 10). The source may be more Celtic than Greek, as in *The Mabinogion*; see Jeffares, *Commentary*, pp. 361–62.

blazing experience in the incongruous setting of "a crowded London shop," an experience he recounted with only slight variation in *Per Amica Silentia Lunae* (*Myth*, pp. 364–65).

Lines 67–69 of the last stanza of section VI clarify the poem's development thus far:

> From man's blood-sodden heart are sprung
> Those branches of the night and day
> Where the gaudy moon is hung.

Yeats has followed the antinomies of day and night, sun and moon, primary and antithetical, intellect and imagination, as evidenced in the masks of bourgeois, lover, man of action, or solitary. And like the Attis worshipper hanging his god's image in the miraculous tree, man hangs a gaudy moon in the branches which spring from his tormented blood-sodden heart. Whether intellectual or emotional, the source remains man's desiring heart. And it is in answer to a somewhat pompous and priggish Soul (later to become Crazy Jane's more obnoxious Bishop), who stresses the purificatory fire on the way to salvation, that Heart replies, "What theme had Homer but original sin?" Heart recognizes love and war, blood and agony, like the Self in "A Dialogue of Self and Soul," as the source of man's torment and man's greatness. Although the ditches are impure, Yeats remains convinced that existence must be celebrated. And though the more tempting Von Hügel[49] in the last section takes over Soul's arguments to represent Christian faith and miracle, Yeats seeks no "relief" for his heart. Rather, he notes

---

49. Yeats's dismissal, "So get you gone Von Hügel, though with blessings on your head" (l. 89), echoes Wordsworth's "Old Cumberland Beggar," "Then let him pass, a blessing on his head!" (ll. 162, 171). Bloom has seen other Wordsworthian legacies and echoes in Yeats's work, despite the harsh words Yeats directed at the Romantic poet (*Yeats*, pp. 63, 111, 208, 216, 286, 355–56, 383, 457).

his allegiance to an older and pagan faith: "Homer is my example and his unchristened heart." Precisely this conjunction of paganism and heart's truth is imaged in Crazy Jane and Tom the Lunatic and runs through the two lyric sequences "A Man Young and Old" and "A Woman Young and Old."

4

The lunatic figures of Yeats's later work—Crazy Jane, Tom the Lunatic, Ribh, and more anonymous wild wicked old men—are all singers of "supernatural songs" and express through paradox the wisdom gained from heart's truth. Their songs have the same gnomic quality as those of Shakespeare's Fool in *King Lear* or of Blake. Fool and madman are emblematic of the crazed heart or disintegrating brain, and Yeats accords them a special place in his system. All are outcasts in one form or another, and range themselves against a world representative of values and behaviour contrary to vision and truth. Their alienation is a variation upon the dichotomy of triumph and solitude expressed in "Nineteen Hundred and Nineteen," while the cyclical pattern to which Yeats becomes resigned there is now voiced in a handy-dandy with distinctively sexual terms, as in "Crazy Jane Talks with the Bishop":

> "A woman can be proud and stiff
> When on love intent;
> But Love has pitched his mansion in
> The place of excrement;
> For nothing can be sole or whole
> That has not been rent."

The dialectic divides but also unites, and the puns to be seen on "sole or whole" (soul or hole) are indeed part of her paradoxical vision.[50] The tragic vision has become translated into sexual terms and is seen in Tom

50. Unterecker, *Reader's Guide*, p. 229.

the Lunatic's songs against the larger cosmic dance. According to Jane's wisdom, gained through suffering and tragedy as well as love, the dead journeyman lover Jack remains more solid than the coxcomb now set out in Bishop's habit. And the perverse nature of the Bishop's position is reflected in his physical deformity, just as Yeats's beautiful women evince a spiritual beauty. Likewise, St. Cellach proclaims Christ's physical perfection in "The Dancer at Cruachan and Cro-Patrick," and Tom the Lunatic asserts the blessedness of existence with a Berkeleyan idealism. Despite age and the "smoking wick" of Nature, despite his vision of the dead Huddon, Duddon, and Daniel O'Leary, previously distinguished for their ranting and randiness, Tom can still firmly uphold his faith:

> "Whatever stands in field or flood,
> Bird, beast, fish or man,
> Mare or stallion, cock or hen,
> Stands in God's unchanging eye
> In all the vigour of its blood;
> In that faith I live or die."

> ("Tom the Lunatic")

No less than Crazy Jane, in "Crazy Jane on God," he recognizes that blessedness derives from the interrelationship of finite and infinite, whether as man and daimon or man and God. He is resigned to loss of vision—the eye image again—in the knowledge that divine perception maintains all things in their blessed existence. The source of all things remains God ("perfection"), and "the self-begotten" are at polar opposites to "fantastic men":

> Things out of perfection sail,
> And all their swelling canvas wear,
> Nor shall the self-begotten fail
> Though fantastic men suppose

Building-yard and stormy shore,
Winding-sheet and swaddling-clothes.

("Old Tom Again")

Yeats's various uses of the term "fantasy" are helpful here. In the five-line lyric "A Meditation in Time of War" at the close of *Michael Robartes and the Dancer* (1921), he declared, "I knew that One is animate, / Mankind inanimate phantasy." That knowledge came in "one throb of the artery," which, as its gloss in *Per Amica Silentia Lunae* explains, brings an end to time, and "is alone animate, all the rest is fantasy . . ." (*Myth*, p. 357). Fantasies are what in section VI of "Meditations in Time of Civil War" we have fed the hearts on, thus brutalizing heart and denying ourselves the Condition of Fire. The irony is all the more heavy since the Bishop, who acts as Jane's spiritual adviser, is the most mistaken of all these figures. The handy-dandy is complete: the supposedly wise is the most ignorant, the apparently lunatic and fantastic is the most perceptive and visionary, the most damned is the most capable of blessedness. The Vision of Evil has come complete circle. Nothing can indeed be made whole that has not been rent, whether that rending take place on a sexual, a psychological, or a spiritual level.

Consequently, in "Crazy Jane Reproved," where the Bishop does most of the talking, interrupted only by the contrary, ridiculing refrain of Jane's *"Fol de rol, fol de rol,"* we find the Bishop failing to recognize those first principles upon which Jane and Tom are most insistent.[51] Indeed, the Bishop's faith, akin to a spiritual blackmail which stresses that morality pays,

---

51. The refrain is neither spoken by the Bishop nor trivial, as Unterecker would have it (*Reader's Guide*, p. 227). Cf. the *"fol de rol de rolly O"* of "The Pilgrim" in *Last Poems*. William York Tindall complicates matters unnecessarily by arguing that

is founded upon the essential duality of God and man in a fallen world.

Refuting the superstitions of sailors—a reckless pursuit when we remember Yeats's elevation of the primitive mind capable of reaching into the *Anima Mundi*—the Bishop denies the sailors' account of thunder. Rather than the common superstition of God's anger, which St. Patrick earlier offered in *The Wanderings of Oisin* (II, 204–6), the Bishop offers a superstition of his own: thunder evidences a casual, almost indifferent, response on God's part. Heaven yawns.

> I care not what the sailors say:
> All those dreadful thunder-stones,
> All that storm that blots the day
> Can but show that Heaven yawns;
> Great Europa played the fool
> That changed a lover for a bull.
> *Fol de rol, fol de rol.*

The verb "yawns" is important: coming as it does at the end of both line and metrical foot, it is given particular emphasis because it serves as a "hinge" or vortex influencing our interpretation of the lines before and after. The act of yawning is seen more clearly against Yeats's gloss in *Autobiographies*, p. 249: "Politics, for a vision-seeking man, can be but half achievement, a choice of an almost easy kind of skill instead of that kind which is, of all those not impossible, the most difficult. Is it not certain that the Creator yawns in earthquake and thunder and other popular displays, but toils in rounding the delicate spiral of a shell?"[52]

---

the speakers' identity is uncertain, in "W. B. Yeats," *Columbia Essays on Modern Writers*, 15 (New York: Columbia Univ. Press, 1966), p. 38. See Brian John, "Yeats's 'Crazy Jane Reproved,'" *Eire-Ireland*, 4, no. 4 (1969), pp. 52–55.

52. Noted by Jeffares, *Commentary*, p. 372.

God, like other creators in Yeats's myth, is fascinated by what is most difficult. What Jane recognizes, however, is what Yeats on other occasions notes: that after sexual intercourse lovers are inclined to stretch and yawn ("On Woman," "Three Things," "News for the Delphic Oracle"). The association leads directly on to Europa's sexual experience with Zeus, an experience the Bishop fails to interpret properly. For the Bishop is a dirty old man, and just as he misinterprets the thunder (associated in classical myth with Zeus), so too does he misinterpret Europa's conjunction with the bull-Zeus. He mistakes the interaction of god and woman, seeing the sexual experience not as a metaphor of the marriage of macrocosm and microcosm but as another piece of promiscuity to be rigorously condemned. Europa was a fool. And in Jane's sense she was: not in mistaking a bull for Zeus but in being elevated to that folly or madness which constitutes the only wisdom. *Fol de rol* indeed, a comment which in its ambivalence directs us to both Europa's wise folly and the Bishop's foolish stupidity.

The same irony is implicit in the second stanza, and again centres on the verb at the end of the fourth line, "crack." The Bishop's emphasis lies not on energy of any kind, which remains the attribute of Jack, but on the fragile delicacy of a shell, a piece of the Creation which in his eyes asserts the supremacy of Heaven.[53] To create the intricacy of the "shell's elaborate whorl" with its labyrinthine design stretched the powers even of God. Jane's preoccupation with a mere "roaring, ranting journeyman" and the sexual labyrinth is thus

53. Yeats's use of the shell image varies considerably (see n.38) but seems related to order and the impulse to construct and contain. Cf. Blake's fountain and cistern (*MHH*, 8: 35). Indeed, it is possible that Yeats might have in mind Blake's Mundane Shell, the material world which contains amongst other things the Twenty-seven false Churches (*M*, 37: 19–43), a suitably fallen Urizenic world for the Bishop to uphold.

misplaced: she should give herself up to a superior spiritual power and follow a different labyrinthine path. However, the timing and positioning of the verb "crack" is crucial, for the verb serves once more as an ironic device. The Bishop draws attention to a condition which he again misinterprets because his mind is closed to the richness of experience. He fails to perceive the world in its wholeness because he in turn, not knowing love, has not been rent or made whole. Jane, however, was cracked in more than one sense. First, she was crazy and called originally "Cracked Mary" (*Var*, p. 507); secondly, she was sexually rent, "cracked," and made whole by her journeyman lover. Moreover, the cracking of heaven's joints suggests the stretching of God's infinite powers but also points to God's love of the world and the world's blessedness. For God's love also was so infinite that He was willing to take upon Himself the supreme task of Creation. The verb "crack" comments upon the situation following it, as the verb "yawn" commented and put in proper perspective Europa's love of Zeus. The Bishop is right to emphasize the heartbreak Jane will experience in loving Jack but wrong in believing in the irrelevance of heartbreak (another instance of "crack") in the tragic process of existence and redemption. Rather than suggesting God's superior powers, as the Bishop argues, the confronting of obstacle even to the point of cracking is the duty of any creator (God, artist, or woman) and is what Jane has known and endured in her love.

Yet again the Bishop offers a wisdom he is too stupid to notice. He warns Jane against hanging her heart on so unfaithful a lover as Jack, whose love brings only misery. But we remember not only Jane's awareness of love's dialectic (*"Love is like the lion's tooth"* in "Crazy Jane Grown Old Looks at the Dancers") or Blake's apothegm favoured by Yeats ("sexual love is founded upon spiritual hate"), but also those occasions in Yeats's work when precisely the action of hanging one's heart brings revelation and fulfilment, tragedy and redemption. The ultimate sacrifice cannot be appreciated by a Bishop whose eyes are closed to tragic irony and supreme wisdom. The refrain *"Fol de rol, fol de rol,"* far from being trivial, is the only response possible, but it includes a tragic sense and a heroic dignity, informing Jane's profound spiritual wisdom, as well as being a scourging satire.

Although Jane remains convinced of the temporal dialectic and therefore of love's tragedy, she is also aware of the eternal consummation incomprehensible to the empirical or rational mind:

"What can be shown?
What true love be?
All could be known or shown
If Time were but gone."
"That's certainly the case," said he.

("Crazy Jane on the Day of Judgment")

The "he," almost certainly the Bishop, agrees with Jane but for the wrong reasons. The Bishop also believes in the eventual judgement of motive and action on the Last Day, but his italicized "last word" suggests a misplaced triumph on his part. For what Jane knows is that the Apocalypse will prove her right. The Bishop, who has known neither love nor tragedy, neither passion nor madness, is ignorant of Jane's wisdom "Learned in bodily lowliness / And in the heart's pride" ("Crazy Jane Talks with the Bishop"). Unlike Jane, who knows the satisfaction of love which takes body and soul, he wants only to denigrate body and insists upon the duality of body and soul.

Despite her continued suffering, Jane can continue in affirmation: "My body makes no moan / But sings on" ("Crazy Jane on God"). With characteristic paradox, however, she knows her sexual satisfaction with

Jack depended upon his being free to leave, so bringing
subsequent suffering, but that her future bliss in eternity will derive from that satisfaction and her ultimate
reunion with her satisfied lover. Their relationship is
thus defined by way of Yeats's recurrent skein or
thread image, which is related once more to the labyrinth, particularly the Daedalus myth involving
Ariadne, granddaughter of Zeus and Europa. Jane sees
the relationship of man and woman as a binding and
unbinding of skeins, just as in the larger pattern of
history "Each age unwinds the thread another age had
wound" (*V*, p. 270). The self's progress in its lifetime
towards passionate intensity dictates the extent to
which it is purged and qualified for redemption. Echoing the situation of an earlier poem, "The Cold
Heaven" in *Responsibilities,* Jane comments on the
dreaming-back process in which lovers walk the earth
seeking each other out if unsatisfied in their previous
existence. The process is described in *A Vision* as one
of six discarnate states which bring the soul to judgement. Because she has not repressed her love and
forged a marriage ring around Jack—a situation Blake
warned against in "The Fairy" (E, p. 466)—Jane has
known bodily ecstasy but, in peculiarly Yeatsian fashion, has also suffered from love's tragedy. Consequently, unlike the lonely ghost who has known no
love, her future life will bring spiritual ecstasy:

> I—love's skein upon the ground,
> My body in the tomb—
> Shall leap into the light lost
> In my mother's womb.

> ("Crazy Jane and Jack the Journeyman")

Without that love which is paradoxically both free and
binding, Jane would suffer torment after death and

walk the roads after Jack. That fate is presumably reserved for the ignorant Bishop.

Now resonant with echoes of Blake[54]—"Did he die
or did she die? / Seemed to die or died they both?" in
"Crazy Jane Grown Old Looks at the Dancers"; "Saw
I an old man young / Or young man old?" in "Girl's
Song"—the dialectic is resolved. Yet even in the more
idealized seven songs following Crazy Jane, the young
man speaks for the vast majority of figures undergoing
heartbreak in Yeats's last work when he knows "That
out of rock, / Out of a desolate source, / Love leaps
upon its course" ("His Confidence"). The confidence
gained from heart's truth is what informs and illuminates these last poems. For Yeats continued in his pursuit of the dialectical course of love, in the knowledge
that he was also pursuing the pattern of existence and
the means to redemption. The source was no less desolate and the path no less rigorous and tragic for all that.

The two lyric sequences "A Man Young and Old"
and "A Woman Young and Old" were originally intended to be published together.[55] While the woman's
sequence provides perhaps the climax, certainly the
conclusion, to The Winding Stair, the man's sequence
cannot be regarded as either climax or conclusion to

---

54. The parallel with Blake's "Mental Traveller" is tempting; Bornstein suggests "Shelley's notion of life as a reverse aging,"
noting also arguments in favour of a neoplatonism familiar
to both Yeats and Shelley (Yeats and Shelley, pp. 105–7). We
might add Blake also.

55. In 1933 Yeats could not remember the details: "A Woman
Young and Old was written before the publication of The
Tower, but left out for some reason I cannot recall" (Var,
p. 831). The reason seems to have been an insufficient number
of poems for the 1929 edition of The Winding Stair
(Unterecker, Reader's Guide, p. 194), which consisted of
poems 248–52. Only the 1933 edition of The Winding Stair
included poems 253–75, Words for Music Perhaps (published
separately 1932), and the woman's sequence.

The Tower. The reason may be found in comparing
the concluding poems of *The Tower* with the man's
sequence. "The Gift of Harun Al-Rashid," while stilted
and not wholly satisfying, is nevertheless meant as a
genuine tribute to Mrs. Yeats;[56] "All Souls' Night"
likewise was eventually subtitled "Epilogue to 'A Vision.'" Yeats preferred to conclude *The Tower* volume
with poems celebrating the new-found security and
wisdom gained from the "mummy truths" his wife's
automatic writing had brought. The man's sequence,
on the other hand, which is even more autobiographical than the woman's, deals in the main with Yeats's
experiences with Maud Gonne and Olivia Shakespear.
Yeats preferred to end *The Tower* not only with a
tribute to his wife and the wisdom their love brought
but on a more positive note than the stoic resignation
which the man's sequence provides.

Nevertheless, considered together, both sequences
pass through a quasi-Blakean journey through youth
to age and conclude with a lyric from a Sophoclean
tragedy. Although several autobiographical references
have been explicated,[57] the sequences are less autobiography than an attempt to chart the mental and physical journeys taken by lovers, male and female, along
the path of the whirling zodiac (the dialectical tension
in love) to the sphere (eternity and resolution of the
antinomies). Personal references or relevance are
merely part of Yeats's recurrent correspondence of the
individual self with the larger cosmic pattern. The
progression of the lover, man or woman, through the
various stages of love, is an attempt to delineate the
nature of love and the consequences for the experienc-

---

56. A draft of "The Gift of Harun Al-Rashid" included the can-
    celled lines, "And that was my first news of her that now Is
    my delight & comfort" (*Yeats: Last Poems*, ed. Stallworthy,
    p. 16). The terms resemble and surely echo Blake's description
    of Catherine as "my sweet Shadow of delight" (*M*, 42: 28).
57. Jeffares, *Commentary*, pp. 309–12, 392.

ing self. The male, however, does not gain anything like as fruitful a wisdom as the female: in the first sequence the man sees love from the position of failure and in the second takes on the Blakean form of the repressive father figure. Moreover, as Unterecker has argued, the first sequence's conclusion directs us to life's bitterness, while that of the second to "love's bitter-sweet."[58] Both conclusions point to the zodiacal nature of things, but the second, following "Words for Music Perhaps" which proclaims the sexual vision of Crazy Jane and Tom the Lunatic, provides a different emphasis: the ecstasy or revelation accompanying love.

In the opening poem of the man's sequence, "First Love," the man's experience leads him to lunacy, when, transfigured by the woman's smile, he discovers "a heart of stone" instead of the expected "heart of flesh and blood." The subsequent four songs (II–V) pursue the youthful experience, the fifth song being pivotal in that it looks both back to the previous encounters and forward, preparing us for the future condition of age. The final song (XI) acts as a commentary upon the whole sequence. The youthful experiences are all equally disastrous for the man—whether becoming "like a bit of stone" himself (II); experiencing the drowning of self in love's "cruel happiness" (III); learning the beloved's preference for another lover (IV); or being driven crazy by the empty cup of love (V). Nevertheless, the second half makes it clear that the experiences have brought a form of wisdom. And we are reminded of a later pronouncement in "After Long Silence" of *The Winding Stair:* "Bodily decrepitude is wisdom; young / We loved each other and were ignorant." At times the man is consoled by memories, as in the sixth song. Age may have broken body, deforming limbs into "twisted thorn" and gaining only women's indifference, "yet there beauty lay." And the

58. *Reader's Guide*, p. 240.

man finds consolation in the stature of his previous love—"The first of all the tribe lay there"—as Yeats draws one more analogy with the Homeric Helen-Maud. Or, in "Summer and Spring," he can adopt a gleeful tone in remembering their past union and how he bettered Peter, another of the woman's lovers. When the man meets up with his previous lovers, Madge and Margery, he learns "The Secrets of the Old," a wisdom which distinguishes between the various achievements in love. The result is laughter and tears ("The Friends of His Youth"), though of a more crazy, hysterical kind than the usual scornful, indifferent response of the hero. Similarly, in "His Wildness," the man bitterly mourns the decline of life and love and ends with his lullaby, reminiscent of Crazy Jane, to a stone. But the lunatic man still dreams of the sphere's eternal rest. The last song, "From 'Oedipus at Colonus,'" puts both the man's desire and that of Yeats in "Sailing to Byzantium" in a final perspective learnt from other poems in the volume:

> Endure what life God gives and ask no longer span;
> Cease to remember the delights of youth, travel-wearied
>   aged man;
> Delight becomes death-longing if all longing else be
>   vain.

The woman's sequence, however, substitutes a "life-longing" in place of the "death-longing" the man must confront with stoic resignation. Her poems pursue love's dialectic, using imagery from "A Dialogue of Self and Soul" with the caustic tone of Crazy Jane:

> How could passion run so deep
> Had I never thought
> That the crime of being born
> Blackens all our lot?
> But where the crime's committed
> The crime can be forgot.

> ("Consolation," ll. 7–12)

Again the fifth song, "Consolation," is pivotal, looking
backward to the first four poems in which love is related to the mask and the dissembling coquetry of self,
and forward to the visionary experiences of the consummated woman. And this song offers the "sages" a
wisdom they are ignorant of. Yeats has consistently
preferred the lunar ignorance of woman to the solar
knowledge of man ("Michael Robartes and the
Dancer"). And precisely the imagery of dragon, mirror,
and shriek, used in the 1921 poem, is taken over in
"Her Triumph," the woman's fourth song. Under the
influence of the dragon, identified in 1921 as the lady's
"thought," the source of which may well be Blake's
Urizen (Intellect),[59] the woman experiences a diminished love: "a casual / Improvisation, or a settled
game." With the advent of real love, however, she is
released from her enchainment—the source of which
is perhaps the repressive father—and granted a form
of revelation: "And now we stare astonished at the
sea, / And a miraculous strange bird shrieks at us." The
experience leads her to an awareness of love's dialectic
in "Consolation"; of the chosen "lot of love" and the
transformation, through sexual union, of zodiac into
sphere in "Chosen." It grants her a wisdom superior
to that which her lover, anxious to leave with day-
break, can have. He rejects her offer of further darkness (the "subterranean rest" of "Chosen"): "I offer
to love's play / My dark declivities" ("Parting").

The remaining songs, VIII–X—the eleventh is once
more a commentary upon the whole sequence—
explore the consequences of the woman's old age. Age

59. Kathleen Raine has argued for such an identification, "Yeats's
Debt to Blake," *Dublin Magazine* (Summer 1966), 39; noted
by Jeffares, *Commentary*, p. 394. Dragons figure prominently
in Blake's myth and are connected with man's enchainment,
spiritual or political. Vala in *The Four Zoas*, Night the Second,
26: 7–13, becomes first a serpent and then a dragon, while the
serpent in *Europe*, 10: 16, is related specifically to thought:
"Thought chang'd the infinite to a serpent."

brings awareness of "love's bitter-sweet" and the tragedy implicit in love: not only love's loss but its intrinsic
conjunction with hatred. "Her Vision in the Wood,"
within the more substantial and ceremonious *ottava
rima*, captures the torment and agony of the woman
now grown old, raging against old age and mutilating
her body to scourge herself of memory. Given the time
(midnight) and the setting (sacrificial sacred wood),
both of which are propitious, her rage brings first a
vision of Adonis. The wounded hero, beloved of
Aphrodite, goddess of love, and mutilated by a wild
boar, places the aged woman's torment in perspective.
For her agony is the result of her wound, given her
by her "beast," which in an earlier poem, "Demon and
Beast," is identified with desire. And the classical analogy, like the references to "Quattrocento painter" and
"Mantegna," "picture," and "coin," simply indicates
the recurrent nature of love's torment and wounding
of self by desire. Moreover, Adonis is seen later as
"That thing all blood and mire, that beast-torn wreck,"
thus relating him to the image of archetypal man in
"A Dialogue of Self and Soul" and "Byzantium." However, the first vision of Adonis is transformed into a
second, of her previous lover, perhaps the anxious man
of the sixth song, and "malediction" turns into
"shriek," sympathy into torment.

> That thing all blood and mire, that beast-torn wreck,
> Half turned and fixed a glazing eye on mine,
> And, though love's bitter-sweet had all come back,
> Those bodies from a picture or a coin
> Nor saw my body fall nor heard it shriek,
> Nor knew, drunken with singing as with wine,
> That they had brought no fabulous symbol there
> But my heart's victim and its torturer.

> (ll. 25–32)

Aphrodite was granted spring and summer to enjoy

Adonis in subsequent years, whereas in her next songs Yeats's woman knows only continued spiritual hatred. In "A Last Confession" she distinguishes between her various lovers and confesses that her deepest and most lasting love was that in which, giving soul as well as body, she "loved in misery." Mere physical love may bring pleasure but not the irrevocable binding of ghost to ghost. The misery of love, however, brings also possession of soul as well as body. And we remember Yeats's remark, "The tragedy of sexual intercourse is the perpetual virginity of the souls."[60] The woman, not in spite of but because of her torment and misery, has known the highest love: "There's not a bird of day that dare / Extinguish that delight."

The tragic irony is completed by her last song, "Meeting": in their final confrontation in old age, the two lovers, "Each hating what the other loved," go through one more exercise in love and hatred, each renouncing the other, each irrevocably bound up with the other. Only if they could discard their masks and "This beggarly habiliment" of body would "a sweeter word" be possible. The irony, however, is that, owing to love's dialectic, their love depends upon their masks, upon their ambivalent love-hatred, and no more within time is possible. Yet in the final song, Yeats-Sophocles can on the one side pray for the total destruction of time and eternity by the "bitter sweetness" imaged in Antigone, while on the other offer compassion in grief and tears for "Oedipus' child" and for all humanity. The characteristic vacillation has come full circle: the impulse to transcendence is once more qualified by the contrary impulse towards time and man:

> Pray I will and sing I must,
> And yet I weep—Oedipus' child
> Descends into the loveless dust.

60. Quoted in Jeffares, *Commentary*, pp. 372, 398, with slight variations.

5

Richard Ellmann is to some extent right to insist that
Yeats is without analogue—that "Yeats is in some present peril everywhere of being swallowed up by the great
whale of literary history" and that it is "time to emphasize the disconnections" between Yeats and his
analogues.[61] Whatever the disconnections between
him and his previous participants in the Romantic
vitalist tradition—and Yeats's divergences were many
and important—nevertheless he constantly judged
himself against his predecessors and defined his own
path by way of his analogues. He insisted that his
myth's eccentricity was apparent rather than real. And
at the centre of that vitalist myth is man's abundant
self, creating those supreme fictions by which he can
measure and define himself and at the same time confront with dignity and courage the overwhelming and
impersonal forces of time and eternity.

With an eye cocked on the glories and grandeur of
the past, Yeats-Ribh in his last supernatural song,
"Meru," can wave the past analogues goodbye. "Egypt
and Greece, goodbye, and goodbye Rome!" The flip-
pancy is ironic, almost bitter, but also necessary when
one recognizes the greater relevance of the destructive
journey man must of necessity take:

> . . . man's life is thought,
> And he, despite his terror, cannot cease
> Ravening through century after century,
> Ravening, raging, and uprooting that he may come
> Into the desolation of reality.

Hermits on Meru, like Ribh and other supernatural
singers, "know / That day brings round the night, that
before dawn / His glory and his monuments are gone,"

61. "Yeats Without Analogue," in *Modern Poetry*, ed. Hollander,
    pp. 395, 398.

but Yeats's vision has provided for that contingency, and he remains undaunted in his recognition of the need to learn the wisdom of daimonic images.

In addressing himself to the supreme question perpetually confronting man—how to live—Yeats could commit any number of follies. He could be tempted into a personal snobbery and arrogance and an unpopular reactionary political faith to scourge an undeserving present. Defiantly rejecting modern science and philosophy, he preferred eccentric occultism and a doubtful historical cyclism. Naïvely seduced by bravura and swagger, he mistakenly elevated violence and war into a cosmic cathartic. George Orwell dismissed all this silliness as Yeats's "rather sinister vision of life."[62]

Nevertheless, in speaking for himself and Ireland he managed to transcend provincial horizons. Though rooted in self and country, his work is limited to neither, ranging through all history, East and West, giving continuity and meaning to man's perpetual search for fulfilment. He shared Lawrence's principle, "Man is a thought-adventurer" (Ph. II, p. 616), and was constantly exploring the boundaries of self and beyond, through crisis and purgation, to future grace and redemption.

Other artists may offer a deeper compassion or a fuller sense of joy, a greater humility or a more commanding intellectual sense. In choosing a different path, however, Yeats provided a vision no less uncompromising, honest, and moving. Tracing a design through time and space, in which man is both victim and victor, he furnished a framework in which justice, truth, suffering, and beauty take on new and vital meaning.

62. *Critical Essays*, p. 129.

CHAPTER FOUR

D. H. Lawrence and the Quickening Word

It is four years since I saw, under a little winter snow, the death-grey coast of Kent go out. After four years, down, down on the horizon, with the last sunset still in the west, right down under the eyelid of the shut cold sky, the faintest spark, like a message. It is the Land's End light. And I, who am a bit short-sighted, saw it almost first. One sees by divination. The infinitesimal sparking of the Land's End light, so absolutely remote, as one approaches from over the sea, from the Gulf of Mexico, after sunset.

I won't pretend my heart was dead. It exploded again in my chest. "This is my own, my native land!" My God, what lies behind that spark of light! ("On Coming Home," *Ph. II,* p. 250)

Such was the reaction in 1923 of D. H. Lawrence, returning to England after four years of travel, first to Italy and then to Ceylon, Australia, the United States, and Mexico. The reaction is distinctively ambivalent: Lawrence is a peculiarly English writer, rooted in English literary and social traditions, yet even from his early years feeling profoundly for England, to the extent of being driven, like Joyce, into necessary, exasperated exile. Moreover, the passage reveals much essential Lawrence. There is his criticism of the sepulchral quality of English life, in terms reminiscent of Alvina in *The Lost Girl* (p. 303) or Richard Somers in *Kangaroo* (p. 264), but there is also his recognition of the potentiality for renewal in the apocalyptic blinking of a light positioned, symbolically enough, at Land's End. With the western sunset paralleling the cultural decline of the West, Lawrence takes on the aspect of the circumnavigating mythic traveller, now returning from the western isles, crossing again the threshold of adventure to renew the spark of life in a wasteland England.[1] He insists explicitly that the light is symbolic, requiring not good eyesight but a keen spiritual sense. He notes the reaction set off in his heart, as he was frequently provoked by his country. Finally, he introduces the implied obligation to investigate England's death-in-life and, like Blake's Los, to awaken the giant Albion from his debilitating sleep. Noteworthy in its fusion of concrete description and symbolic character and its interaction of traveller and scene, the passage portrays a dying universe and its saviour bringing resurrection and life everlasting in "the Eternal Now" (Blake, "Annotations to Lavater," E, p. 581).

In a similar essay, "Return to Bestwood" (written 1926), the focus is more limited. Yet Eastwood-Bestwood life he knew most intimately and cared about perhaps even more deeply. "The darkish Midlands" were "exactly the navel of England" (*CL*, p. 552); in the metaphorical as well as geographical sense, "the heart of England," as Sir Clifford says in *Lady*

1. The appropriateness to Lawrence's work of Joseph Campbell's terms, *The Hero With a Thousand Faces* (1949), has been noted by Jascha Kessler, "Descent into Darkness: The Myth of *The Plumed Serpent*," in *A D. H. Lawrence Miscellany*, ed. Harry T. Moore (Carbondale: Southern Illinois Univ. Press, 1959), pp. 239–61.

Chatterley's Lover (p. 44). Here the heart is sick and heavy: the coal strike has superseded whatever was left of the vital life of the mining community Lawrence had known in his childhood. The sense of alienation hurts all the more because the roots are deeper and more necessary for continued growth:

> I feel I hardly know any more the people I come from, the colliers of the Erewash Valley district. They are changed, and I suppose I am changed. I find it so much easier to live in Italy. And they have got a new kind of shallow consciousness, all newspaper and cinema, which I am not in touch with. At the same time, they have, I think, an underneath ache and heaviness very much like my own. It must be so, because when I see them, I feel it so strongly.
>
> They are the only people who move me strongly, and with whom I feel myself connected in deeper destiny. It is they who are, in some peculiar way, "home" to me. I shrink away from them, and I have an acute nostalgia for them. (*Ph. II*, p. 264)

Whatever the changes in Eastwood social life, and they are more than superficial ones in Lawrence's eyes, the extent of his involvement, not just with England but particularly with Eastwood and the Nottinghamshire coalfield, is clear. The colliers' problems are only apparently social and economic; essentially, they are ones of "shallow consciousness," of a failure to live or to achieve contact or relationships among themselves and with the world. They are as out of touch with the vital life force as they are with Lawrence himself. Indeed, at his most arrogant Lawrence tends to identify himself with that force: the destinies of village (or country) and native son are thus irrevocably intertwined, much as the aesthetics of both Blake and Yeats were affected by their sense of responsibility, the one for Albion's spiritual death, the other for modern Ireland's lack of culture.[2] And whatever the logical counterarguments, Lawrence with his "female intellect" knows-feels the truth of his perception.[3] His work constitutes in part explanation and elaboration of that destiny but proceeds further to the larger hope and responsibility of the promised salvation.

Unlike Yeats, however, Lawrence did not normally uphold a tragic vision of life; his fundamental optimism is closer to Blake or Carlyle, who likewise believed in the eventual victory of good over evil. The declaration "Ours is essentially a tragic age," with which *Lady Chatterley's Lover* begins, is in some ways more peculiarly Connie's view than his own. This is not to say that Lawrence remained ignorant of the modern calamitous state: his very deep despair and wounding of spirit during World War I are evidence enough to contradict the charge of myopic idealism. Rather, his optimism, while denying any Yeatsian tragic vision, was retained only after he had overcome the temptations of cynicism, withdrawal, disillusionment, and despair. His faith was a severely tested one, though all the firmer because of those tests; his vitalism all the more gloriously affirmed because he saw the deathly and evil nature of modern mechanism. The distinction applied earlier to Blake holds true for Lawrence also: he had as vivid an awareness of evil as any modern artist, but he did not uphold a Yeatsian Vision of Evil. Admitting the tragic nature of the modern world, he nevertheless rejected tragedy; admitting evil, he likewise defined "the real principle of Evil" as "anti-life" (*Not I*, p. 272). Similarly, he regarded the

2. Frank Kermode has also noted "a sort of Blakean patriotism," in "Lawrence and the Apocalyptic Types," *Critical Quarterly*, 10 (1968), 22.
3. Paul West, *The Wine of Absurdity: Essays on Literature and Consolation* (University Park: Pennsylvania State Univ. Press, 1966), p. 34.

tragic as fundamentally a northern or Greek myth, antithetical to his preferred Etruscans (*Ph*, pp. 57, 164), and concluded: "Strictly, there is no tragedy. The universe contains no tragedy, and man is only tragical because he is afraid of death" (p. 58). The parallel between the last clause and Yeats's affirmation in "Death" that "Man has created death" is only apparent. "Tragedy ought really to be a great kick at misery," he wrote (*CL*, p. 150); "Death's not sad, when one has lived" (p. 851). As Frieda herself has stated, "He [Lawrence] was not tragic, he would never have it that humanity, even, was tragic, only very wrong, but nothing that true wisdom could not solve" (*First Lady Chatterley*, p. viii). His whole life and art were dedicated to elucidating and communicating that wisdom, by way of "the quickening word . . . that will deliver us into our own being" ("Study of Thomas Hardy," *Ph*, p. 434).

1

The prophetic mask, worn with varying success by Blake, Carlyle, and Yeats, is then adopted once more by Lawrence. Even at the outset of his career he attracted disciples and demanded conversion, while detesting the conformity requisite to any system of belief. As one of those first disciples, Jessie Chambers, put it, "He was prepared to assault the cosmos" (*PR*, p. xxxix). Although, like Yeats, he could occasionally be tempted to provide a more formal system of belief— as in his *Psychoanalysis and the Unconscious* (1921), *Fantasia of the Unconscious* (1922), and *Apocalypse* (1931)—he was, like Yeats, first and foremost an artist. While his "pollyanalytics" (*Fan*, p. 57) are as intellectually suspect as Yeats's *Vision*, he is in E. M. Forster's terms "the greatest imaginative novelist of our generation."[4] In his "Study of Thomas Hardy" (1914), "which has turned out as a sort of Story of My Heart, or a *Confessio Fidei*" (*CL*, p. 298), his judgement upon the earlier novelist is peculiarly appropriate to himself: "It is not as a metaphysician that one must consider Hardy. He makes a poor show there." "His feeling, his instinct, his sensuous understanding is, however, apart from his metaphysic, very great and deep, deeper than that, perhaps, of any other English novelist" (*Ph*, p. 480). Aware of the dangers of subduing his "art to a metaphysic," he nevertheless wrote "because I want folk—English folk—to alter, and have more sense" (*CL*, p. 204). In "Surgery for the Novel—or a Bomb" (1923), he advocated the coming together of philosophy and the novel, to prevent the first from going "abstract-dry" and the second from being "sloppy" (*Ph*, p. 520).

Indeed, to the novel as a literary form he ascribed a "vast importance," as he argued in the now famous statement in *Lady Chatterley's Lover:* "It can inform and lead into new places the flow of our sympathetic consciousness, and it can lead our sympathy away in recoil from things gone dead. Therefore, the novel, properly handled, can reveal the most secret places of life: for it is in the *passional* secret places of life, above all, that the tide of sensitive awareness needs to ebb and flow, cleansing and freshening" (p. 104). He provided a similar definition of the novel's task in several essays, while his own fiction suitably illustrates his practice. Faced with the dual obligation to cleanse and freshen, Lawrence concentrated upon "our sympathetic consciousness," to enable us to undertake that "thought-adventure" necessary to our spiritual growth (*Ph. II*, p. 628). We must cast off the old and deathly and embrace the vital and alive or "*passional.*" With

4. Letter to *Nation and Athenaeum*, 29 Mar. 1930, quoted by F. R. Leavis, *D. H. Lawrence, Novelist*, p. 10.

such a moral, even puritanical, conception of his art, he took his duties very seriously. Yet, recalling his father's reaction to *The White Peacock*, he tells how his father "struggled through half a page, and it might as well have been Hottentot," only to express amazement at the amount his son had been paid. "'Fifty pounds!' He was dumbfounded, and looked at me with shrewd eyes, as if I were a swindler. 'Fifty pounds! An' tha's niver done a day's hard work in thy life'" (*Ph*, p. 232). Perhaps his ascribing to literature a moral purpose may be in part derived, as in the case of Carlyle, from his Non-Conformist conscience that he should do "a day's hard work." Certainly he regarded his books as "the trophies . . . of man's eternal fight with inertia" (p. 235).

While he may share with Carlyle and Yeats a corresponding faith in action and be drawn to dreams of leadership, power, and social change, he never shared their denigration of literature, never belittled the novel as a form. He may in rare instances become impatient with writing, or more frequently resent the abuse he received from an ignorant and hypocritical public. "If there weren't so many lies in the world," he declared, "I wouldn't write at all" (Nehls, III, 293). But upholding the Carlylean principle of veracity, he argued for the novel not only as a form but as pre-eminently suited to the elucidation and solution of modern man's spiritual dilemma. Using one of his central images, the rainbow, he insisted in his essay "Morality and the Novel": "The novel is a perfect medium for revealing to us the changing rainbow of our living relationships. The novel can help us to live, as nothing else can: no didactic Scripture, anyhow" (*Ph*, p. 532). That rainbow vision is no dream world but a very real enlightenment about the phenomenal paradise: "If you're a parson, you talk about souls in heaven. If you're a novelist, you know that paradise is in the palm of your hand, and on the end of your nose, because both are alive;

and alive, and man alive, which is more than you can
say, for certain, of paradise. Paradise is after life, and
I for one am not keen on anything that is *after* life"
("Why the Novel Matters," pp. 533–34). The definition
of paradise echoes Blake's "Auguries of Innocence,"
and the novelist is elevated, like Blake's visionary artists, for his integrated vision. He is, indeed, "superior
to the saint, the scientist, the philosopher, and the
poet, who are all great masters of different bits of man
alive, but never get the whole hog" (p. 535). "The novel
is the one bright book of life"; "In this sense, the Bible
is a great confused novel" (p. 535). Like characters in
a novel, "we . . . have got to live, or we are nothing"
(p. 537), and in this the novel can help cultivate our
feelings and contribute to our necessary wholeness
("The Novel and the Feelings," pp. 755–60). In that
most Carlylean of essays, "Climbing Down Pisgah,"[5]

5. Cf. Raymond Williams, who also argues for affinities between
   Lawrence and Carlyle, noting particularly this essay, in *Culture
   and Society, 1780–1950* (London: Chatto and Windus, 1959),
   pp. 199–200. Cf. also Graham Hough, *The Dark Sun: A Study
   of D. H. Lawrence* (London: Duckworth, 1956), pp. 3–4; George
   Ford, *Double Measure: A Study of the Novels and Stories of
   D. H. Lawrence* (New York: Holt, Rinehart, and Winston, 1965),
   pp. 12, 33; Edward Alexander, "Thomas Carlyle and D. H.
   Lawrence: A Parallel," *University of Toronto Quarterly*, 37,
   no. 3 (1968), 248–67; Robert O. Preyer, Introduction, *Victorian
   Literature, Selected Essays*, ed. Robert O. Preyer (New York:
   Harper & Row, 1967), p. xv. F. R. Leavis, on the other hand,
   has emphatically denied Lawrence's affinities with Carlyle but
   does not define the nature of his objection, in *D. H. Lawrence,
   Novelist*, p. 17; Eugene Goodheart sees Lawrence within a European tradition including Blake, Nietzsche, Freud, and Rilke,
   rather than Leavis' English tradition or Williams' social thinkers,
   in *The Utopian Vision of D. H. Lawrence* (Chicago: Univ. of
   Chicago Press, 1963), pp. 1–3, 7–8, 136–37; while Colin Clarke
   prefers English Romantic poetry to any debt to organicist social
   philosophers (Coleridge, Carlyle, Ruskin), in *River of Dissolution: D. H. Lawrence and English Romanticism* (London: Routledge and Kegan Paul, 1969), p. 16.

the novel is related to the last but most important adventure left to modern man, conqueror of air and polar ice caps, "the venture of consciousness" (p. 741), or, as he put it in the "Foreword to *Women in Love*," "the passionate struggle into conscious being" (*Ph. II*, p. 276).

While he ascribed a profound significance to the novel, Lawrence distinguished that significance from didacticism, or putting one's "thumb in the pan" ("Morality and the Novel," *Ph*, p. 532). He insisted that "the greatness of the novel" lay in its rejection of "didactic lies" of the kind he found offensive in Tolstoy ("The Novel," *Ph. II*, p. 417). "The novel is a great discovery: far greater than Galileo's telescope or somebody else's wireless. The novel is the highest form of human expression so far attained. Why? Because it is so incapable of the absolute" (p. 416). The absolute is static and dogmatic, while the novelist-with-a-purpose is not only untruthful but egocentric and self-conscious: the objection to egotistic self-consciousness is again reminiscent of Carlyle. The novel itself has a purpose larger than mere self and more dynamic than any absolutism: to catch the "quick" of life, the vital essence of men and the universe, through revelation. Faithful to the three essential characteristics of the novel—quickness, organic interrelation of its parts, and honourableness—the novelist will reveal "the oldest Pan-mystery" (p. 426). Moreover, that mystery is indeed Pan-like—inclusive and various—and, despite the rather Yeatsian "flame," is joyfully exultant rather than tragically gay. "God is the flame-life in all the universe; multifarious, multifarious flames, all colours and beauties and pains and sombrenesses" (p. 426). Lawrence rejects the "God with a pair of compasses!" (p. 421), Blake's Urizenic Nobodaddy, in favour of the "quick" or "God-flame" who is the real hero in every great novel (p. 419). In his insistence upon mystery, however, he commits the Blakean sin

of consorting with Vala, the Shadowy Female, who is
one instance of the Female Will he himself abhorred.
However, he again defined art along quasi-Blakean lines
in "Making Pictures" (1929) as religious in impulse,
expressing and celebrating the particularity of objects
with which the artist identifies. The result is "delight,"
a variation upon Blake's Joy: "Art is treated all wrong.
It is treated as if it were a science, which it is not.
Art is a form of religion, minus the Ten Command-
ment business, which is sociological. Art is a form of
supremely delicate awareness and atonement—meaning at-oneness, the state of being at one with the object.
But is the great atonement in delight?—for I can never
look on art save as a form of delight" (p. 605).

This religious sense, honouring the vital spark in
one's being and appreciating its participation in the
larger life force in all things, constitutes the supreme
consummation to which Lawrence wished to bring
man. It accounts for his recurrent motifs of sleep and
arousal, of death and rebirth, and for his central theme
of interchange or relationship between men, the universe, and the God-like Force. It results in the distinctively Lawrencean joyfulness and sense of heightened
aliveness, and in the Blakean version of the Christian
myth to which he was brought (*CL*, p. 301–4). It also
explains why, like the other vitalists we have seen,
Lawrence saw modern man's spiritual dilemma as an
epistemological one: change the way in which men see
and one will change also the nature and constitution
of their presently fragmented selves. Men will once
more live freely and at-one in a radiantly iridescent
and, in the best sense, fictive world, constructed by
their creative liberated selves. As he argued in *Fantasia*,
"We have got to get back to the great purpose of manhood, a passionate unison in actively making a world"
(p. 144). Art, particularly the novel, is of inestimable
value in this redemptive process.

What then is man to be saved from, awakened to,

and how is he to proceed? Lawrence's entire career was spent attempting to answer these questions, diagnosing the modern disease and offering his curative alternatives. In this task he takes his directions from the central Romantic preoccupation with the fulfilment of the individual self, seeing man as searching after unity and completeness in a world distinguished for its disunity and fragmentation. Although Lawrence's roots are Romantic and vitalist, he felt, on the other hand, that the quest for permanence, a prime consideration of poets like Wordsworth and Keats, was a mistaken striving after the chimera of absolutes. Rather, the world's very mutability is to constitute the organic matrix out of which man's real immortality is to come. Similarly, the individual self, which may prove either static and dead or creative and vitally alive, is to be both battleground and victor.

While Lawrence may be indebted to both Blake and Carlyle, who proved early and lasting influences, the parallels in his work are the result partly of direct influence and partly of participation in the common Romantic vitalist tradition. And despite an antipathy to the artificiality of the early Yeats, Lawrence shared with him a particular hatred of the nineteenth century, seeing it as the most immediately harmful: "Fight the great lie of the nineteenth century, which has soaked through our sex and our bones. It means fighting with almost every breath, for the lie is ubiquitous" ("Pornography and Obscenity," *Ph*, p. 185). But he knew with Yeats that no one century is solely responsible for such life-denial. Indeed, for both writers the disease had been growing cancerously for the past three thousand years. Hence, Lawrence interprets history to give the Christian myth of the Fall and Redemption of man a vitalist colouring, inheriting the cosmic scope and proportions characteristic of the other three writers. Though he may deal with microcosms like Eastwood or Taos, those microcosms reflect and involve the larger world of time and space, history and redemption, as do the microcosms of Blake, Carlyle, and Yeats. He takes sides with the abandon of the amateur historian, much as they do, praising the Etruscan or the Mexican Indian cultures as vital and organic, while condemning the Roman, Christian, and modern as fundamentally mechanistic. In his own *Movements in European History* (1921) he reveals not only a Carlylean insistence upon the momentous and dramatic occasion or heroic figure, concluding with a faith in the emergence of a future great leader, but in characteristic fashion recreates the imaginative appeal of the vast and dark German forests and sees the greatness of modern Europe as resulting from the fusion of the fair Teutonic and the dark Roman bloodstreams. In this way, Lawrence's own recurrent motifs—of the dark man rousing sleeping females to involvement in the passional life, as he affected Frieda Weekley, as Mellors revived Connie, or as Christ is converted to a warmer, instinctive Dionysian vision—are seen as historical and archetypal in relevance. The same interchange of personal and cosmic we have seen in the other vitalists.

No matter how persistent and deeply felt was their condemnation of mechanism and mechanical death-in-life, neither Blake nor Carlyle was a Luddite, seeking to destroy machines in a quaint but futile attempt to put back the clock. Certainly Carlyle could sometimes promote a medievalism, just as both Yeats and Lawrence could praise past communities for possessing a superior spiritual life. And while his own Rananim resembled an updated pantisocracy, Lawrence firmly set his mind against the Pre-Raphaelite temptation of escape into the temporally distant. He might compare the Taos pueblo to a medieval European monastery ("Taos," *Ph*, p. 100), but was too much a "child of the present" to feel happy among such medievalism ("Introduction to *Memoirs of the Foreign Legion*," *Ph. II*, p. 318). His stay at Monte Cassino with Maurice Magnus, for example, reminded him of the Tithonus myth—a fearful stasis lasting eternally—and near-wounded his spirit (p. 319). Besides, he constantly rejected "artyness" and sentimentalism, and Victorian medievalism contained elements of both. He might from time to time seek withdrawal from the world—to Cornwall or Taormina or Taos—as in his fiction do characters like Lou in "St. Mawr." But such moments were only necessary resting times before venturing forth into the battle he conceived life to be, whereas withdrawal into the past was as negative and life-denying as the rejection of the dialectical battle and of contact and relationship, which withdrawal from society involved. Nevertheless, he distinguished between contact and the submersion of the individual in the mass. Mass ideas, like Blake's chiaroscuro, blur the individual outline or the Minute Particular, and are equally mechanistic. The masses were, like Parliament, "a grunting *schweinerei*" (*QR*, p. 112; cf. *Ph*, p. 606), like Carlyle's *schwärmerei*, incapable of anything but mechanical ideas and values: "The seed is not in the masses, it is elsewhere" (*CL*, p. 424). Indeed, the existence of the masses depended upon their ability to destroy the individual in all its forms. Lawrence's individualist faith normally sought the dialectical tension of selves, in contact but not in subservience, while also leading him to the paradoxical extreme of the political leader who demanded both contact and subservience.

Lawrence's opposition to mechanism was more to a state of mind or being than to mere machinery or mass production. The modern sickness goes beyond increasingly complicated machinery and higher productivity, as he shows in men like Gerald Crich or Sir Clifford Chatterley, to the crucial and damning loss of contact, whether between employer and worker or between workers and their work. Though on one momentous occasion Rupert Birkin may ride in a car like a modern pharaoh, the curse of our age is usually epitomized in machinery like the motorcar. Tourists driving through the Arizona desert to the Hopi snake dance struck him as like "a funeral cortège" with the appearance of black beetles (*MM*, p. 62), and reflect the modern plague. The beetle or insect imagery he applied frequently to spiritual death, whether to actual machines or to mechanical minds like Bertrand Russell. Hence in *Lady Chatterley's Lover* (p. 230), Mellors' objection to men being turned into "labour-insects" and his desire to "wipe the machines off the face of the earth again, and end the industrial epoch absolutely, like a black mistake" are Lawrence's own. Although Lawrence makes Mellors admit this is impossible, against the machine and the perversion of organic being he pits his dark men or dark forces, stallions like St. Mawr who cannot be ridden safely by the Ricos of this world.

Yet an industrial society need not entail perversion of being; not always are workers mere hands to run machines or machines inevitable manipulators of men's souls. Mourning the loss of the small mining companies, whose contact with and concern for the men give way to the new abstract and impersonal regimentation of nineteenth-century industrialists (*Sons and Lovers*, chap. 1), Lawrence prefers the smaller social unit, whether the village or the Rananim community. For only within such a unit can real intimacy and real individualism flourish—again the characteristic Lawrencean dialectical impulse, towards contact and towards independence. Although there might be an element of sentimentalism here, his sister, Ada, has warned against it: "He never pretended that there was something artistically picturesque about the rotting roof of a miner's home" (*YL*, p. 6). Yet mining life involved a Hardy-like confrontation and battling of "man against nature and man against fate" (Nehls, II, 417), and, in "Nottingham and the Mining Countryside" (1930; *Ph*, pp. 133–40) and elsewhere, Lawrence showed the hold possessed over his imagination by men working underground in a plutonic underworld. The old agricultural instinctive England was still retained in the fulfilment, by instinct, touch, and communion, of miners working underground. Just as the blood life could still be guaranteed to bring salvation to the conscious self from the dark unconscious levels to which the blood led, so too could going underground redeem the miner from the drab inadequacy of his above-ground diurnal existence. This it is which has allowed critics to point to Lawrence's Persephone myth and apply it to the formative experiences of his childhood in a mining community. His dark men and dark gods thus become reflections of the miners.[6] Be this as it may, it illustrates further his distinctive ambivalence, granting his central positives to mine workers while maintaining a persistent attack upon the disabling ugliness of modern industrial life.

Lawrence's vitalist rejection of machines is then a reflection of his larger objection to mechanism of any kind. Machinery is merely an outward manifestation of an internal spiritual blight, reducing man to "no more than the little god in the machine." Rather than being master of his fate and captain of his soul, man becomes an "engine-driver" (*Psy*, p. 12). In *Apocalypse*, where Lawrence, like Yeats, severely criticized the Christian Church for its contribution to the predominance of mechanism, he provides the historical perspective:

> There are flashes throughout the first part of the Apocalypse of true cosmic worship. The cosmos became anath-

ema to the Christians, though the early Catholic Church
restored it somewhat after the crash of the Dark Ages.
Then again the cosmos became anathema to the Protes-
tants after the Reformation. They substituted the non-vital
universe of forces and mechanistic order, everything else
became abstraction, and the long, slow death of the human
being set in. This slow death produced science and machinery, but both are death products. (p. 48)

The argument resembles Yeats's gnomic and Blakean
account, "Locke sank into a swoon; / The Garden
died; / God took the spinning-jenny / Out of his side"
("Fragments").

Although such anti-mechanism, now made respect-
able because of crusaders like himself, often provoked
Lawrence to savage but well-directed irony, his vitalist
preferences could at other times decline into absurdly
oversimplified conclusions. Finding no comfort in a
Tennysonian vision of the ringing grooves of change,
he asked in "Pan in America": "Which is truer, to live
among the living, or to run on wheels?" (*Ph*, p. 26).
But the choice is simplistic: whether to warm one's
loins, Indian-fashion, around a fire or to turn up the
thermostat in one's centrally heated living room. Likewise, in "Education of the People," where he argues
for the destruction of all weapons to create a happy
world, his argument is founded not on pacifism but
upon his hatred of machines. Consequently, he objects
to war-by-machine as rendering the enemy "abstract
and invisible," but approves of hand-to-hand fighting
as enabling enemies to come into contact. He may be
right in noting the impersonality of killing when the
instruments of death become technologically refined,
but he is foolish to believe that issuing swords and
shields will result in "a rare old lively scrap, such as
the heart can rejoice in" (pp. 660–61). A similarly
perverse faith in violence is to be found in Carlyle and
Yeats, their vitalism betraying them into a misguided
emphasis upon physical action, which has little to do

with the spiritual conflict epitomized in Blake's Mental Fight.

Yet a dialectical mental conflict he saw from the beginning as desirable, welcoming the "opposition" Frieda represented (Nehls, I, 71), even if he was also to berate her for it on other occasions. His mother too described his early life as "battle, battle, battle" (III, xii), while he himself continually characterized the faith of his friends, the Brewsters, in the Eastern meditative life as a retreat. "All truth—and real living is the only truth—has in it the elements of battle and repudiation"; "My business is a fight, and I've got to keep it up"; "The world must be fought, not retreated from" (CL, pp. 933, 980, 984). But the smashing of lies, which he ascribed to Attila the Hun, made him, like Attila, "a man of peace" (CP, II, 227). In 1919 certainly he felt "happier now the war is fought with the soul, not with filthy guns" (CL, p. 587). Such views, as we will see, involve a Blakean and vitalist dialecticism.

The real targets, as for the other vitalists, are modes of behaviour and thinking, ways of doing, seeing, and being. Man no longer sees the universe as mysteriously vital and unpredictably blossoming, but explicable, predictable, not only knowable but more or less known. Similarly with man's self: controlled, outmanoeuvred, and rendered passive, its individuality is being ruthlessly eradicated. Such were Lawrence's objections to psychoanalysis, in which the cold abstract and indistinguishable mass replaces the sensuously concrete and individually particular.[7] "He hated the very word *abstract*" (Nehls, III, 45). But whatever form

7. See Frederick J. Hoffman, "Lawrence's Quarrel with Freud," in his *Freudianism and the Literary Mind* (New York: Grove, 1959), chap. 6. Cf. Lawrence's own objections: "I am not Freudian and never was—Freudianism is only a branch of medical science, interesting" (CL, p. 291); "You know I think 'complexes' are vicious half-statements of the Freudians: sort of can't see wood for trees" (p. 475). See also *Mem*, p. 388; Nehls, I,409.

mechanism might take—whether science, rationalism, or abstraction—another of its damnable features is its incompleteness. It takes a half and makes it the whole explanation. As we have seen, the great value of the novel is that it gets "the whole hog."

Whether within the individual self where intellect, passions, senses, and intuition interact vitally and dialectically; or whether between people, man and man, man and woman; or whether between perceiver and cosmos—in all cases the emphasis lies upon totality and harmony, what in "A Propos of *Lady Chatterley's Lover*" (1930) he calls the way of knowing which is "togetherness" (*Ph. II*, p. 512). The abstract and scientific substitute a way of knowing which separates rather than unifies, destroys rather than creates, or, in Blakean terms, contracts rather than expands. Vitalism is an inclusive vision which portrays a vibrant, quick, dynamically alive world, but, far from dispensing with intellect and rational processes, *redeems* them. Despite Lawrence's persistent attack upon science and scientific methodology, his vitalism envisages a creative mode of knowing which harmonizes the dialectical and quaternary nature of the self (cf. *CL*, pp. 374–75). And if, like Blake at the end of *The Four Zoas*, "sweet Science reigns" (IX, 139: 10), it is a science quite distinct from the limited rationalistic analysis destructive of the vital life.

In terms of knowing, Lawrence's vitalism prefers a supra-logical reliance upon blood, instinct, intuition, or the unconscious to an arid intellectualism. His two long essays *Psychoanalysis and the Unconscious* and *Fantasia of the Unconscious* are devoted to his promotion of these means. The "new science," he proclaims, will require the abandonment by science of outmoded intellectualism and the embracing of "the old religious faculty" in which "we can begin to live from the spontaneous initial prompting, instead of from the dead machine-principles of ideas and ideals." Science, however, "does not thereby become less scientific, it only becomes at last complete in knowledge" (*Psy*, pp. 16–17). As such, he appeals to "the great pagan world of which Egypt and Greece were the last living terms" (*Fan*, p. 54), a culture which relied upon a subjective science, universal in scope, mythic and vitalist in vision, intuitive in method, symbolist in form. As Berkeley, much to Yeats's delight, dismissed English empiricism with "We Irish do not hold with this,"[8] so Lawrence denied modern scientific explanations with "I do not believe" (pp. 181–82). Instead of deathly myopia, man desperately needs to regain the old pagan vision. Though neither was a primitivist, Lawrence could share Yeats's pagan preference, "Homer is my example and his unchristened heart" ("Vacillation"), praising a similar Greek quality in the Sicilian novelist Giovanni Verga (*Ph*, p. 229), and calling for "the old Homeric aristocracy" (p. 121). Although Frieda has argued against any paganism in Lawrence ("He was too English for that," *Mem*, p. 294), the parallel with Yeats is close. Even Lawrence's declaration, "Primarily I am a passionately religious man, and my novels must be written from the depth of my religious experience" (*CL*, p. 273), resembles that of Yeats (*Auto*, pp. 115–16). While he might argue, like Yeats, that he found Christianity "insufficient," a "has-been" (*CL*, p. 466), his early religious upbringing retained a more lasting effect upon him than in Yeats's case. Graham Hough is probably correct to characterize Lawrence's paganism as "haunted by Christianity" and so differing from a pre-Christian one.[9] The distinction is less appropriate to Yeats's paganism. Similarly, wanting "people to be more Christian rather than less" (p. 465), Lawrence rewrote the Christian vision in "The Man Who Died" and *Apocalypse*, in order that men might go beyond the negative limitations of historical Christi-

---

8. *The Senate Speeches of W. B. Yeats*, ed. Donald R. Pearce (Bloomington: Indiana Univ. Press, 1960), p. 172.
9. *Dark Sun*, pp. 189–90.

anity to the real Christian fulfilment, which is to acknowledge and practise the sacredness and wonder of
life in "the Eternal Now." The plan resembles Blake
more than Yeats.

Hence, in "A Propos of *Lady Chatterley's Lover*,"
Lawrence made an impassioned plea against abstraction and in favour of the pagan religious sense. Buddha,
Plato, and Jesus are named as the sources of death—"all
three utter pessimists as regards life"—responsible for
"the tragic *excursus*" (*Ph. II*, p. 511). "The universe
is dead for us," he declares, "and how is it to come
to life again?" "How . . . are we to get back the grand
orbs of the soul's heavens, that fill us with unspeakable
joy?" Instead of the reductive world of science, let us
have "Apollo, and Attis, Demeter, Persephone, and the
halls of Dis." Distinguishing "the two ways of knowing," the scientific *apartness* and the poetic *togetherness*, Lawrence provides a historical perspective analogous to Blake's Fall, Carlyle's Everlasting No, and
Yeats's widening gyres. "The Christian religion lost, in
Protestantism finally, the togetherness with the universe, the togetherness of the body, the sex, the emotions, the passions, with the earth and sun and stars"
(p. 512). The religious and cosmic character of this
view goes beyond the epistemology of Eliot's dissociation of the sensibility and gives it a distinctive
Lawrencean colouring: "When we know the world in
togetherness with ourselves, we know the earth hya-
cinthine or Plutonic."

Although his entire work leads to the exultant
affirmations of *Apocalypse* and other late novels, stories, and essays, Lawrence's faith in the physical wisdom known to the unified self is present from the
beginning. In 1913, for example, he wrote to Ernest
Collings: "My great religion is a belief in the blood,
the flesh, as being wiser than the intellect. We can go
wrong in our minds. But what our blood feels and
believes and says, is always true. The intellect is only
a bit and a bridle. What do I care about knowledge.

All I want is to answer to my blood, direct, without fribbling intervention of mind, or moral, or what-not" (*CL*, p. 180). This is what to W. E. Hopkin he characterized as "physical vision" (Nehls, I, 74), or what Lady Cynthia Asquith described as his thinking with the solar plexus (I, 442). And below the navel, especially the phallus, is indeed ascribed a special intelligence. Lawrence thus translates the central Romantic faith in an intuitive, supra-logical intelligence into a more peculiarly physical vision, cultivating a more extreme sexual sense than is involved in Keats's axioms of philosophy being proved upon our pulses. Consequently, we get such moments as Connie Chatterley feeling with her womb, Parkin in *The First Lady Chatterley* knowing in his shoulders of her pregnancy, or the volcanic mountains in *The Plumed Serpent* being heard along the blood. The aboriginal blood and vertebrate consciousnesses are constantly preferred over the mental-spiritual. The Mexican Indian, like the Etruscans or the old agricultural English, is in fuller contact with life. Hence, "a true thought . . . comes as much from the heart and the genitals as from the head" (*Ph*, p. 279), and Kant and Spinoza are rejected for failing to think with the blood (p. 732).

Yet Lawrence envisages a fusion, even if only in the future, of the whole self—blood *and* intellect. The modern world is tragically disintegrating because of the bifurcated nature of the modern self: "the self divided against itself most dangerously" (p. 281). In this case, what Yeats turned to advantage, Lawrence found, like Blake, cause for despair. In noting his stress upon the instinctive and sexual, Lawrence's critics have thus often tended to overlook his incorporation of intellect:[10]

10. The most abusive criticism perhaps came in Wyndham Lewis, *Paleface* (1929) and in T. S. Eliot, *After Strange Gods* (1934), refuted firmly by F. R. Leavis, *The Common Pursuit* (Harmondsworth: Penguin, 1962), pp. 233–39, 240–47, 255–60; and *D. H. Lawrence, Novelist*, pp. 22–27. Later critics have

> Any creative act occupies the whole consciousness of a
> man. This is true of the great discoveries of science as well
> as of art. The truly great discoveries of science and real
> works of art are made by the whole consciousness of man
> working together in unison and oneness: instinct, intui-
> tion, mind, intellect all fused together into one complete
> consciousness, and grasping what we may call a complete
> truth, or a complete vision, a complete revelation in sound.
> ("Introduction to These Paintings," pp. 573–74)

For these reasons also he recognized not only the worth
of the aboriginal experience but its limitations. Wyndham Lewis' virulent attack in *Paleface* is thus not only
hysterical but misplaced. Despite his admiration for
the Mexican Indian's instinctive contact and pagan
vision, Lawrence no more wanted a primitivism than
he did a medievalism or a crusade against industrialism. He rejected the Romantic notion of the innocent,
whether Tolstoy's peasant, Wordsworth's Lucy, or
Yeats's Fool (p. 246; *Ph. II*, p. 624). Man's obligation
is to unite mind and emotion, and blind elevation of
the nonmental or ignorant, whether in the Romantic
innocent or primitive, Lawrence found limiting. The
totality of one's perception depends upon the self's
totality: the basic Romantic and vitalist principle.
"And we cannot return to the primitive life, to live
in tepees and hunt with bows and arrows" (*Ph*, p. 31).
Besides, the unwashed Apache offended his nostrils (p.
95); savages could be a burden (*Letters*, p. 636; Nehls,
II, x); and despite the immense significance of the

---

been able to see more clearly, after Leavis, that Lawrence was
in fact seeking a union of the whole consciousness: Ford,
Double Measure, pp. 56–57; Harry T. Moore, *The Intelligent
Heart: The Story of D. H. Lawrence* (Harmondsworth: Penguin, 1960), p. 184. Indeed, John Bayley has even gone to the
other extreme and criticized Lawrence for overintellectualiza-
tion, in *The Characters of Love* (London: Constable, 1960),
pp. 24–29.

Mexican experience to him, he eventually thought "of Mexico with a sort of nausea: . . . really I feel I never want to see an Indian or an 'aboriginee' or anything in the savage line again."[11] In fact, his position closely resembled that of Lou in "St. Mawr": "I don't want to be an animal like a horse or a cat or a lioness, though they all fascinate me, the way they get their life *straight*, not from a lot of old tanks, as we do. I don't admire the cave man, and that sort of thing. But think, mother, if we could get our lives straight from the source, as the animals do, and still be ourselves" (p. 46). The caveman is "a brute, a degenerate. A pure animal man would be as lovely as a deer or a leopard, burning like a flame fed straight from underneath." He would be possessed of wonder. And Lou's cry, "I want the wonder back again, or I shall die" (p. 47), is Lawrence's own.

The whole imagination is to be preferred because its perceptions are founded on the creative, quickening self, vitally alive in itself and among its various parts and in wondrous touch with the cosmos. The ugly modern industrial world, on the other hand, is, like Blake's London, the product of a limited, unfulfilled, mechanistic self. The vicious circle continues when that uncreative environment proceeds to stunt men's creative selves. Salvation depends upon one's capacity to break out of this circle; to cultivate that capacity was one function of the novel. When, in his "Study of Thomas Hardy," Lawrence puts such views into an historical context, he can account for the greatness of the Renaissance in terms reminiscent of both Blake and Yeats. Capable for a time of a "union and fusion of the male and female spirits" (*Ph*, p. 454), Renaissance art in the hands of Botticelli and Correggio conveys a vision based on knowledge. "Truth," after all,

11. Lawrence to Eduardo Rendón, 21 May 1925, quoted in Moore, *Intelligent Heart*, p. 421.

is "that momentary state when in living the union between the male and the female is consummated" (p. 460). While also achieving consummation, Raphael and Michelangelo in their different ways—the one leading towards geometrical abstraction and the other to rage against the transitory nature of the consummation—indicate the movement towards dissociation, towards Rembrandt, Turner, and modern art. Lawrence returned to the history of the bifurcated self in "Introduction to These Paintings" (1929), postulating in the Elizabethan age "the grand rupture . . . in the human consciousness, the mental consciousness, recoiling in violence away from the physical, instinctive-intuitive" (p. 552). Hence Hamlet is horrified by sexuality; Restoration comedy makes sex dirty; Swift and Sterne become excrementalists; while the Romantics, excepting Burns, are "post-mortem poets." He has not forgotten Blake, however, for whom he reserves especial praise:

> Blake is the only painter of imaginative pictures, apart from landscape, that England has produced. And unfortunately there is so little Blake, and even in that little the symbolism is often artificially imposed. Nevertheless, Blake paints with real intuitional awareness and solid instinctive feeling. He dares handle the human body, even if he sometimes makes it a mere ideograph. And no other Englishman has even dared handle it with alive imagination. (p. 560)

The most impressive and moving expression of the creative whole self is caught best in that constant assertion of life which distinguishes Lawrence, an assertion which is religious, almost mystical, in tone and source. His early reading was extensive—Blake, Coleridge, Schopenhauer, Nietzsche, Whitman, Carpenter, Carlyle—but the source was ultimately his very being. His friends constantly attested to this quality in him; Jessie Chambers, for example, wrote:

He was always to me a symbol of overflowing life. He seemed able to enter into other lives, and not only human lives. With wild things, flowers and birds, a rabbit in a snare, the speckled eggs in a hole in the ground he was in primal sympathy—a living vibration passed between him and them, so that I always saw him, in the strictest sense of the word, immortal. (*PR*, pp. 222–23)

Jessie's "strictest sense" coincided with Lawrence's own in this respect: "To be perfectly alive is to be immortal" (*Ph. II*, p. 266). The resemblances to both Blake and Yeats are striking:

Immortality is not a question of time, of everlasting life. It is a question of consummate being. Most men die and perish away, unconsummated, unachieved. It is not easy to achieve immortality, to win a consummate being. It is supremely difficult. It means undaunted suffering and undaunted enjoyment, both. And when a man has reached his ultimate of enjoyment and his ultimate of suffering, *both*, then he knows the two eternities, then he is made absolute, like the iris, created out of the two. Then he is immortal. It is not a question of time. It is a question of being. It is not a question of submission, submitting to the divine grace: it is a question of submitting to the divine grace, in suffering and self-obliteration, and it is a question of conquering by divine grace, as the tiger leaps on the trembling deer, in utter satisfaction of the Self, in complete fulfilment of desire. ("The Crown," pp. 410–11)

There are in Lawrence's entire work innumerable instances which express and define this vision. "The only unforgivable sin," in Brewster's words, was "to deny life" (Nehls, III, 134), for no matter how disillusioned and embittered he might become—and the years in Cornwall during the First World War resemble a dark night of the soul—the miracle of life always contradicted his despair. At the advent of spring or after harvest he could always be made aware of the

regenerative process of life itself: "There is another
world of reality, actual and mystical at once, not the
world of the Whole, but the world of the essential now,
here, immediate, a strange actual hereabouts, no before
and after to strive with: not worth it" (*QR*, p. 123).
"Life is ours to be spent, not to be saved" (p. 237),
and to everyday living, as his friends attest, he brought
a vitality and a sense of physical awareness which are
reflected in his work.

We need to germinate, as he frequently tells us, and
recognize the dialectical nature of that process. Though
such germination brings eventual decay and death,
man should not out of cowardice "refrain from plant-
ing a seed" nor lament this "cycle of all things created": "given courage, it saves even eternity from stale-
ness" ("On Human Destiny," *Ph. II*, p. 629). We have
seen Blake too ascribing a dialectical dynamism to
eternity itself. Lawrence thus objected to Shelley and
Keats for writing poetry of "exquisite finality" rather
than of "the immediate present." His own was "the
seething poetry of the incarnate Now," which seeks
not "the qualities of the unfading timeless gems" but
"the whiteness of the seethe of mud, . . . that incipient
putrescence which is the skies falling, . . . the never-
pausing, never-ceasing life itself" (*Ph*, pp. 218–20). His
very vocabulary, with its recurrent "heave" and
"quick," "blossoming" and "ripening," captures that
essence, while essays like "The Crown" (1915) or *Reflections on the Death of a Porcupine* (1925) are full
of this dialectic. In the latter, for example, he offers
a marvellously anthropomorphic dance of the seed in
the sun. Meant allegorically as well as quasi-literally—
for this is the dance towards blossoming all things
(dandelions, men, creatures, races) engage in—his
definition establishes this exultant theme: "Blossoming
means the establishing of a pure, *new* relationship with
all the cosmos. This is the state of heaven. And it is
the state of a flower, a cobra, a jenny-wren in spring,

a man when he knows himself royal and crowned with the sun, with his feet gripping the core of the earth" (*Ph. II*, p. 471). Throughout his prose, particularly of the last years, Lawrence returns constantly to this nec-essary and dynamic correspondence of man and cos-mos which creates a regenerated world, a new heaven and a new earth. His "daring," however, was, in Philip Rieff's words, "not only to place the self at the centre of the universe but to imagine it literally as the hot creative stuff from which even the remotest cold stars derive."[12] In doing so, he may have showed his willing-ness to challenge the rationalism of his age but he revealed also his essential Romantic vitalism.

As Yeats in "The Tower" and elsewhere asserted man's "bitter soul" as the matrix out of which all things, including Paradise, come, so too Lawrence in-sists upon a similar Berkeleyan epistemology:

> England is what I know it to be. I am what I know I am. And Bishop Berkeley is absolutely right: things only exist in our own consciousness. To the known me, nothing exists beyond what I know. True, I am always adding to the things I know. But this is because, in my opinion, knowledge begets knowledge. Not because anything has entered *from the outside*. There *is* no outside. There is only more knowledge to be added. ("On Being a Man," p. 617)

Additional knowledge enables the individual psyche to grow so as to become God-like. The "breast to breast [contact] with the cosmos" (*Apo*, p. xxviii) is thus founded upon the creative self: "When man changes his state of being, he needs an entirely different de-scription of the universe, and so the universe changes its nature to him entirely" (*Ph*, p. 301). "We become, alas, what we think we are" (*Apo*, p. 31), a conclusion

12. Introduction to *Psychoanalysis and the Unconscious* and *Fantasia of the Unconscious*, p. xi.

not very different from Blake's "he became what he beheld" (*FZ*, IV, 53: 24; *M*, 3: 29). Brewster recollected that while in Ceylon Lawrence declared, "Man himself created the sun and the moon" (Nehls, II, 118–19). Similar arguments are present in *Psychoanalysis and the Unconscious* and *Fantasia of the Unconscious:* "The fixed and stable universe of law and matter, even the whole cosmos, would wear out and disintegrate if it did not rest and find renewal in the quick centre of creative life in individual creatures" (*Psy*, pp. 19–20). Or again: "Even the sun depends, for its heartbeat, its respiration, its pivotal motion, on the beating hearts of men and beast, on the dynamic of the soul-impulse in individual creatures" (*Fan*, p. 163; cf. *MEH*, p. xii).

Insisting constantly upon the individuality of life, Lawrence refuses to accept scientific laws and explanations and offers instead a fantastic mythic account. He admits he does not always, indeed cannot, explain how certain things happen. But that they do, he is unshakable: "The Cosmos is nothing but the aggregate of the dead bodies and dead energies of bygone individuals. The dead bodies decompose as we know into earth, air, and water, heat, and radiant energy and free electricity and innumerable other scientific facts. The dead souls likewise decompose—or else they don't decompose. But if they *do* decompose, then it is not into any elements of Matter and physical energy. They decompose into some psychic reality, and into some potential will. They re-enter into the living psyche of living individuals" (*Fan*, p. 182). Evolution is thus discounted: "The individual soul originated everything, and has itself no origin" (p. 190; cf. *CL*, p. 518). Man is both "battle-ground and marriage-bed"; "the God-quick" in him is timeless and created each time consummation takes place ("The Crown," *Ph. II*, p. 411). "It is true of a man as it is true of a dandelion or of a tiger or of a dove" (p. 412). Living in a world bursting like that of Blake's New Jerusalem, man will see the sun, not as it appears to be but as it is—"something tingling with magnificence" (p. 415). However, although this transformed world resembles that which Blake envisaged once the senses had been sufficiently cleansed, it remains intrinsically phenomenal while at the same time infinite and miraculous. Nevertheless, it was a more persistent affirmation than Yeats's moments of blessedness, and never depended upon a contrary disparagement of the temporal as "the frog-spawn of a blind man's ditch" ("A Dialogue of Self and Soul").

The logical corollaries of Lawrence's position are to deny, like Blake, the existence of an external God—external to man and to the universe; to see with expanded vision the world as paradisal; and to recognize the ultimate goal of the growing consciousness as divinity. That vision was implicit from the beginning and Lawrence's entire work constitutes its multifarious revelation. And although the present critical consensus is to regard Lawrence's final phase as a decline, producing fiction inferior to the major novels (*The Rainbow* and *Women in Love*), it is in precisely this last phase that the vision is most exultantly affirmed. The wonder which man must acknowledge is central, whether to the political and religious realm of *The Plumed Serpent* or to the phallic consciousness of *Lady Chatterley's Lover*. As I intend to show by a closer examination of this final phase, Lawrence's art continued to grow, proceeding to chart new thought-adventures and new ways of expression.

2

With his departure from England in 1919 and the publication in the following year of *Women in Love*, a new stage in Lawrence's career begins. The novels following soon after—*The Lost Girl* (1920), *Aaron's Rod* (1922),

Kangaroo (1923), and *The Plumed Serpent* (1926)—
have been labelled his "leadership" novels. *Lady Chatterley's Lover* (1928), on the other hand, promotes a
new attitude, of "tenderness," and the antithesis of the
two concepts, leadership and tenderness, has been supported further by Lawrence's own statements. To Rolf
Gardiner, who had recently been converted to disciple-
ship by such views on leadership, he wrote (4 March
1928):

> I'm afraid the whole business of leaders and followers is
> somehow wrong, now. Like the demon-drive, even Leader-
> ship must die, and be born different, later on. I'm afraid
> part of what ails you is that you are struggling to enforce
> an obsolete form of leadership. It is White Fox's calamity.[13]

13. For the following information concerning the identity of
    White Fox I am much indebted to Mr. S. C. Gardiner, son
    of the late Rolf Gardiner, who kindly quoted from his father's
    unpublished autobiography. Rolf Gardiner wrote: "White Fox
    was: John Hargrave, a prominent Scout Commissioner for
    woodcraft and camping who revolted against the military as-
    pects of Scout Head Quarters and formed his own movement:
    'The Kibbo Kift Kindred'. This breakaway fraternity exercised
    a formative influence on the style of the German Bünde.
    Hargrave or White Fox became a name famous in European
    youth circles. A Quaker, Dr. Westlake, also founded a similar
    life-bond: the order of Woodcraft Chivalry, with head quarters
    in the New Forest. Leslie Paul, one of Hargrave's original band,
    split off from the Kibbo Kift to establish a Socialist movement;
    the Woodcraft Folk.
        "Working for a while with Hargrave I [H.R.G.] had tried to
    bring all these movements together on a European basis. The
    campaign to achieve this lasted from 1923–25. But Hargrave was
    not an easy man to serve under. D. H. Lawrence summed him
    up [quotes letter of 4 Mar. 1928 in text].
        "In the summer of 1925 I [H.R.G.] had broken away from
    Hargrave and the Kibbo Kift. Hargrave had, inter alia, adopted
    social credit and in a few years his following was known as the
    'Green Shirts' and was committed to the Socialisation of the
    Banks and the Just Price" (letter to me, 26 July 1972).
        Other references to Hargrave (or White Fox) and to his novel
    Harbottle (1924) occur in *Letters*, pp. 604, 606, 697–700, and in-
    dicate Lawrence's dissatisfaction with the Kibbo Kift. A useful

When leadership has died—it is very nearly dead, save for Mussolini and you and White Fox and Annie Besant and Gandhi—then it will be born again, perhaps, new and changed, and based on reciprocity of tenderness. The reciprocity of power is obsolete. When you get down to the basis of life, to the depth of the warm creative stir, there is no power. It is never: There *shall* be light!—only: Let there be light! (*Letters*, pp. 704–5)

Similarly, a week later (13 March 1928) to Witter Bynner, who was considerably more sceptical of Lawrence's theories of leadership and power, he reaffirmed the need for continued fighting, not in any military or political sense but "for the phallic reality." "The hero is obsolete, and the leader of men is a back number." "And the new relationship will be some sort of tenderness, sensitive, between men and men and men and women, and not the one up one down, lead on I follow, *ich dien* sort of business" (*CL*, pp. 1045–46).

On the strength of such declarations critics have tended to overemphasize the nature and degree of Lawrence's changing views.[14] Change there certainly

---

anthology of the writings of Rolf Gardiner has recently been published, *Water Springing from the Ground*, ed. Andrew Best (Shaftesbury, Dorset: Springhead, 1972).

14. Daniel Weiss sees Lawrence moving from a maternal to a paternal authority, in *Oedipus in Nottingham: D. H. Lawrence* (Seattle: Univ. of Washington Press, 1962), p. 109; David Cavitch sees Lawrence making "a psychological adjustment" towards reduced sexual desire, in *D. H. Lawrence and the New World* (New York: O.U.P., 1969), p. 189; Julian Moynahan argues that the novels show a "very real loss of moral focus," in *The Deed of Life: The Novels and Tales of D. H. Lawrence* (Princeton: Princeton Univ. Press, 1963), p. 113; Mark Spilka notes "a remarkable relaxation and shift of emphasis" in the late period, in "Lawrence's Quarrel with Tenderness," *Critical Quarterly*, 9 (1967), 363–77. A notable exception is H. M. Daleski, who sees change but also continuity in Lawrence's development, in *The Forked Flame: A Study of D. H. Lawrence* (Evanston, Ill.: Northwestern Univ. Press, 1965). Indeed, Daleski's study takes its point of departure from the two semi-

was, but what the letter to Gardiner indicates is also the continuity between the dialectic of concepts, power and tenderness. Leadership will be reborn, based now on tenderness, and the change is one of emphasis rather than of direction. Given his dialecticism and belief in mutability, change was both inevitable and desirable. His Paradise, considerably more earthy and phenomenal than Blake's, was similarly organic and steadfastly opposed to any kind of stasis. The Eternal Now, like Blake's Moment, pulsated with dynamic life. The change in feeling Lawrence himself underwent in his last years was one he sought for the world at large. In *Apocalypse,* however, he expressed that kind of reconciliation of the dialectic which qualifies any impression of distinct change, and in arguments strongly reminiscent of Carlyle and Blake: "Jesus was an aristocrat, so was John the Apostle, and Paul. It takes a great aristocrat to be capable of great tenderness and gentleness and unselfishness: the tenderness and gentleness of *strength.* From the democrat you may often get the tenderness and gentleness of weakness: that's another thing. But you usually get a sense of toughness" (pp. 16–17). Calling for a reassessment of Jesus, as did Blake in *The Everlasting Gospel,* the argument is more peculiarly Carlylean in its necessary conjunction of strength and tenderness. The real tenderness will be strong rather than tough, as the only strength is tender: the paradox proved the basis of Carlyle's troublesome conjunction of might and right. The "one great chosen figure," to whom modern Europe must turn, will be "some hero who can lead a great war, as well as administer a wide peace" (*MEH,* p. 344). It was an argument to which Lawrence returned frequently in the last years (*CL,* p. 1035); love and power, rather than being

---

nal essays, "The Crown" and "Study of Thomas Hardy," discusses Lawrence's dualism, and is a valuable contribution to Lawrence scholarship.

antithetical, are the two modes of behaviour by which "the soul *learns* and fulfils itself" ("Democracy," *Ph*, p. 707). Lawrence may indeed vacillate between leadership and tenderness, power and gentleness, but the theme of the consummation of the creative self runs throughout and depends ultimately, not upon the polarities of love and power nor their reconciliation, but upon their balance.

The Plumed Serpent is not a favourite novel even among Lawrence admirers: F. R. Leavis regards it "the least complex of all Lawrence's novels . . . and . . . the only one that I find difficult to read through"; Julian Moynahan sees it as "undeniably bad," objects to "the insane proliferation of ritual detail," and regards the leadership novels generally as reflecting "a temporary breakdown in Lawrence's morale." Critics feel "very uneasy" (R. P. Draper), describe it as "a curiously mixed work" (Graham Hough), but have to weigh also the author's own comment: "I consider this my most important novel, so far" (*CL*, p. 845; cf. pp. 844, 860).[15]

15. Leavis, *D. H. Lawrence, Novelist*, p. 66; Moynahan, *Deed of Life*, pp. xvi, 112–13; Ronald P. Draper, *D. H. Lawrence* (New York: Twayne, 1964), p. 102; Hough, *Dark Sun*, p. 135. For a summary of the diverse critical opinions on the novel, see L. D. Clark, *Dark Night of the Body: D. H. Lawrence's 'The Plumed Serpent'* (Austin: Univ. of Texas Press, 1964), pp. 8–12. Few share the enthusiasm of William York Tindall, who finds *The Plumed Serpent* Lawrence's "most brilliant" novel, surpassing *The Rainbow* and *Women in Love* whose "beauties are lost among the sermons"—a strange judgement considering the sermonizing of the later novel. *Forces in Modern British Literature, 1885–1956* (New York: Vintage, 1956), p. 226. In Tindall's eyes, however, *The Plumed Serpent* is "one of the most wonderful novels of our time" (p. 299). L. D. Clark, who admits it is "the most perplexing of D. H. Lawrence's novels" and "a flagrant piece of propaganda" (pp. v, 4), provides a more balanced and useful discussion. Daleski, *Forked Flame*, and Keith Sagar, *The Art of D. H. Lawrence* (Cambridge: C.U.P., 1960) are useful. John R. Harrison, on the other hand, tends to substitute jeers for intelligent criticism (*The Reactionaries*).

However, artists are not necessarily the best judges of their own work, and Lawrence was constantly inclined to regard a newly completed work as his finest to date. Nevertheless, Lawrence's novels are rooted in autobiography, not only in the numerous couples who are Frieda and Lawrence but in that way in which Blake's Prophetic Books or Yeats's dialogues of Self and Soul have their source in and take their directions from the dialectic within the creator's self. Similarly, *The Plumed Serpent* is important partly as an expression of Lawrence's religious sense, now taking the rather sadistic form of revived Aztec sacrificial religious practices, but more importantly as evidencing through Kate Leslie his own ambivalence about Mexico and the aboriginal experience, about his principles of power and leadership, and about the hold European culture possessed over him. For Lawrence is present in more than one character in the novel: parts of him are included in the Mexican leaders, Don Ramón and Don Cipriano, but other parts are present in Kate Leslie, the widowed Irishwoman, who is also at times a thinly disguised Frieda. The novel does not resolve these various parts, and reconciliation comes only with Lawrence's own return to Europe and his revived interest in a Christian myth, to be given distinctive and new expression in his last work.

The antithesis of *The Plumed Serpent* and *Lady Chatterley's Lover*, played out also in the shorter stories like "The Woman Who Rode Away" and "The Man Who Died," bears some resemblance to the vacillation in Yeats's later work, between *The Tower* and *The Winding Stair*. On a smaller scale within *The Plumed Serpent*, the dialectical vacillation is central to Kate Leslie and her ambivalent attitudes towards the prophetic role and faith of Don Ramón. We might expect the favourite Lawrencean motif, of a woman roused from a sleeping existence to full consciousness and totality of self, to apply yet again. And in certain obvious ways it does; that Lawrence should deliberately manipulate the motif in a new way suggests in part his own inability to sort out his true feelings. According to Aldous Huxley, Lawrence had ceased to believe in the novel even before finishing it.[16] Some, though not all, of the novel's failings are thus viewed as the consequence of the author's spiritual confusion. However, in a novelist whose own marriage often took the pattern of battle and repudiation and who extended that dialectical pattern to life itself, such vacillation is perhaps more calculated. While the overall impression is of a not wholly unified work, its real unity consists not in reconciliation but constant repudiation, not only reflecting Lawrence's own ambivalence towards Mexico and the principle of leadership but, as Keith Sagar has argued, offering a means by which he can explore and weigh "the possibilities of experience."[17]

The novel begins in Mexico City with the superb evocation of a bullfight, a resoundingly boring tea party of American tourists, and even sideswipes at the art created by the new socialist revolution in Mexico—all that Kate's cousin, Owen Rhys, calls "LIFE" (p. 14). The intense disgust Kate feels, however, whether towards the unruly mob in the arena, or the cowardliness of the encounter between bull and effeminate toreador, or the anarchical socialism of the revolutionary frescoes, establishes her real strength. "Her breeding and her natural pride were outraged" (p. 11). But the tea at Mrs. Norris' offers no preferable alternative: the American couple, Judge and Mrs. Burlap, are rude and bloodless, and Kate is relieved only by her awareness of the dark blood of the Mexicans, Don Ramón and Don Cipriano.

These opening scenes have been deemed more satis-

---

16. Moore, *Intelligent Heart*, p. 417.
17. *Art of D. H. Lawrence*, p. 160.

fying than much of the novel; certainly they establish convincingly the emptiness, aridity, and automatism of American lives in a country still in touch with its ancient, aboriginal, instinctive past. Kate is thus placed in the dilemma of rejecting the American present as mechanistic and dead; preferring the Mexican soul as vital, alive, vibrantly thrilling, and fascinatingly distinct; but also in her proud European individualism—what Blake and Lawrence called Female Will—rejecting the Mexican world of power, leadership, blood, and instinct as too male, cruel, and destructive to her old self. Hence, Lawrence describes her at Don Ramón's dinner party in the following way:

> Kate felt she was in the presence of men. Here were men face to face not with death and self-sacrifice, but with the life-issue. She felt for the first time in her life, a pang almost like fear, of men who were passing beyond what she knew, beyond her depth.
>
> Cipriano, his rather short but intensely black, curved eyelashes lowering over his dark eyes, watched his plate, only sometimes looking up with a black, brilliant glance, either at whomsoever was speaking, or at Don Ramón, or at Kate. His face was changeless and intensely serious, serious almost with a touch of childishness. But the curious blackness of his eyelashes lifted so strangely, with such intense unconscious maleness from his eyes, the movement of his hand was so odd, quick, light as he ate, so easily a movement of shooting, or of flashing a knife into the body of some adversary, and his dark-coloured lips were so helplessly savage, as he ate or briefly spoke, that her heart stood still. There was something undeveloped and intense in him, the intensity and the crudity of the semi-savage. She could well understand the potency of the snake upon the Aztec and Maya imagination. Something smooth, undeveloped, yet vital in this man, suggested the heavy-ebbing blood of reptiles in his veins. That was what it was, the heavy-ebbing blood of powerful reptiles, the dragon of Mexico. (p. 62)

Lawrence's characterization is always most vivid when he is intent on exploring the struggle in a soul, and certainly Kate Leslie is the only character in the novel whose portrait is full and real. The others—Don Ramón and Don Cipriano, essentially, for the rest are minor characters—are quite shadowy and undeveloped, stock figures whose full natures, for all their mystic maleness, are never developed or conveyed. Yet the burden of conversion to their revived cult of Quetzalcoatl is borne by these two men, who are at best given those value-terms Lawrence reserved always for his heroes: dark, quick, vital, alive. When Don Ramón, however, defines freedom as serving "the God that gives me my manhood" (p. 68), he distinguishes the Quetzalcoatl cult from both the new socialist Mexico of President Montes and the old colonial Mexico. The latter depend upon bullying. Kate, on the other hand, whose pride and will continue to the end, is usually unable to see the distinctly male character of Ramón's cult as anything more than bullying also. Her dilemma is whether to stay in Mexico alone, once Owen and Villiers have left, to go with them to the United States, or to return to Ireland and her children. The dilemma reflects the spiritual conflict, the battle within Kate's self, between her European will and her increasing awareness of a womanhood blossoming in her through further contact with Don Ramón and Don Cipriano. Though it is never sufficiently developed to become convincing, Kate's Irishness is deliberate: the Mexican and Celtic remain aware of the instinctive life to an extent denied to the European and American.

While Lawrence is describing Kate's spiritual struggle, he holds our attention, as he does also with his superb powers of description. Indeed, he convinces us of the Mexican vitality in his descriptions of Kate being rowed across the lake to Orilla, of the man of Quetzalcoatl who stops them for a tribute to his god, or of the boatman suddenly swooping down into the shallow water to fish out an old earthenware pot used previously to provide food offerings for the dead gods in their sleep of death. We are made more directly aware of what Lawrence's vitalist faith entails than we do through the eccentric, protofascist ritualism and heavy didacticism of the later chapters. In a similar fashion, the Saturday plaza dance at Sayula and its effect upon Kate are also vividly caught. Effeminate *fifis* and empty flappers, suitably enough "the motor-car people from town" (p. 110), are superseded by the ancient Quetzalcoatl men. At first preferring no contact, Kate is eventually drawn in to the dance, to experience her womanhood and to reject mechanical time: "She would not look at her watch. She would lay her watch face down, to hide its phosphorus figures. She would not be timed" (p. 128). The concrete details take on a symbolic significance more convincing than the abstract didacticism to be found in the cult and in some of Lawrence's essays: "We must take up the old, broken impulse that will connect us with the mystery of the cosmos again" (p. 134).

Likewise, during Kate's first visit to Ramón's hacienda, we are given considerable description of the Quetzalcoatl cult—of the craftsmen making the various paraphernalia (symbols, serapes, sandals) for the cult; of the prayers and hymns written by Ramón; his spiritual exercises and salutes—but again the didacticism is heavy, the imagery foreign and remote, and the forms and rhythms of the hymns reminiscent of bad Whitman. The vital life is more forcefully and vividly communicated in the description of the sudden storm than in these ceremonies.

> The lake was quite black, like a great pit. The wind suddenly blew with violence, with a strange ripping sound in the mango trees, as if some membrane in the air were being ripped. The white-flowered oleanders in the garden

below leaned over quite flat, their white flowers ghostly, going right down to the earth, in the pale beam of the lamp—like a street lamp—that shone on the wall at the front entrance. A young palm tree bent and spread its leaves on the ground. Some invisible juggernaut car rolling in the dark over the outside world. (p. 198)

The simile of the pit, with which the description begins, immediately points towards that imaginative fusion of coal mines and plutonic underworld which Lawrence used constantly to characterize the dark instinctive life force. Both the rising wind assaulting the landscape and the concluding image of the juggernaut car, with its implied reference to the Hindu myth of Krishna, complete the sense of impending cataclysm. But the imagery is sexual also: the prolific wind is also the devourer and tears at the air as if at a membrane. In its dual aspect the wind image is clearly related to Shelley's West Wind, Yeats's Second Coming, and includes rebirth as well as destruction. Indeed, in Ramón's words, to "turn to life" one turns "from the clock to the sun and the stars, and from metal to membrane" (p. 359).

Similarly, though a minor, faceless figure, Dona Carlota, Ramón's Catholic wife who strongly disapproves of her husband's new paganism, is a more recognizable character in the novel than Don Ramón himself. Despite the fact that her religion is one of death and that she is not portrayed as an attractive person, her contradictory nature is a less desirable version of Kate's own vacillation and she keeps our attention. Capable of adoring Ramón while possessed of a moral conscience that rejects his cult, she is damned with that Lawrencean sin, a very definite female will, which is the furthest extreme of Kate's own position. The opposite extreme is taken later in the novel by Teresa, who gladly submits to and glorifies Ramón. Carlota's love, however, is destructive of Ramón's manhood, and on

one occasion she is described as tearing at his bowels
(p. 203), paralleling on a personal level Mexico's spiritual death-in-life epitomized by the disembowelling at
the bullfight in the opening chapter. Carlota's struggle
is placed with the physical attack upon the hacienda—one a murdering with the spirit, the other with
knives—but both are given a larger significance, as
struggling for the Mexican soul in the figure of Ramón.

When Kate feels it would be oppressive not to be
able to leave Mexico, she is expressing more than
Frieda's anxiety to return to London and her children.
For despite Lawrence's deep attachment to their New
Mexico ranch and the profound religious awareness he
experienced in the Southwest, his own disinclination
to settle anywhere for any length of time and his frequent dissatisfaction with where he was presently living are present in Kate's feelings. Whether or not such
feelings derive from Lawrence's need to pursue his
mystic journey, it was a recognizable phenomenon
throughout his life. The "monstrous and cruel"
(p. 216) elemental nature of the Mexican world proved
both fascinating and horrifying to Kate, Frieda, and
Lawrence himself.

Meanwhile, despite the opposition of the Catholic
Church, Ramón's Quetzalcoatl cult spreads, offering a
more purely Mexican alternative to the foreign colonial religion. Yet the Mexican desire is "sloppy inertia"
(p. 275), a disastrous state in the light of Lawrence's
work ethic which regarded his fiction as "trophies
against man's inertia." The turning point in Kate's own
conversion is the attack on Ramón's hacienda by the
fascist Knights of Cortes.[18] Dead to everyday existence,
Kate feels her soul can live only with Ramón and

18. Cf. Clark, Dark Night of the Body, p. 65; Kessler, in D. H.
    Lawrence Miscellany, ed. Moore, p. 251. Although the attack
    on the hacienda is important in effecting Kate's conversion
    and Ramón's resurrection, nevertheless Kessler does not meet
    Father Tiverton's objections to Lawrence's descriptions "as a
    sensational, Western-type piece of action-writing, as something

Cipriano, the latter proposing both marriage and elevation as the goddess Malintzi. While the relationship
between Kate and Cipriano blossoms, Carlota becomes
increasingly deranged and finally dies in her attempt
to counter Quetzalcoatl with Jesus. On a later occasion
when, in a further ritual, Cipriano is to lose himself
in order to adopt the identity of Huitzilopochtli, Kate
refuses to be "swallowed up" in this foreign religion
and, reasserting herself again, cries to herself:
"Malintzi! I am Kate Forrester, really. I am neither Kate
Leslie nor Kate Tylor. I am sick of these men putting
names over me. I was born Kate Forrester, and I shall
die Kate Forrester. I want to go home. Loathsome,
really, to be called Malintzi" (p. 369). And certainly her
disgust and alienation are forcibly communicated to
her when, during the Huitzilopochtli ceremony,
Ramón's betrayers are summarily executed, either by
having their necks broken or by being stabbed in the
heart.[19]

Kate continues to be troubled by her individualism
and will, a position Lawrence found wrongheaded and
spiritually deadening in most modern women. The

---

to make Zane Grey blush with envy." The episode is crucial,
as Kessler rightly argues, but Father Tiverton was objecting to
the quality of the writing. However, Leavis specifies this description as one of the "good things" in the novel (*D. H.
Lawrence, Novelist*, pp. 66–67).

19. The summary execution has rightly been criticized: Daleski
argues that the "travesty of a trial" is accompanied by a forced
quality in the writing and concludes: "Lawrence is deliberately
forcing himself to be demonic in the interests of making a
grand male assertion" (*Forked Flame*, p. 228 ff.). Cf. Harry T.
Moore, "The Plumed Serpent: Vision and Landscape," in *D. H.
Lawrence: A Collection of Critical Essays*, ed. Mark Spilka
(Englewood Cliffs, N.J.: Prentice-Hall, 1963), pp. 66–67. That
the men would have been executed in most countries today
seems a specious argument (Clark, *Dark Night of the Body*,
p. 97; Sagar, *Art of D. H. Lawrence*, p. 165). The objection
is surely that Lawrence is willing, in the name of Ramón's
illegal authority, to give the executions an air of legality.

alternative position in the novel, that of Kate submitting to the male will epitomized in the Quetzalcoatl
cult, was also too peculiarly a Mexican alternative to
be wholly acceptable to him. Richard Aldington's comment has considerable relevance here: Lawrence, "who
through all his transformations and 'battlings' with
himself remained as English as a wet Sunday in Hull,
was considerably rattled by all this."[20] Like Kate, Lawrence could cry out *"Noli me tangere"* (p. 415) and,
like her, was drawn back to Europe. The Aztec cult
might satisfy the Mexican psyche but the malevolence
inherent in the country was also antagonistic to Lawrence himself. While he might rise to the new vitalism
being practised, Lawrence could recognize, with Kate,
Cipriano's naïveté and childishness (p. 391). He might
make Ramón proclaim Natural Aristocracy (p. 245), as
he himself had done, yet it is the narrator and not Kate
who offers the following judgement: "The whole country was thrilling with a new thing, with a release of
new energy. But there was a sense of violence and
crudity in it all, a touch of horror" (p. 419). Ramón's
advice, through Kate, to the Irish is surely Lawrence's
too: "Let them find themselves again, and their own
universe, and their own gods. Let them substantiate
their own mysteries" (pp. 424–25). Such an argument
flows naturally from Lawrence's subjectivist belief in
man creating his own world. But what was appropriate
to the Mexican psyche might not prove suitable for the
European: Lawrence's frequent moves, which disturbed
Frieda and which has suggested to some critics a debilitating restlessness, are a necessary exploration of different states. Exploration, if not total acceptance, of the
Mexican malevolence and horror was thus as obliga-
tory for Lawrence as the vacillation between antithetical poles was for Yeats. In the case of both men, their
restlessness was based on honesty and their sense of
responsibility to a spiritual quest.

20. Introduction to the Phoenix ed. of *The Plumed Serpent*, p. viii.

While Kate is brought to a greater awareness of the power and sacredness of sex, her insistence "I must have both" (p. 438)—"the greater sex" (p. 437), which allows her body to blossom, *and* her ego and individuality—suggests more than nagging wilfulness. It suggests also the inadequacy of Ramón's male assertiveness, which demands subservience, not individuality, and she is given the position which Lawrence will adopt in place of Ramón's cult—namely, the vitalist phallic consciousness and philosophy of tenderness climaxed in *Lady Chatterley's Lover.* Tenderness is mentioned on several occasions in *The Plumed Serpent* (pp. 66, 309, 320) and is seen as consistent with the Quetzalcoatl cult. Yet the tenderness is felt in Kate or Cipriano; it is Ramón who represents the "impassive male cruelty" which makes him "changeless as a stone idol" (p. 154), while changelessness had never been a feature of Lawrence's philosophy, as his remarks on the poetry of Shelley and Keats have indicated. Moreover, when Ramón remarries and Kate deliberates on his relationship with his young wife, Teresa, Kate's conclusion represents the transitional nature *The Plumed Serpent* is characterized by. The argument that "Teresa is the ideal of womanhood toward which Lawrence's heroines struggle but whose perfection they seldom attain"[21] is not borne out by either her inadequate characterization or Kate's objections. And though we might credit Kate with a deathly wilfulness, she nevertheless offers valid Lawrencean objections.

Kate is made angry by the "harem" slavery and "self-prostitution" demanded of Teresa by Ramón and argues for precisely that strength which avoids bullying but includes also tenderness, defined later in *Apocalypse* (pp. 16–17):

> Was it right? Kate asked herself. Wasn't it degrading for a woman? And didn't it make the man either soft and

21. Clark, *Dark Night of the Body,* p. 70.

sensuous, or else hatefully autocratic?

Yet Kate herself had convinced herself of one thing, finally: that the clue to all living and to all moving-on into new living lay in the vivid blood-relation between man and woman. A man and a woman in this togetherness were the clue to all present living and future possibility. Out of this clue of togetherness between a man and a woman, the whole of the new life arose. It was the quick of the whole.

And the togetherness needed a balance. Surely it needed a balance! And did not this Teresa throw herself entirely into the male balance, so that all the weight was on the man's side? (p. 397)

However, she agrees to a civil marriage with Cipriano and, although her conflicting feelings last through to the end of the novel, she experiences that "mindless communion of the blood" (p. 422) celebrated in the last novels and stories. Her experience with a snake, like that of the woman and child in "Sun" or of Lawrence himself in his poem "Snake," is characterized by a sense of "reconciliation" (p. 423). And we are constantly reminded in the novel of the snake symbolism intrinsic to the Quetzalcoatl cult and to Mexico itself. Both the country and the cult, however, proved a horror and a fascination, and *The Plumed Serpent* reveals precisely this duality throughout. Even the last words are suitably ambiguous: "You won't let me go!" (p. 443). Cipriano's hold over Kate is indeed considerable, but whether or not she will return to Ireland remains unclear. She maintains to the end her equivocation towards the male will, and her final remark is anything but plainly submissive.

Discussing the conclusion to the novel which Lawrence himself "wished he had finished . . . differently" (*Not I*, p. 149), L. D. Clark argues rightly that the final version "seems perfect for a book that depends so much on attraction and repulsion for its force." However, his further argument tends to underestimate Lawrence's own irresolution and the embryonic rejection of Quetzalcoatl and Mexico which the novel itself reveals: "This protest of acceptance, while less affirmative than Mrs. Bloom's 'Yes', is no less fervent in committing the speaker to the world the book has made. Its ambiguity is only apparent; it is the affirmation of a woman who has manipulated events so as to be asked to stay involved in an emotional situation that she has no intention of abandoning."[22] To reject Clark's view is not to accept the alternative of F. R. Leavis, who sees "a failure in Lawrence to convince himself that the conquest [of Kate's repugnance] would ever have been achieved."[23] Rather, the equivocation is deliberate on Lawrence's part, an instance of that recurrent refusal to commit himself to the tyranny of absolutism. His thought-adventurers are always on the high seas, never quite arrive at Rananim, but their dialectical vacillation is more truthful and valid than a more static dogmatism would permit.

There is no such equivocation in "The Woman Who Rode Away" (written in the summer of 1924 between drafts of *The Plumed Serpent*) and the sacrifice is all the more frightening and horrifying. The single-mindedness Lawrence displays, while making the story more unified than *The Plumed Serpent*, makes it also all the more inhuman and objectionable, though we must beware of attributing a realistic meaning to a work which is essentially fable in nature. The woman is the Californian wife of a one-time owner of a silver mine, now breeder of pigs, in Mexico. The details already begin to take on a symbolic meaning. The husband is incapable of fully rousing his wife, and their life together is inadequate in its incompleteness. Provoked, however, "by a foolish romanticism more unreal than a girl's," the wife now feels it is "her destiny

22. *Dark Night of the Body*, pp. 47, 73–74.
23. *D. H. Lawrence, Novelist*, p. 69.

to wander into the secret haunts of these timeless, mysterious, marvellous Indians of the mountains" (p. 549), especially of the tribe of Chilchuis who still practise the ancient Aztec religion. Riding off alone into the mountains, during her first night under the stars she feels "like a woman who has died and passed beyond. She was not sure that she had not heard, during the night, a great crash at the centre of herself, which was the crash of her own death. Or else it was a crash at the centre of the earth, and meant something big and mysterious" (p. 552). Drawn on through a landscape increasingly menacing and fatal, she is met by three Indians, the inevitable dark men, while her powerlessness before them indicates the extent to which her Western female will is being eradicated. Her spiritual pilgrimage has most certainly taken new and important directions and the story adopts the character of a mythic journey. Angry but also exultant, "she knew she was dead" (p. 556).

The journey over the mountains takes her to the Chilchuis living in a remote and magical valley. She declares her intention to serve their gods, and, dressed in Indian clothes and given Indian food and drink, she undergoes a quasi-mystical experience described in obviously Romantic terms: "She felt as if all her senses were diffused on the air, . . . she could distinguish the sound of evening flowers unfolding, and the actual crystal sound of the heavens, as the vast belts of the world-atmosphere slid past one another, and as if the moisture ascending and the moisture descending in the air resounded like some harp in the cosmos" (pp. 565–66). Her self-consciousness, womanhood, and will are being increasingly annihilated, and she gains further extra-sensory perceptions: "She *heard* the little dog conceive, in her tiny womb, and begin to be complex, with young. And another day she could hear the vast sound of the earth going round, like some immense arrow-string booming" (p. 568). Such treatment

is the Indians' preparation of the woman for the supreme sacrifice, which is to give herself up to their gods
so that the world will be remade by them and that of
the white man will disintegrate. Hence, the woman
becomes the sacrificial white woman and, in "that
other state of passional cosmic consciousness" (p. 574),
as "some mystic object" (p. 577) she is carried cere-
monially to a cave in the mountains. When the sun's
rays penetrate to the innermost reaches of the cave,
where she lies naked on the stone altar, the old priest-
chief will "strike home, accomplish the sacrifice and
achieve the power" (p. 581).

The story ends there with the acknowledgement in
the final sentence of "the mastery that man must hold,
and that passes from race to race." The parallels between the story and *The Plumed Serpent* are obvious,
whether in the Mexican location and sacrificial male
cult or in the vitalism which enables the woman to
achieve a mystical awareness of the cosmic life force.
But the woman is a far cry from Kate: her loss of will
is complete, and in her unequivocal pilgrimage she
never experiences the doubts constantly troubling a
Kate Leslie. She resembles more Teresa, who similarly
gives herself completely to Quetzalcoatl. Likewise,
Lawrence himself offers no equivocation or comment:
the only judgement passed—of her "foolish romanticism" (p. 549)—might apply only to her initial motiva-
tion, for it is never repeated nor are the Indians described in anything but favourable terms. To describe
the story as Lawrence's "completest artistic achievement" and "his profoundest comment on the world
of his time," as Graham Hough has done,[24] seems remarkably wide of the mark. Certainly the story's heart-
lessness is somewhat lessened when we treat it as fable,
while the woman's progression to heightened consciousness is persistent and unambiguous. She learns

24. *Dark Sun*, p. 146.

the need to submit to the dark gods, and her sacrifice symbolizes a death to that arid mechanism predominant in the Western psyche. In this respect Hough's analogy with Yeats might be better appreciated if, instead of comparing it with "The Second Coming," as he does, we substitute "Two Songs from a Play," discussed in the previous chapter. For in the latter poem there are similar sacrificial deaths, centring upon the gift of heart, though the cosmic proportions are greater because the protagonists are Dionysus and Jesus; a similar sense of renewal and rebirth; a similar welcoming of a future consciousness antithetical to the present dead Christian one; but also a tragic sense and a heightened dignity granted to the lesser protagonists, the human lover, painter, soldier, and herald. Yeats's version is not only larger in scope but more compassionate towards the inadequacies of individual men. It is in this last respect that Lawrence's story takes on a heartless ruthlessness, which both Yeats's poem and Lawrence's subsequent story, "St Mawr," manage to avoid.

"St. Mawr" (written, like "The Woman Who Rode Away," during the summer of 1924 between drafts of *The Plumed Serpent*) promotes several tenets of Lawrence's passional faith while suggesting a more complex attitude than is evident in the previous fable. The story explores the effect of a Welsh stallion, St. Mawr, upon yet another inadequate marriage, between Lou Witt, an American girl from Louisiana, and Rico Carrington, an Australian amateur painter and heir to a baronetcy. Their marriage is based on wilful domination and their lack of physical relationship is disruptive. While Lou has the advantage of being rootless, an outsider, like a gipsy—qualities which Lawrence can turn to advantage—she is also the dominating American female, possessed of a disastrous will. Rico, on the other hand, is a "young poser" (p. 4), capable of philandering— never a virtue in Lawrence's strict puritanical eyes—

and lacking in real artistic talent and taste. Lou's mother, Mrs. Witt, is no better: even more wilful than Lou and scathing in her criticism of Europe, she is acidly ironic, conceited, and, worse, aristocratic-democratic, anxious to cut an impressive figure on London's Rotten Row.

Lou is first made aware of Rico's essential weakness when she sees St. Mawr, the stallion which she eventually buys for him. The horse has an immediate effect upon her: she falls instantly in love with it, is moved by the dark fire and hostile threat it seems to exude, and its demonic quality forces her not only to admiration and love but also to worship. The stallion achieves her submission in a way her husband had failed to do; it rouses her to an awareness of a darker, more splendid, and vital world than she had previously known and of the banalities of the fashionable world. And, suitably enough, the horse, which has proved its wilfulness with two riders already, proves unmanageable to Rico, who treats it as a piece of fashion. St. Mawr, which Lawrence compares to a snake and later describes as "one of the kings of creation" (p. 70), terms of distinction repeated in his snake poem, is symbolic of that vital instinctive life which Don Ramón in *The Plumed Serpent* pontificated over. Consequently, the half-breed Navajo, Phoenix, and the dark-bearded Welshman, Lewis, who are themselves aware of and participate in that life, are the only two men capable of handling the stallion. Both men through their blood have closer contact with the aboriginal world, whether of Mexican Arizona or Celtic Wales, though Phoenix possesses also a "categorical hatred" (p. 38), which distinguishes him from Lewis.

The vitalism expressed in "St. Mawr" is generally more acceptable than the inflated seriousness of *The Plumed Serpent*, partly through the presence of a considerable irony and satire, and partly through an inclusiveness of vision offered in the final pages. Only the opening chapters of that novel contain such a tone and purpose, and the remainder settles down to the more pompous matter of communicating a new religion. Indeed, one of Kate's great strengths is her redeeming humour and satirical eye, which Ramón and Cipriano almost totally lack. Lawrence's setting of the Shropshire village in "St. Mawr," based on his own visit to his friend Frederick Carter (the Cartwright of the story), allows him also to range over ground more intimately known than the deserts of Mexico. Even the minor characters in the village come alive—the subservient Mr. Jones, the postmaster, or the Anglican Dean Vyner with his semi-invalid wife, whose Christian theology seems based on death and destruction of the vital life. But Lawrence's most scathing irony and sarcasm are reserved for Mrs. Witt: so empty-headed herself yet admiring only men who are capable of thought; so full of busyness but incapable of real work; so supposedly lively but in fact dead at the core; so democratic in her American spirit yet overwhelmingly snobbish and domineering. Surrounded by Rico and Mrs. Witt, Lou can experience a sense of wonder only through contact with St. Mawr, and it is she who is given the Lawrencean positives. Opposing her mother's portrait of animal man as mere caveman, she argues in favour not of brute degeneracy but of "pure animal man" (p. 47).

Despite the satirical treatment of Mrs. Witt in the first third of the book, Lawrence grants her an understanding and realization Rico never attains, and she responds favourably to Mr. Cartwright's talk of the Great God Pan. Indeed, during the subsequent ride to the Welsh border her relationship with Lewis, the Welsh groom, is clearly being established and the demarcation lines are being drawn: on the one side are the vitalists, Lou, St. Mawr, Lewis, and now Mrs. Witt, and on the other, led by Rico, the believers in a good time, "so entirely contained within their card-

board let's-be-happy world" (p. 25), confident in their
aliveness and superiority, and well-read, like Flora
Manby, in H. G. Wells's *History* (p. 60). It is against
the latter group that the wild stallion rears, throwing
his rider, Rico, and kicking at Edwards' face. The stallion's action, appropriately enough when they are en
route to the Devil's Chair,[25] is interpreted by Lou as
part of a pattern of evil which she sees sweeping over
all mankind in some apocalyptic flood. For her, none
of the modern political alternatives proves worthy: in
different ways, both bolshevism and fascism participate
in the fearful evil. And recognizing the need for destruction, with an apocalyptic sense shared by the previous vitalists, Lawrence asks himself through Lou:

> What's to be done? Generally speaking, nothing. The
> dead will have to bury their dead, while the earth stinks
> of corpses. The individual can but depart from the mass,
> and try to cleanse himself. Try to hold fast to the living
> thing, which destroys as it goes, but remains sweet. And
> in his soul fight, fight, fight to preserve that which is life
> in him from the ghastly kisses and poison-bites of the
> myriad evil ones. Retreat to the desert, and fight. But in
> his soul adhere to that which is life itself, creatively de-
> stroying as it goes: destroying the stiff old thing to let the
> new bud come through. The one passionate principle of
> creative being, which recognises the natural good, and has
> a sword for the swarms of evil. Fights, fights, fights to
> protect itself. But with itself, is strong and at peace.
> (pp. 66–67)

The problem of communication, posed in this passage,
is one which confronted Lawrence throughout his ca-

25. As noted by Kingsley Widmer, "Our Demonic Heritage: D. H.
Lawrence," in *D. H. Lawrence Miscellany*, ed. Moore, p. 20. I
find farfetched Cavitch's argument that the horse's falling on
Rico is evidence of "a male fear of coitus that could only be
Lawrence's own" (*D. H. Lawrence and the New World*, pp.
157–58). His reading of the entire story I find unacceptable.

reer and corresponds to the Mental Fight which Blake's mythological figures, Carlyle's heroes, or Yeats's personae engage in. Disillusioned by the masses' inability to learn from the destruction they promote, Lawrence felt that the only alternative was temporary retreat. There in isolation the individual self awaits rebirth, which, because of Lawrence's fundamental optimism, will be forthcoming. The dialectical tension will swing in the goodness of time in more positive directions; life itself, which requires such a destruction and a dialectic, remains sweet. Meanwhile, the individual must fight to retain for himself and for future man "the living thing."

What distinguishes this last phase of Lawrence's career is the dialectic of power and tenderness. Just as for Yeats there was a false and a true mask, so too for Lawrence there was a false and true power, a false and true tenderness. The true power for Mexico might be the male Quetzalcoatl cult, but the principle of leadership could too easily decline into the bullying authoritarianism of fascism. The destruction of the old must be creative and not "Mere anarchy . . . loosed upon the world." If St. Mawr is merely mean, then he must be shot; if he is indeed "one of the kings of creation," then he represents that vital energy constantly being annihilated by modern man, whose faith lies in machines and mechanistic subservience. Hence, the arch-proponents of the plan to destroy or geld St. Mawr—Rico, the Vyners, and Flora Manby—epitomize "our whole eunuch civilisation, nasty-minded as eunuchs are, with their kind of sneaking, sterilising cruelty" (p. 84), while Mrs. Witt is redeemed to some extent by her plan to retreat to America, with Lou, the two grooms, and St. Mawr. However, although recognizing Lewis' strength and proposing marriage to him, Mrs. Witt is still unable to appreciate his characteristic Lawrencean pantheism which sees the vital life in himself and the world outside. Lewis is one of "the aristocracy of the invisible powers, the greater influences, nothing to do with human society" (p. 110), and he remains unable to marry or have contact with women. Although he is a precursor of Oliver Mellors in *Lady Chatterley's Lover*, his wounding remains unhealed and he disappears in the last part of the story. Lou, on the other hand, can appreciate the vitalism of St. Mawr, believes also in the retreat from contact to a desert wilderness, but upholds the new insistence upon tenderness. It is upon her that Lawrence concentrates in his conclusion.

> It seems to me [Lou says to Lewis] men and women have really hurt one another so much nowadays that they had better stay apart till they have learned to be gentle with one another again. Not all this forced passion and destructive philandering. Men and women should stay apart till their hearts grow gentle towards one another again. Now, it's only each one fighting for his own—or her own— underneath the cover of tenderness. (p. 111)

The despair Lou and Mrs. Witt experience on their return to America is superseded only when they buy a ranch in the Southwest. Lawrence's superb descriptive powers take over in the last twenty pages of the story, and his vitalist faith is convincingly conveyed, surpassing the rather stilted and contrived aboriginal vision Lewis articulated earlier on the ride to Merriton. Critics have been quick to appreciate the malevolence of the landscape—for the spirit of the place is wild, cruel, even threatening—and also the considerable lyricism of Lawrence's descriptions, a lyricism which reflects his deep attachment to his own ranch. However, objecting to the solution to the problems of modern civilization posed by these final pages, Graham Hough insensitively reduces Lawrence's position thus: "If you don't like men any more, go and live in New

Mexico with a horse."[26] This *reductio ad absurdum* is a gross misreading of the tale and particularly of these final pages. Nor are these pages, as another critic has argued, "a digression" and "a vivid, unassimilated description."[27] Rather, F. R. Leavis is correct in refusing to see Lou's flight to the ranch as a retreat ("Back to Nature") and in regarding the conclusion as "superficially so inconsequent and tailing-off, essentially so germane, so *belonging* to the significance."[28] For Lou's desire for peace is constantly being denied: her annihilation must be as complete as the symbolic sacrificial death in "The Woman Who Rode Away." Consequently, even St. Mawr now ceases to have any hold over her and is seen as an "illusion" (p. 127), while Phoenix is reduced to making unwelcome sexual overtures: the limitations of both stallion and Indian are now recognized. Her new world is, instead, presexual in character: Lawrence's famous pine tree, for example, is described as "a passionless, non-phallic column, rising in the shadows of the pre-sexual world" (p. 134). Indeed, the predominant imagery is of both column and circle: "the circling guard of pine trees"; "The desert swept its great fawn-coloured circle around"; daylight, like the eagles, "made the vast turn" or "vast, eagle-like wheeling" (p. 135); "The great circling landscape lived its own life" (p. 137). Presexual or not, the dialectic of images—column and circle—is sexual by implication, and the sexual relationship of a man and a woman is merely one instance of a fundamental cosmic pattern which the landscape reflects.

Yet the New England wife of the previous owner sought to establish there a "paradise on earth," a "New England belief in a world ultimately all for love" (p. 141). Her vision depended upon a belief in man's

26. *Dark Sun*, p. 184.
27. Clark, *Dark Night of the Body*, p. 42.
28. *D. H. Lawrence, Novelist*, p. 244.

capacity to "master" a world more cruelly dialectical than she could ever acknowledge. The ranch, after all, had been used to rear goats, animals appropriate enough to the Pan-like, inclusive vision Lou must now cultivate. Likewise, we must avoid misreading the lyricism of Lawrence's descriptions as the New England wife misread the beauty of the landscape. "Ah, that was beauty!—perhaps the most beautiful thing in the world. It was pure beauty, *absolute* beauty! There! That was it. To the little woman from New England, with her tense, fierce soul and her egoistic passion of service, this beauty was absolute, a *ne plus ultra*" (p. 135). But such beauty is that Romantic chimera of absolutes which Lawrence constantly opposed, and the woman's vision is defeated by the destructive nature of that very world she was entranced by. Animals die off, pack rats invade, lightning strikes, weeds overtake— the menacing battle at all levels of existence breaks her spirit and her unreal vision.

The dialectic both destroys and re-creates, and Lou's struggle is analogous to that which "every civilisation, when it loses its inward vision," must take upon itself (p. 141). It is a struggle analogous also to Lawrence's own purpose as novelist and visionary, a cleansing of "an Augean stable of metallic filth" (p. 142). At the conclusion of the story there is no resolution, no explicit progression: Mrs. Witt remains critical, unbelieving, and concerned about the price Lou has paid for the ranch. Lou, on the other hand, is aware of another kind of price—a cheapness of self and sex—which her struggle with the wild spirit there will redeem. That such redemption is conceivable in the case of Lou rather than of the New England woman is due to the regenerative process set in motion by the stallion, St. Mawr, but also to Lou's new awareness, through the wild spirit of the place, of the existential dialectic which includes cruelty as well as love, tenderness as well as power. That awareness is more fully developed

in Lou than in Kate Leslie and represents a further
advance in the development of Lawrence's last work.

3

Whatever Lawrence's feelings for his ranch, for the
Southwest, or for wild America as a whole, his worsen-
ing tuberculosis dictated that his last years be spent
in Europe. After returning from Mexico in 1926, he
undertook in the following March a tour of Etruscan
tombs with his friend Earl Brewster. As early as 1920
he had planned to write on the Etruscans (*EP*, p. v)
and in the following year was asking Catherine Cars-
well about "the secret of the Etruscans" (*CL*, p. 668).
The 1927 tour proved significant, not merely in enabling him to produce *Etruscan Places*, one of his most
memorable pieces of travel writing, but also in helping
to provide the transition from the emphasis upon male
power and sacrifice of female will to the theme of
phallic tenderness, which is at the heart of his last
works. America, for all its wildness, posed the problem
of the female will to a much greater degree than
Europe: in a very personal way America meant Mabel
Dodge Luhan. *Etruscan Places*, then, together with
stories like "The Virgin and the Gipsy" and "The Man
Who Died," prepares us for Lawrence's last major
novel, *Lady Chatterley's Lover*.

Etruscan Places (published 1927–28; in book form,
1932) is full of Lawrence's acute powers of observation
and description, not only of the tombs but of the people he meets on his way: the local guide, people at the
hotel and railway station, the German archaeological
student. We are also constantly made aware of the
interpenetration of time—past, present, and, by implication, future. Consequently, we recognize both the
timeless quality of Etruscan art and the relevance of
its vision to contemporary and future man.

The Etruscan culture is distinguished from the
Roman along lines Yeats used to distinguish between

Greek and Roman: the one is subjective, organic, vital, and alive; the other, objective, mechanistic, and dead. Consequently, Italian fascism, to which Lawrence objects most strongly here, is attacked for its authoritarianism and bullying, its reliance upon brute force, and its myopic elevation of things Roman.[29] His own unpleasant experience with the "spy-lout" who insists on examining his passport confirms him in his furious opposition (pp. 21–22). By contrast, the tombs reveal a people's perception and acknowledgement of the "quick" of all things, in which they too participate. Such a vision inevitably centres on that characteristically Lawrencean positive, touch:

They really have the sense of touch; the people and the

29. Lawrence's objections here and elsewhere to fascism are clear, yet because of his deep distaste for modern liberalism and democracy and corresponding promotion of leadership, shared by Carlyle and Yeats, he too has been accused of either adherence to fascism or promotion of fascist elements. William York Tindall, *D. H. Lawrence and Susan His Cow* (1939), and Bertrand Russell (Nehls, III, 283–84) and *Autobiography of Bertrand Russell*, II (London: Allen & Unwin, 1968), pp. 20–24, have led the accusers. The attack has been continued more recently by Harrison, *The Reactionaries*, p. 189, and Frank Kermode, *New York Review of Books*, 13 Aug. 1970, pp. 31–33. Reviewing Philip Rahv's *Literature and the Sixth Sense*, in which Rahv dismissed Russell's charges, Kermode argues otherwise: "I myself think this defense goes wrong, that 'blood-consciousness' does have something to do with 'racial . . . purity of blood,' which Rahv denies. It is true, though, that Fascists found no use for Lawrence in their propaganda." However, other critics have defended Lawrence against such charges (among them, Moore, in *D. H. Lawrence*, ed. Spilka, pp. 66–67, and Daleski, *Forked Flame*, p. 228 ff.), while Frieda Lawrence herself made a spirited defence against both Tindall and Russell (*Mem*, pp. 277, 445, 448), dismissing the charges as "bunk" and "pure nonsense." The categories of communist and fascist did not fit: "Those concepts were too tight for his purely human outlook" (*First Lady Chatterley*, pp. x–xi). And although Frieda might be naturally partial in her defence, there is a considerable truth in her rebuttals.

creatures are all really in touch. It is one of the rarest
qualities, in life as well as in art. There is plenty of pawing
and laying hold, but no real touch. In pictures especially,
the people may be in contact, embracing or laying hands
on one another. But there is no soft flow of touch. The
touch does not come from the middle of the human being.
It is merely a contact of surfaces, and a juxtaposition of
objects. This is what makes so many of the great masters
boring, in spite of all their clever composition. Here, in
this faded Etruscan painting, there is a quiet flow of touch
that unites the man and the woman on the couch, the
timid boy behind, the dog that lifts his nose, even the very
garlands that hang from the wall. (pp. 45–46)

Here is no inclination to shout, like Kate Leslie or
Jesus, *Noli me tangere* and retreat into the desert or
to the Taos ranch; no debilitating insistence upon sacrifice or upon assertion: *"Thou shalt acknowledge the
wonder"* (*MM*, p. 53). Simply, there *is* the wonder, in
terms Wallace Stevens might have used: "content with
just a sense of the quick ripple of life" (*EP*, p. 35). The
Etruscan symbolism, moreover, disproves any sentimental idyllicism. Taking over Blake's terminology in
The Marriage of Heaven and Hell, Lawrence notes that
the symbolism evidences a dialecticism: the prolific
(lamb) and the devouring (lion) (p. 57). Indeed, Lawrence refers to Blake when discussing an Etruscan
Typhon (p. 73), and praises the "clear outline" of
Etruscan art and vision (p. 68). Similarly, the Etruscan
vitalism and belief in a great soul or *anima* is communicated in a Blakean anthropomorphism:

> To the Etruscan all was alive; the whole universe lived;
> and the business of man was himself to live amid it all.
> He had to draw life into himself, out of the wandering
> huge vitalities of the world. The cosmos was alive, like
> a vast creature. The whole thing breathed and stirred.
> Evaporation went up like breath from the nostrils of a
> whale, steaming up. The sky received it in its blue bosom,
> breathed it in and pondered on it and transmuted it, before

breathing it out again. Inside the earth were fires like the heat in the hot red liver of a beast. Out of the fissures of the earth came breaths of other breathing, vapours direct from the living physical under-earth, exhalations carrying inspiration. The whole thing was alive, and had a great soul, or *anima:* and in spite of one great soul, there were myriad roving, lesser souls: every man, every creature and tree and lake and mountain and stream, was animate, had its own peculiar consciousness. And has it today. (p. 49)

That such a vision is possible not only in Etruscan Italy but in twentieth-century England is expressed in "The Virgin and the Gipsy" (written 1926; published 1930). Back in his familiar village situation, Lawrence draws an obvious parallel between his own elopement with Frieda and that of the vicar's wife in the story. The scandalized family is ruled by a domineering aged grandmother; the runaway wife is reduced to the status of "She-who-was-Cynthia" (p. 5); while the children grow up spiritually wounded and deformed. Into such an obviously negative and life-denying situation comes the inevitable dark man, the gipsy, whom Yvette, the virgin daughter, falls in love with. The story revolves around the clash of wills—that of the matriarchal Mater whose "dead old hand" rules everyone's lives (p. 7), and whose power derives from "a toad-like self-will that was godless, and less than human" (p. 65); that of Yvette, who rebels against her family and loses herself in the gipsy's will; and finally that of the gipsy. In an apocalyptic-like climax, the gipsy saves Yvette from the rising flood of water from the broken reservoir dam, and in her near-disintegrated home warms her to life.

A similar resurrection is the central theme of "The Man Who Died" (written in 1927 between drafts of *Lady Chatterley;* published as "The Escaped Cock" in 1928, and in expanded form in England only in 1931). The story is a more ambitious attempt in that Lawrence

rewrites the Resurrection story and conceives a revitalized Christianity. The parallel with Blake's own rewriting of the Christian myth in *The Everlasting Gospel*
is obvious.[30] Clearly Lawrence's Congregational background in Eastwood remained influential, and Graham
Hough is right to distinguish Lawrence in this way:
"Unlike Yeats, who seems never to have had any particular orientation to Christianity, Lawrence is haunted
by it."[31] Provoked by his recent reading of Moffat's
translation of the Bible, Lawrence reasserts the Christian myth, though reformed according to his vision.
The new Christianity will centre not on transcendence,
self-sacrifice, self-denial, and compulsion—the "nice
cul de sac" of Murry's Jesus (*CL*, p. 861)—but upon
consummation of self through a deepened appreciation
of life, through delight, tenderness, and touch.

"The Man Who Died"—the earlier title of "The
Escaped Cock" more stridently asserting a phallicism—traces the life of Christ as he awakes in the
tomb, not to a transcendent resurrection in Heaven but
to a revitalized life on earth. Tied, like the peasant's
cockerel, and waking up from a Blakean sleep in the
tomb, the man (who is never named Christ in the
story) stirs back into consciousness, regains his will to
live, and is taken in by the same peasant whose cock
has awakened him.[32] Drawn out of his loneliness and
apartness by the warmth of the sun, the man is provoked to recognition of life around him:

> The man who had died looked nakedly on life, and saw
> a vast resoluteness everywhere flinging itself up in stormy
> or subtle wave-crests, foam-tips emerging out of the blue
> invisible, a black and orange cock or the green flame-

30. Vivian de Sola Pinto, "William Blake and D. H. Lawrence,"
    in *William Blake*, ed. Rosenfeld, p. 104.
31. *Dark Sun*, p. 56.
32. Cf. Patricia Abel and Robert Hogan, "D. H. Lawrence's Singing
    Birds," in *D. H. Lawrence Miscellany*, ed. Moore, pp. 204–14.

tongues out of the extremes of the fig tree. They came
forth, these things and creatures of spring, glowing with
desire and with assertion. They came like crests of foam,
out of the blue flood of the invisible desire, out of the
vast invisible sea of strength, and they came coloured and
tangible, evanescent, yet deathless in their coming. The
man who had died looked on the great swing into existence of things that had not died, but he saw no longer
their tremulous desire to exist and to be. He heard instead
their ringing, ringing, defiant challenge to all other things
existing. (p. 10)

The passage moves from the general to the particular
and returns to the general. Lawrence gives the impression he is describing several particular natural phenomena: the colours and the sense of movement dominate. Yet in particular and only incidentally he is
describing the cock or the fig tree's new leaves. Instead
of the particular, the passage centres on conveying the
overall pattern of existence as it returns to life in the
spring. There is more than mere movement; there is
above all the battle for life. And part of the force of
the writing here surely depends upon Lawrence's
awareness of his own impending death. Yet true to his
vision, he refused to submit to life-denial and proceeded to make perhaps his most personal affirmation
of all, to draw an analogy between himself and the
Christ that should have been. "The doom of death was
a shadow compared to the raging destiny of life, the
determined surge of life" (p. 11). From all accounts
such a faith did much to keep Lawrence alive in the
last few years.

Meeting Mary Magdalene in the garden, Christ informs her that his public life as saviour and teacher
is over, his faith in transcendence broken. He recognizes that it is possible to give too much and take too
little, a point reminiscent of Blake's song "The Clod
& the Pebble," but too subtle for Mary's sacrificial

ethic. Seeing the peasant woman's breasts sway, he can appreciate her desire for him and the limitation and exclusiveness of his previous chastity. Lawrence's arguments against virginity here are again paralleled in Blake, who in turn influenced Yeats. Christ's chastity hitherto was a form of greed: he gave but never took. Similarly, when on the road to Emmaus and appreciative of "the seethe of phenomena," "this infinite whirl," he recognizes the "narrow belief" of his disciples (pp. 20–22). Christ finds on the shores of the Mediterranean a temple dedicated to Isis and served by a priestess whose obligation is to search for the fragmented body of Osiris. When she reassembles his broken body, he will come alive again and impregnate her. She has known both Caesar and Anthony in her youth. Appropriately enough, the Roman emperor had repelled her with his rapaciousness, and the golden Anthony had been unable to stir her womb to life. However, being "touched on the quick" by the man who died (p. 30), she feels he is the lost Osiris. Christ, on the other hand, is still not sufficiently revitalized and is loath to give himself up to the touch and contact of the priestess. Though *Noli me tangere* still holds his self in selfish isolation, he is struck by her tenderness: "More terrible and lovely than the death I died—" (p. 33). He acknowledges, nevertheless, the need for reunion of god and man and the presence of "all-tolerant Pan" (p. 34). When the priestess comes to him later that night, Christ rejects his previous teaching, centred on death of body and self, in order to embrace the priestess's life-affirming flame. In their sexual consummation he is reborn in tenderness and desire, his wounds no longer hurting but burning like suns. "This is the great atonement, the being in touch. The grey sea and the rain, the wet narcissus and the woman I wait for, the invisible Isis and the unseen sun are all in touch, and at one" (p. 44).

The outside world of men, however, has not

changed: the priestess's mother is wilful and seeks dominion over her; the slaves are capable of hurt and destruction, raping a female slave and informing against the escaped prisoner, Christ; while the union of gods and men remains incomplete in the lives of the majority of men. Although he has impregnated the priestess with Osiris, the man who died must leave to preserve their mutual consummation and prevent further death at the hands of Roman justice. The tale ends with the Christ figure rowing out to sea, carried by the currents, but welcoming now the dawning of a new day. The conclusion is infinitely more hopeful than that of a comparable story, "Sun," where "the fatal chain of continuity" remains unbroken (p. 545). In "The Man Who Died," however, through his rewriting of the Resurrection, Lawrence could rely upon a more nearly allegorical treatment to express the Christianity of phallic tenderness he would have preferred. In "Sun" he was limited by the contemporary scene and by modern men and women. *Lady Chatterley's Lover* attempts to combine both concerns in its application of his new insistence upon tenderness, not to a Mediterranean Christ-Osiris, priestess-Isis, but to the Eastwood which constituted the *heart* of his England.

4

Of the first draft of *Lady Chatterley's Lover*, begun in 1925, Lawrence said: "They'll say as they said of Blake: It's mysticism, but they shan't get away with it, not this time: Blake's wasn't mysticism, neither is this. The tenderness and gentleness hadn't enough punch and fight in it, it was a bit wistful" (*First Lady Chatterley*, p. vi). Frieda herself has described the novel as something Lawrence wanted all his life to write, and has convincingly argued: "Only an Englishman or a New Englander could have written it. It is the last word in Puritanism" (p. v). Lawrence himself denied it was "a dirty sexual novel," distinguishing between sex and phallicism: "Sex is a thing that exists in the head, its reactions are cerebral, and its processes mental. Whereas the phallic reality is warm and spontaneous" (*Letters*, p. 710). Or again, to the unbelieving young, he said in "A Propos of *Lady Chatterley's Lover*," "Sex means just plainly and simply, a lady's underclothing, and the fumbling therewith" (*Ph. II*, p. 496). Yet the "abuse and hatred" (*Not I*, p. 193) he himself predicted and received have not always been replaced by the critical understanding and appreciation the novel deserves. F. R. Leavis relegates *Lady Chatterley's Lover* to the status of the lesser novels, preferring the greater tact of "The Virgin and the Gipsy."[33] Few critics share the enthusiasm of Julian Moynahan: "More clearly and more persuasively than in any previous novel, Lawrence brings the reader into touch with that vision [of the world's aliveness], the mystery which, as one suspected from the beginning, was only of life itself."[34]

The novel is indeed flawed. Leavis is right to stress its calculatedness, though that is a flaw inherent in Lawrence's prophetic role. Certainly his art could at times suffer from the didactic purpose he took upon himself. The first draft, however, which in many ways indicates a quite different novel from the third and final version, is noticeably lacking in preaching: the moralizing passages are almost entirely absent. Closer to the novels of Mrs. Gaskell from whom Lawrence in part comes, the first draft reveals a novel concerned essentially with class rather than with the nature of sexual-spiritual fulfilment. The first draft, like "The

33. *D. H. Lawrence, Novelist*, pp. 293–94, cf. p. 70, and *Anna Karenina and Other Essays* (London: Chatto and Windus, 1967), pp. 235–41. Cf. Bayley, *Characters of Love*, pp. 15, 24–25; Cavitch, *D. H. Lawrence and the New World*, p. 197 ff.; Moore, *Life and Works of D. H. Lawrence*, pp. 264, 282.

34. *Deed of Life*, p. 172; cf. Hough, *Dark Sun*, pp. 151–52, and Mark Spilka, *The Love Ethic of D. H. Lawrence* (Bloomington: Indiana Univ. Press, 1966), pp. 177–200.

Virgin and the Gipsy," is more akin to Lawrence's earlier stories and lacks the solidity and depth of the major novels. The final version more fittingly provides the climax to his life-long pilgrimage towards a vision of affirmation, towards that consummation which constitutes the fullest expression the creative self is capable of. He might have turned full circle in returning to the Nottinghamshire country life he knew best, but except for his earliest work he is anything but a regional novelist. Rather, the novel explores the spiritually diseased state of England, the secret worm gnawing away at the heart of the sick rose. While the symbolism, as Lawrence once wrote (*Ph. II*, p. 514), is unconscious rather than deliberate, all the characteristic Lawrencean targets are quite calculatingly set up: the generation of Englishmen lacking contact amongst themselves and with their world; the attitudes of death and life-denial replacing the vitalism and organicism necessary for growth; the disharmony and fragmentation of self and society; the mechanism and mammonism; the arid intellectualism; the refusal to live fully in a world as animated and as essentially based on the creative self as any Romantic cosmos; the perversion of sex to appetite; the domination of the female will; and the fundamental cruelty and bullying that replaces the warmth, gentleness, and exuberance of feeling and living by which consummation is to be attained. The reliance upon phallic tenderness is central, but only because it is at the heart of a larger vitalism which places the sexual experience in the cosmic pattern of growth and change and rebirth. In the same way, while focusing upon Sir Clifford and Lady Constance Chatterley and Oliver Mellors, Lawrence comments upon the present impotence and potential strength which lies at the heart of the English psyche. He remained as quintessentially English as Blake and sought a similar regeneration of Albion, the Giant Man, in the figure of his all-tolerant Pan.

The novel traces the familiar Lawrence motif of a

woman awakened to a fuller consciousness through the presence of a dark man. Beginning with the state of sleep, it proceeds to the awakening, to the dawning of a fuller awareness, and concludes with the anticipated regeneration in the spring. Just as the Isis priestess in "The Man Who Died" seeks to reassemble the fragmented Osiris, who had been put to death by an antagonistic world, so too Lawrence seeks the renewal of the English psyche after its disintegration at the hands of the nonvital forces within and without. Consequently, we are shown the extremes of the dialectic when not held in a proper synthesis or balance. Sex is reduced to animal appetite or cheap thrills, as in Connie's and Hilda's lovemaking in prewar Dresden; such imbalance within the self gives rise either to assertion of will, taking the form of male cruelty or female domination, or to the cerebral sex of a Tommy Dukes. Denied access to the instinctive life, Sir Clifford cultivates a social group of friends who promote a cold intellectualism and engage in artificial, calculated "creativity." Because he has lost contact, whether within his own polar self or with other people and things, Sir Clifford maintains an isolation, both physical and spiritual, which increases his dilemma and reduces the robust Connie to a restless, wasting woman. The various parts within the self are being pushed further into extreme and separate entities, in the manner of Blake's Zoas. Like the Christ figure whose wounds are healed into suns by the priestess, even Mellors needs a Connie to heal the wounding he received at the hands of his wife.

The proper harmony within the self—between mind and body—is stressed in Lawrence's own essay "A Propos of *Lady Chatterley's Lover*," which remains the best introduction to the novel:

> The mind has to catch up, in sex: indeed, in all the physical acts. Mentally, we lag behind in our sexual

thought, in a dimness, a lurking, grovelling fear which belongs to our raw, somewhat bestial ancestors. In this one respect, sexual and physical, we have left the mind un-evolved. Now we have to catch up, and make a balance between the consciousness of the body's sensations and experiences, and these sensations and experiences them-selves. Balance up the consciousness of the act, and the act itself. Get the two in harmony. It means having a proper reverence for sex, and a proper awe of the body's strange experience. It means being able to use the so-called obscene words, because these are a natural part of the mind's consciousness of the body. Obscenity only comes in when the mind despises and fears the body, and the body hates and resists the mind. (*Ph. II*, p. 490)

Or again:

Life is only bearable when the mind and body are in harmony, and there is a natural balance between them, and each has a natural respect for the other. (p. 492)

Similarly, Lawrence no more wanted to overthrow marriage—"perhaps the greatest contribution to the social life of man made by Christianity" (p. 502)—than he wished "to suggest that all women should go run-ning after gamekeepers for lovers" (p. 490; cf. *CL*, p. 1111). He wished, indeed, to retain marriage, as he did sex, because both involved on an individual level the fundamental principles of relationship, contact, or touch. To be married or to make love to another person required an exchange of selves, a dialectical movement between two people, without destroying the individ-uality of either person. Marriage and lovemaking touch upon the fundamental dialectic in the life force. Both experiences depend for their success upon a harmony within the self, while at the same time strengthening and extending that harmony beyond the limits of the individual self. Hence, "Sex is the balance of male and female in the universe"; "Marriage is the clue to

human life" (*Ph. II*, p. 504). Similarly with the world
around us: we must get back the great relationships
which our mental consciousnesses in disequilibrium
have attempted to destroy and keep apart. Our failure
will be not only our spiritual death but, on a social
level, "class-hate and class-consciousness," as evidenced in the "civil strife" (p. 513) he had seen around
him in Eastwood during the General Strike. Again the
sexual relevance of this novel is extended to include
even the social, economic, and political life of England,
and the organic and inclusive character of Lawrence's
vision, like that of Blake, is evident. A situation takes
on added and symbolic dimensions when we are made
to see it in terms which are at the same time metaphysical, ethical, political, social, epistemological as
well as sexual.

The novel begins with the dilemma of Connie, married to Sir Clifford who returned from the Great War
paralysed from the hips down and impotent. The symbolism, as Lawrence acknowledged, is obvious and perhaps even unfair (p. 514), but the age is, nevertheless,
wounded and impotent, dead to the instinctive, passional life. And, as Frieda has argued, "The terrible
thing about Lady C. is that L. identified himself with
both Clifford and Mellors; that took courage, that
made me shiver, when I read it as he wrote it" (*Mem*,
p. 389). The dialectic within the self is then, for some,
irrevocably damaged and will require considerable re-
adjustment to be restored to health, unity, and equilibrium. Although this disastrous state has become aggra-
vated because of the war, Connie's prewar Dresden
experiences with Hilda indicate that even then she was
possessed of the modern disease. The sexual relations
she and her German student lovers knew were founded
on greed and selfishness, taking and not giving. The
results were either appetite or male cruelty or female
will. The imagery Lawrence uses is peculiarly appropriate—"One was less in love with the boy afterwards,

and a little inclined to hate him, as if he had trespassed on one's privacy and inner freedom" (p. 7)—and is picked up later by Sir Clifford. Sitting in his wood, "the heart of England," "the old England," Clifford expresses his wishes in imagery deliberately sexual in implication: he wants to keep the wood "intact," "untouched"; "I want no one to trespass in it" (p. 44), he says, and is particularly angry that it was denuded by his father during the war. On the other hand, he fails to notice the intrusion of noisy colliery hooters; the industrial situation, even when he becomes closely involved with his mines later in the novel, offers merely machines to be refined or efficiency to be improved. He shrinks from contact with real people, seeing the miners "as objects rather than men" (p. 16), a peculiarly Carlylean situation. Similarly, the literal and symbolic appropriateness of the wood as the setting for Connie's warming to life is obvious. To push the irony further, Lawrence makes the trespasser who touches Clifford's wife a real Pan dryad figure, Mellors, whose job as gamekeeper is to protect Sir Clifford's game from trespassing poachers.

The Chatterleys, for all their exclusive, ancient, aristocratic breeding, represent England's particular dilemma.[35] Even the running of Wragby Hall takes on a symbolic relevance: the house lacks "warmth of feeling" which would unite it "organically" (p. 18). Their friends too fail to provide that spiritual leadership England needed from her "natural aristocrats," as Lawrence frequently called them. Connie's father, despite

35. Daleski is probably right to object that *Lady Chatterley's Lover* lacks "the spaciousness of *Women in Love.*" Consequently, "Wragby, clearly, cannot equal the combined weight of Shortlands, Breadalby, and the Pompadour, just as Clifford, its owner, cannot be made to possess the substantiality of a Gerald *and* a Hermione, to say nothing of a Halliday" (*Forked Flame*, p. 267). What is remarkable, in my opinion, is that Lawrence should try and indeed almost succeed.

his positive qualities, advises promiscuity in the face of her ailing body and spirit; Clifford is so anxious to provide Wragby with an heir that he encourages her to have a child by another man, while prostituting himself to "the bitch-goddess," success (p. 53). Likewise, among Clifford's set, Tommy Dukes is given certain Lawrence principles to express—a faith in the whole self and a phallicism, an organicism, and even a liberal distribution of four-letter words. Perhaps this is why Mellors reminds Connie of him. Yet Tommy remains a "mental-lifer" (p. 41), as he admits; his heart and penis are inclined to droop, and he is all talk (pp. 77–78). The other friends are even more arid in their intellectualism, ridiculing Tommy's views. The generation is summed up by Connie after she has escorted Mellors' upset child home to his cottage:

> All the great words, it seemed to Connie, were cancelled for her generation: love, joy, happiness, home, mother, father, husband, all these great, dynamic words were half dead now, and dying from day to day. Home was a place you lived in, love was a thing you didn't fool yourself about, joy was a word you applied to a good Charleston, happiness was a term of hypocrisy used to bluff other people, a father was an individual who enjoyed his own existence, a husband was a man you lived with and kept going in spirits. As for sex, the last of the great words, it was just a cocktail term for an excitement that bucked you up for a while, then left you more raggy than ever. Frayed! It was as if the very material you were made of was cheap stuff, and was fraying out to nothing. (p. 64)

It is perhaps not coincidental that the previous vitalists—Blake, Carlyle, and Yeats—also used such clothes imagery to describe spiritual states, and that, when liberated, both Connie and Mellors dance naked in the life-bringing rain.

The spiritual impotence epitomized by Wragby Hall both causes and reflects the same state in society outside. With savage irony Lawrence declares that faith in St. George has been replaced by faith in Lloyd George. Just as England lacks its natural aristocrats— those visionaries who will give the country the spiritual leadership it requires—so too the working classes are rapidly losing what connections they possessed in the old agricultural England, connections amongst themselves and with the natural world around them. Industrialism, as we have seen earlier, is not the simple villain: the problem is how to reconcile technology with people without reducing persons to the status of things and without substituting a mechanical for an organic process. The problem was central to Blake and Carlyle; it proved fundamental also to Lawrence. Hence, to Mellors the nighttime industrial landscape takes on a symbolic status like Blake's world of Experience: "Even in its sleep it was an uneasy, cruel world, stirring with the noise of a train or some great lorry on the road, and flashing with some rosy lightning-flash from the furnaces. It was a world of iron and coal, the cruelty of iron and the smoke of coal, and the endless, endless greed that drove it all. Only greed, greed stirring in its sleep" (p. 149). And echoing arguments from *Past and Present*, Lawrence makes Connie aware of the loss of old England with its organic connections and relationships when she visits Shipley Hall and sees the colliers' semi-detached houses turning the former estate into a "no-man's-land" (p. 165). The image is appropriate in its wartime connections, for the peace in 1919 brought no end to the war between the old and the new, agricultural and industrial, organic and mechanical, aristocratic and democratic, alive and dead. She becomes increasingly aware of Clifford's contribution to such fearful industrialization evident in the ugliness and degradation of Tedershall village. The problem is one of a Carlylean mammonism, as Mellors argues in his letter at the end of the novel, though his vision of men wearing scarlet trousers, dancing, singing, carving, and embroidering has nothing of the force and persuasiveness which Lawrence's perception of the problem possesses.[36] Indeed, one of the finest pieces of writing in the novel is the famous description of Connie's visit to Tevershall.

As the car picks its way through village and landscape, the setting, so richly and realistically evoked, becomes highly symbolic: there is a very real sense of a Hell through which Connie is descending as a necessary part of the educating process she undergoes throughout the novel. Just as we are given the positive alternatives in the lovemaking scenes in the wood, so the negative pole of Experience is revealed in this and other industrial landscapes.

> The car ploughed uphill through the long squalid straggle of Tevershall, the blackened brick dwellings, the black slate roofs glistening their sharp edges, the mud black with coal-dust, the pavements wet and black. It was as if dismalness had soaked through and through everything. The utter negation of natural beauty, the utter negation of the gladness of life, the utter absence of the instinct for shapely beauty which every bird and beast has, the utter death of the human intuitive faculty was appalling. The stacks of soap in the grocers' shops, the rhubarb and lemons in the greengrocers! the awful hats in the milliners! all went by ugly, ugly, ugly, followed by the plaster-and-gilt horror of the cinema with its wet picture announcements, "A Woman's Love!", and the new big Primitive chapel, primitive enough in its stark brick and big panes of greenish and raspberry glass in the windows. The Wesleyan chapel, higher up, was of blackened brick and stood behind iron railings and blackened shrubs. The Congregational chapel, which thought itself superior, was built of rusticated sandstone and had a steeple, but not a very high one. Just beyond were the new school buildings, expensive pink brick, and gravelled playground inside iron railings, all very imposing, and mixing the suggestion of a chapel and

36. Cf. Moynahan, *Deed of Life*, p. 172.

a prison. Standard Five girls were having a singing lesson, just finishing the la-me-doh-la exercises and beginning a "sweet children s song". Anything more unlike song, spontaneous song, would be impossible to imagine: a strange bawling yell that followed the outlines of a tune. It was not like savages: savages have subtle rhythms. It was not like animals: animals *mean* something when they yell. It was like nothing on earth, and it was called singing. Connie sat and listened with her heart in her boots, as Field was filling petrol. What could possibly become of such a people, a people in whom the living intuitive faculty was dead as nails, and only queer mechanical yells and uncanny will-power remained? (p. 158)

"It was an under-world" (p. 159), as Connie realizes, stunting physical and spiritual growth in its inhabitants and its landscape.

The industrial world takes on the aspect of a "vast evil thing," "the malevolent Thing" (pp. 123, 124), motivated by greed and mammonism, functioning by mechanism, destructive in nature, and capable of producing only ugliness, degradation, vulgarity, and spiritual death. Like the age itself, Clifford's movements depend upon a machine, which he laughingly compares to a "foaming steed" or Plato's "two-horse chariot" (p. 186). The analogies are chosen for their ironic inappropriateness: Clifford is no knight capable of wooing a Lady or searching for the Grail to redeem the wasteland, nor can the soul's chariot of Plato's *Phaedrus* be compared to his wheelchair or a Ford car. He might have faith in his wheelchair but he requires the help of a Mellors, who knows nothing about mechanical things, to climb a particularly steep incline. And picking up the disembowelling imagery of *The Plumed Serpent*, Lawrence makes Mellors murmur, "You'll rip her inside out," when Clifford abuses the gears (p. 196). The incident makes Connie painfully aware of her hatred of Clifford and of his lack of concern for Mellors whom he has bought. Mrs. Bolton's

crude misplaced faith, "the more machines, the more
people" (pp. 109–10), suitably enough inspires Clifford
to transfer his ambitions from literature to industry,
sets his mind working, and in a sense makes "a man
of him" (p. 111). But Clifford awakens to a sense of
power, a principle Lawrence by March 1928 had found
obsolete and superseded by tenderness, while his dependence upon Mrs. Bolton and subsequent kissing of
her breasts indicate his decline into an infantile emotional state. Mellors, on the other hand, who makes
a woman of Connie, admits to her the impossibility
of his desire to "wipe the machines off the face of the
earth again, and end the industrial epoch absolutely,
like a black mistake" (p. 230). Unlike Clifford's, however, Mellors' vision of the future is based on tenderness, a relationship which requires both contact between individual selves and acknowledgement of their
individuality.

Instead of a world as machine, Lawrence offers a
vision of an organic, quick, dynamic world, into which
Mellors initiates Connie. From his first meeting with
her in chapter 5 he impresses her with a vitality of
action, gesture, movement, and finally vision, which
arouses her passional self, hitherto unawakened and
hardened into female will. Her dissatisfaction with life,
of which Clifford is unaware, is sensed by Mellors, who
proves a more satisfying lover than the previous
Michaelis. The descriptions of their lovemaking,
though important to Lawrence's theme, are less successful in conveying his vitalism than other scenes,
where Connie tenderly holds the new-born pheasant
chicks or when she sees Mellors washing outside, both
reminiscent of similar scenes in *Sons and Lovers*. The
effect upon Connie is dramatic in her new contact and
relationship with things around her. "Today she could
almost feel it in her own body, the huge heave of the
sap in the massive trees, upwards, up, up to the bud-
tips, there to push into little flamey oak-leaves, bronze

as blood. It was like a tide running turgid upward, and spreading on the sky" (p. 126). With her sense of touch renewed and her tenderness replacing the previous selfish cruelty of will, she is reborn. But the commitment to life affects also Mellors, whose prophetic gloom is considerable and whose wounding is deep and bitter. The man's natural aristocracy has been offended by the class structure which antagonizes him so much that he is deliberately rude to Hilda and cool with Sir Clifford. His pride has been hurt by his wife's running off with another man, and he has suffered from her female will. The class consciousness, however, which was central to the first draft, has been relegated in importance and seen as one of several aspects of the same life-denial which the novel seeks to oppose.

Yet not all the descriptions of the lovemaking are soberly didactic or clumsily symbolic: "the phallic hunt of the man," "the jungle of herself" (p. 258). While Lawrence has been criticized for precisely that cerebral sex he himself deplored, his humour has been considerably underestimated. The marvellously funny exchange, for example, when Connie stays overnight at Mellors' cottage, is superbly handled and the irreverent quotation of Psalm 34 clearly relished:

> The man looked down in silence at the tense phallos, that did not change.—"Ay!" he said at last, in a little voice. "Ay ma lad! tha're theer right enough. Yi, tha mun rear thy head! Theer on thy own, eh? an' ta'es no count o' nob'dy! Tha ma'es nowt o' me, John Thomas. Art boss? of me? Eh well, tha're more cocky than me, an' tha says less. John Thomas! Dost want *her*? Dost want my lady Jane? Tha's dipped me in again, tha hast. Ay, an' tha comes up smilin'.—Ax 'er then! Ax lady Jane! Say: Lift up your heads o' ye gates, that the king of glory may come in. Ay, th' cheek on thee! Cunt, that's what tha're after. Tell lady Jane tha wants cunt. John Thomas, an' th' cunt o' lady Jane!—" (p. 219)

And later, when they dance naked in the rain, they place forget-me-nots in their pubic hair in another deliberately funny routine.[37] Out of context the scenes could be misinterpreted as crude or ridiculous; placed against Lawrence's affirmation of the vital life and against the evil Thing of science and industry and greed, both passages serve a necessary function. To Clifford, "the life of the body . . . is just the life of the animals," and unless one can accept Connie's faith in the "lovely, lovely life in the lovely universe, the life of the human body" (p. 245), the descriptions prove only dirty or calculatingly shocking. One must acquire the courage of one's own tenderness, as Lawrence makes Connie assert (p. 290), in the "battle against the money, and the machine, and the insentient ideal monkeyishness of the world" (p. 292). Lawrence has made sexual the Romantic assertion of the instinctive and irrational as means by which the visionary life of the consummated self is to be attained. Yeats's description of "the coarse language" as "a forlorn poetry uniting their [Connie and Mellors] solitudes, something ancient, humble and terrible"[38] is one more instance of Yeats's habit of refashioning authors according to his own vision. The description is more suited to his own tragic figures than to anything in Lawrence.

The novel centres then upon the theme of phallic tenderness as fulfilled in the relationship of Connie

---

37. Leavis has been foremost in arguing for Lawrence's humour, though not in this particular scene (*D. H. Lawrence, Novelist*, p. 13). Indeed, the scene would probably be, with the "obscene vocabulary," one of those "offences against taste" to which he objects (pp. 293–94). Other critics have singled out this scene as "ridiculous" (Hough, *Dark Sun*, p. 161) or "downright silly" (Moynahan, *Deed of Life*, p. 164). Daleski's position is closer to my own (*Forked Flame*, pp. 298–99 and 299 n.1).

38. Yeats to Olivia Shakespear, 22 May 1933, in *Letters*, p. 810.

and Mellors, but the scope of the novel expands beyond the individual fulfilment of these two. And despite their planned escape from the mechanized way
of life, epitomized by the industrial society of Tevershall and the decaying heart of Wragby Hall, there is
no retreat on Lawrence's commitment to England and
to saving the English soul. The novel is indeed not
optimistic, and perhaps individual fulfilment is all that
can be hoped for at the moment. However, the regeneration in the coming together of Connie and Mellors
in the future spring is strengthened by the conception
of their child, who may grow up avoiding the contemporary deformity and perversion. Moreover, the larger
relevance of the novel is evident in the manner in
which Lawrence continually sees the plight of particular people—Clifford, Tommy Dukes, Mrs. Bolton,
Bertha Mellors—against the vaster landscape of English
society, its attitudes, and values. As much as Blake or
Carlyle, Lawrence was attempting to redeem the giant
Albion from his blindness and misconceived wilfulness. While his faith in a sexual vision and his prophetic role could lead him to a didacticism which is
sometimes heavy-going, it could also enable him to
write a novel which combines his precise powers of
description of natural phenomena with his remarkable
ability to capture the battle within a person, and to
transform an everyday event or trivial action into a
situation resonant in its symbolism and its relevance
to a whole way of life. What has proved problematical
to Western man over the last three thousand years has
been brought to a fearful hellish climax in contemporary England: "the mortal and terrestrial divinity of
man" (*Apo*, p. 104). Yet it is precisely this which is
given to Mellors to affirm; it is the conclusion to which
Lawrence's entire work leads. Like Blake, he could be
motivated by love of his fellowman, as Frieda has argued, but he could also use his England—"And I am

English, and my Englishness is my very vision" (*CL*,
p. 371)—as reflecting the awful plight of contemporary
man.

5

The final affirmation which Lawrence is capable of
offering us is impressive in its sanity, wholesomeness,
and maturity of judgement. What informs and in-
tensifies that affirmation is a profound compassion and
humanity, rebelling against man's fearful misuse of
life, against his indifference towards that quickness
which transforms the world in which he lives from a
spiritual wasteland into a creative (or fictive) world of
the Eternal Now. In case that suggests a vague mysticism, we must remind ourselves, in Frieda's words, that
Lawrence's "love for his fellowmen" was "not a sentimental, squirchy, superficial love, but a dry hard one
to make people sit up and tackle their job of living."[39]
For love of life acknowledges the wondrously ecstatic
contact between man and his self, his fellowman, and
his world, that for Lawrence constituted the larger
redemption to which he would bring us.

> For man, the vast marvel is to be alive. For man, as for
> flower and beast and bird, the supreme triumph is to be
> most vividly, most perfectly alive. Whatever the unborn
> and the dead may know, they cannot know the beauty,
> the marvel of being alive in the flesh. The dead may look
> after the afterwards. But the magnificent here and now
> of life in the flesh is ours, and ours alone, and ours only
> for a time. We ought to dance with rapture that we should
> be alive and in the flesh, and part of the living, incarnate
> cosmos. I am part of the sun as my eye is part of me. That
> I am part of the earth my feet know perfectly, and my
> blood is part of the sea. My soul knows that I am part
> of the human race, my soul is an organic part of the great

39. Quoted by West, *Wine of Absurdity*, p. 38.

human soul, as my spirit is part of my nation. In my own very self, I am part of my family. There is nothing of me that is alone and absolute except my mind, and we shall find that the mind has no existence by itself, it is only the glitter of the sun on the surface of the waters.

So that my individualism is really an illusion. I am a part of the great whole, and I can never escape. But I *can* deny my connections, break them, and become a fragment. Then I am wretched.

What we want is to destroy our false, inorganic connections, especially those related to money, and re-establish the living organic connections, with the cosmos, the sun and earth, with mankind and nation and family. Start with the sun, and the rest will slowly, slowly happen. (*Apo*, pp. 199–200)

Lawrence's greatness as a novelist is in part that, with his quickening word, he can reveal that process happening and can convince us not only of its actuality but of its necessity and rightness.

Index